PAINT IT WHITE

PAINT IT WHITE

Following Leeds Everywhere

Gary Edwards

MAINSTREAM
PUBLISHING

EDINBURGH AND LONDON

First published in Great Britain in 2003 by
MAINSTREAM PUBLISHING COMPANY (EDINBURGH) LTD
7 Albany Street
Edinburgh EH1 3UG

ISBN 1 84018 729 8

A catalogue record for this book is available from the British Library

Typeset in Baskerville and Civet
Printed and bound in Great Britain by
Mackays of Chatham plc

To Wub and Spoon

Acknowledgements

I would like to thank all the following. Lesley (Wub), the special one in my life, without whom there is no doubt whatsoever I would not have been able to pursue my 35-year adventure. Vicky (Spoon), my daughter for 25 years, whose constant help with the infuriating technicalities of my PC was invaluable. Neil Jeffries, for the countless days and hours of help on the book, also for the expert guidance he gave me through my first literary minefield. Alan Osborne, for having the original idea for this book and his tireless work in ensuring its inception. Bill Campbell, Will Mackie, Graeme Blaikie, Tina Hudson and Becky Pickard at Mainstream. Gary Inman for instigating my contribution of a a monthly column in the *Leeds Leeds Leeds* magazine, which eventually led on to this project. I'm grateful, too, for the helpful input from Martin 'Slugger' Jackson. To Don Revie's Leeds United for giving me the privilege of witnessing the club's finest hours and Rod Johnson (Leeds United 1962–68) for his valuable insights on Revie. My dad for introducing me to Leeds United – although I'm sure he didn't envisage the obsession it would develop into. And my ma and sister Julie for sitting up half the night sewing dozens upon dozens of Leeds patches on my jeans, scarves and jackets. Finally, huge thanks go to Joshua Tetley's for helping me through the '80s.

Contents

Foreword by Alan Osborne

I am a Londoner and a supporter of West Ham United. When I first moved to Kippax, near Leeds, some 20 years ago I was somewhat reticent about moving into a Leeds United homeland. I had no need to worry, for I met a great bunch of lads, all strong supporters of Leeds United, who said, perhaps with tongue in cheek, that they respected West Ham United – probably because they win in most encounters.

One man was, I found out, probably the most avid supporter of any football club. This man was Gary Edwards, whom I now like to call my mate. I thought then, and still think, that it must be some record if he has attended every game, home and away, in Europe and even the Far East and elsewhere in pre-season tours, in fact everywhere, for some 35 years.

You may think after reading this book that he is obsessed with his club, and you may be right, but it is a story of a supporter's experiences and not about Leeds United, and the tales of his travels have made very good listening.

I hope readers of this extraordinary account get as much delight and laughter from it as I have. Helping Gary compile this story has been a real pleasure.

I hope that readers will not think Gary Edwards is all 'laughs', as his work for local people and charities shows that he has a serious side as well.

Good luck, Gary. Keep up the good work.

– 1 –

Better Dead than Red

As long as I can remember I've hated red. I was offered a really cheap van once, by a guy who was emigrating to Australia. But I had to go over and paint it white on the drive with a brush before I could get in to drive it.

For me, supporting Leeds United is a full-time occupation. But when I do get time to relax, there is nothing I enjoy more than hating manchester united. I hate them so much I can never bring myself to use capital letters for their name. I hate them with a passion. In fact, let's nail my colours to the mast right now: for me, hating them almost as much as I love Leeds is a full-time occupation, too.

Some people put it down to jealousy. They could not be further from the truth. You have to admire something to be jealous of it. More importantly, I hated them in the '60s and '70s, when Leeds used to beat them almost every time they played them, knocking them out of two FA Cup semi-finals along the way.

To be honest, it's difficult to pinpoint any single reason for my hatred of the club, but high on the list is their arrogance. I hate the fact that everything has to be done to suit them. No matter how much Mr Ferguson says the opposite, it is extremely rare for a penalty to be awarded to their opponents, and almost unheard of at Old Trafford. I believe they dictate to the Football Association and when they object to a particular referee, you can rest assured that that official will not take charge of their games. David Elleray is a case in point. Now, in my opinion, Mr Elleray is not the best referee in Harrow, let alone England, but since he had the audacity to award a free-kick against manchester united, he has not taken charge of any of their games. There's a Fair Play trophy on permanent display at Old Trafford, but this must be some kind of joke.

Another thing I really hate is the 'United' thing. Commentators, pundits and newspapers constantly refer to them as 'United'. There is only one United and take it from me, it certainly isn't them.

Oh, and I hate the colour of the shirts they normally wear.

I run a small decorating company and we refuse to use red paint. Word of this has spread and it has actually increased business. We even offer a discount for the removal of red paint. The bus stands in Kippax, the village where I live just to the east of Leeds, were once painted red. Until one morning, bright and early, I had three of my men undercoat and gloss them in brilliant white. They looked much better and no one complained.

Another day I came out of my house and there was a huge hole at the bottom of my drive, with two gas board workmen down it. Surrounding them was a little red-and-white fence. While they worked I got some white undercoat from the van and painted their fence. The men looked up at me in disbelief but said nothing. When I had finished I told them I'd be back that afternoon to gloss it and then drove off. Sadly, when I returned home, they had gone and so had the fence. I hate leaving jobs unfinished.

My aversion to red paint has attracted much attention from the media and I have been visited regularly by the BBC, ITV and Channel 4, as well as appearing in the national press. I once even made an appearance in manchester united's *Red Issue* fanzine. Which was odd.

I, like most Leeds fans, never wear any red clothing. However, I believe in honouring our war dead and always wear a poppy on Remembrance Sunday. I once made a terrible mistake, though, when

I tried to adapt this fine tradition. I bought a whole box of poppies and thought it would be worth re-styling them. I enlisted the help of my wife Lesley and daughter Vicky, who stayed up nearly all night painting the poppies white. Lesley didn't mind. Vicky (who I call Spoon because, well, I once thought she looked like one – although she doesn't these days) was game for a laugh. I thought they looked grand but Lunge, one of my friends, was attacked by several senior citizens while wearing one. They came up to him wielding their walking sticks and branding him a 'pacifist bastard'.

I can't help it. I really like white. And I love the team that plays in it.

There is a pub in Kippax called The White Swan. In 1994 I was asked to decorate it inside and out. A couple of weeks later the job was just about complete – all that remained was the re-painting of the pub's name in big letters over the main door. These are set in stone and the date below them reads 1915, four years before Leeds United's formation. The name was set against a dark blue background and once that had dried, I set about picking the letters out in white. Then I had an idea. I would paint all the letters except the last three. I then stood across the road and admired my work. 'THE WHITE S' stood out as clear as day. It looked brilliant.

The landlord, Gary Carver, and his wife Kath, inspected the finished decorations and pronounced themselves very pleased. I could not believe they had failed to notice my alteration to the letters above the door. That evening I called in for a pint with 6 ft 5 in. Gary, fully expecting a rollicking – at least. To my surprise, he never mentioned it. Days and many more pints passed but there was still no comment. I was amazed. Surely someone would have told him by now? Then, just as I thought I had got away with it, I noticed that Gary could hardly keep a straight face while pulling my ale. As he set it down he began laughing out loud and I realised then that he knew. He had known all along. I was delighted that he thought it so funny and left it alone for another two weeks before giving his pub back its rightful name. He and Kath now have premises at The Board Inn in Skipsea, but when we meet we still have a laugh about it.

I like to go bowling occasionally but this presents a problem. I always refuse to wear the house bowling shoes because they are red. I used to get on fine wearing my ordinary trainers until a bowling alley jobsworth had me barred. After that Lesley bought me my own pair of bowling shoes, in light blue. The only problem is that when I put them on, everyone notices and decides I must be either a poseur or an expert. That usually ends when they see my first bowl.

My hatred of red has more than once upset my family. Around 1987, when my daughter Vicky was 11, she upset me by announcing she wanted to buy a red jumper.

'Spoon,' I explained, 'I will not allow it!'

Although we didn't quite resolve our differences, I went out for the evening feeling much better. When I returned home I was horrified, therefore, to see a brand new red coat lying on the telephone table. I was furious and slung the coat out onto the lawn. The grass was wet and muddy following hours of torrential rain but this encouraged me. I jumped up and down on the coat until satisfied I'd done enough to teach her a lesson. Then I picked up the slimy rag that had once been a coat and put it back on the telephone table. Early the next morning, I was awakened by Spoon, who was looking rather puzzled.

'Have you seen the coat that was in the hall?' she asked.

I was just about to give her both barrels when she continued. 'It's Claire's – she stayed last night.'

I slunk back under the covers until disturbed by Claire's almighty scream. I bought her a new coat – a more stylish blue one – but it cost me a lot more in humble pie over the next couple of weeks.

I hate Alex Ferguson. I know I'm not alone in that. I am also very patriotic and have a large picture of the Queen hanging in my lounge. However, when she knighted him, I took her down. I put her in the cupboard under the stairs, and told her in no uncertain terms that she would remain there for two weeks. After the second week I opened the cupboard door and told her I was still angry and she would remain there for another week. Her eyes were half closed as I exposed her to the lounge light, a week later. She is now back on the wall and I'm sure she will think twice before doing anything as stupid in future.

I hate to gloat, but . . . on Christmas Eve, 1995, Leeds beat manchester united 3–1 at Elland Road. I was so elated. Even better, I was taping the Sky broadcast while I watched the game from my place on the Gelderd End. (It's called the Revie Stand these days, and although many still refer to it as The Kop, I'm a traditionalist and prefer to call it by its oldest name, derived from the main road a few hundred yards to the north.)

When I returned home I took the cassette out of my video recorder and wrapped it in Christmas paper. Imagine my excitement, as I rushed downstairs on Christmas morning, at finding under the tree a present bearing a tag that read: 'To Gary, Merry Christmas, hugs and kisses, love Gary'.

I hate not being able to do anything about manchester united but . . . on my home computer I have the *Championship Manager* game. I was bored winning everything as manager of Leeds United, so I applied for the manager's job at Old Trafford. I got it, and the software duly announced me as the new man in charge to a full house before their first game of the season. I quickly got down to work, and by the end of August I had sold the entire team, except Nicky Butt, who I put in goal. The entire team was then reassembled with goalkeepers bought from teams up and down the country. Mervyn Day, on his debut at centre-forward, was sent off. Not surprisingly, the computer was totally confused and asked if I was sure I wanted to sell Eric Cantona to York City for £500,000. I clicked 'yes' and went right through to March without winning a single point. On 17 March, an announcement appeared on the screen: 'Gary Edwards has been sacked from manchester united'. I could not have cared less. They were 26 points adrift at the foot of the table and doomed to relegation.

I am often asked what colour my blood is. That's an easy one – blue. If you look at your veins through your skin, you can see this is true. Blood only turns red when you cut yourself and expose it to the air. As it is leaving you, it doesn't make any difference.

I hate the red of Lancashire . . . In the '70s I had a job as a driver and my route took me across the Pennines on the M62 every Friday. I used to take with me a can of brilliant white spray car-paint and, around four o'clock each morning, on the way there, stop on the

Yorkshire border to re-style the red rose of Lancashire to a proper colour – white. My handiwork would typically last for a couple of weeks and then someone would return it to red, so I'd set off again armed with my can and rectify the problem once more. If they hadn't introduced so many security cameras in the area I'd still be doing it today. And I have history on my side . . .

Palm Sunday, 29 March 1461. The 24-hour Little Chef at King's Lynn was bristling. The Duke of Norfolk was bringing thousands of soldiers marching up the A1 to meet up with other Yorkists at Pontefract to complete a force of 36,000. The soldiers' journey would take them to Towton Dale, three miles south of Tadcaster, where they were to engage 40,000 Lancastrians, under the overall command of the Duke of Somerset. On the way they passed close to my house. I wasn't in but I'm sure they would have all touched my brass Leeds United shield mounted on the front for good luck.

The battle would be the bloodiest of the Wars of the Roses. In fact, the bloodiest ever fought on English soil. The day before, Lord Clifford of Skipton, fighting on the Lancastrian side, was killed, along with hundreds of his followers, by a large mounted body of Yorkist archers near Saxton. These archers, under the command of Lord Fauconberg, now awaited the rest of the Yorkists still on their way up the A1. The Duke of Norfolk and his men had been hampered by road works and so he telephoned Edward, the Black Prince (commander-in-chief of the Yorkists and a staunch Leeds United supporter) to tell him to delay the kick-off. The weather in Pontefract was bitterly cold with the promise of snow. Edward looked at the skies and decided to start without Norfolk. He led his army north through Sherburn.

The Lancastrians, led by the Earl of Northumberland, were in a strong position. With the Yorkist rearguard still stuck in traffic they easily outnumbered the main division of their foe as it advanced towards them, led by the Earl of Warwick.

Edward set up his standard of a black bull with gold hooves and horns. Though not yet 19, he was an accomplished soldier and watched proudly as the Yorkists' vanguard of Fauconberg's archers came within 400 yards of the Lancastrians and a body of archers equal in number. Whichever side took the offensive would have to advance into the dale to bring their archers into range.

The snow began to fall, driven by a southerly wind, striking the backs of the Yorkists and blowing in big white gusts towards the Lancastrians. It was the opportunity that Edward was waiting for. Trumpets signalled the advance into Towton Dale and as they came within 300 yards Fauconberg's men let loose a single flight of arrows. With the wind behind it, that opening volley carried deep into the Lancastrian ranks, killing many. Volley after volley the Lancastrians returned, but their arrows flew blindly into the snow and fell short into the wind while the Yorkists retired a short distance and waited. Then, when they were sure the Lancastrian arrow supply had run out, Fauconberg's men gathered them up and advanced again.

Thousands of steel-headed shafts struck down the Lancastrian bowmen. The Yorkists advanced further until they were among the fallen Lancastrian arrows which they collected and returned with deadly effect. The Yorkist advance continued well into the Lancastrian lines.

His archers decimated, Somerset ordered his knights, men-at-arms and billmen into the no man's land of Towton Dale. For 400 yards they walked into a renewed storm of Yorkist arrows. A group of Yorkist handgunners wreaked further havoc. Beyond the halfway point the Lancastrians were slowed by the rising ground and planted arrows. Soon the two armies were fighting at close quarters – axe to axe, sword against sword – hacking and cutting. The ranks of the dead and the dying formed banks over which both sides had to clamber to reach their adversaries. All the while the snow continued to fall.

The battle continued for many hours and as the day grew on, the Yorkists did give ground, almost to the southern end of the battlefield. Then Edward's mobile phone rang. It was Norfolk – they were minutes away and would take the field direct from their long march. This was to be the turning point.

Bringing pressure from the east, Norfolk's men began to turn the Lancastrian left flank back on itself. The Lancastrian army then began to give way all along its front. Men came pouring back over Towton Dale. From here there was no escape.

By late afternoon the open landscape was a place of utter confusion and carnage. Without leadership, the Lancastrians, still in their thousands, broke up, mercilessly harried by the Yorkist knights on horseback. Here and there groups of Lancastrians rallied, but fell before the Yorkist cavalry.

The Yorkists continued to drive the retreating Lancastrians back through Towton and down the steep valleys towards the river known as Cock Beck. Cock Beck was swollen with winter rains and the valley was flooded. Now, panic stricken Lancastrians dropped their weapons and ran into the valley. As they reached the water, the first of them attempted to turn, but the thousands behind them forced them on. The Cock had a powerful current, sweeping exhausted men off their feet to drown in their armour. Where men did reach the far bank to continue to Tadcaster, it was over the bodies of their drowned comrades. From Towton Dale to below Cock Bridge the river was choked with corpses. At Stutton, three miles downstream, where Cock joins the larger river, the waters ran red with the blood of Lancastrians. The Yorkists had triumphed. Yorkists flags bearing the black boar and the white rose fluttered proudly. Don Revie would have been delighted, too.

The snow that fell that day heralded a period of severe cold. When the sun returned, releasing winter's grip from the frozen soil, the land thawed and blood once again trickled down into Cock Beck. The Burnet Rose, growing in abundance in the area, was renamed the Towton Rose, for its white petals appeared tinged with the red from blood still within the soil. The last of Towton Roses disappeared many years ago and, sadly, are no longer found on the battlefield.

The Yorkist commanders Fauconberg and Warwick are reputed to have stayed at the original Crooked Billet pub, very close to the battlefield, on the eve of the battle. The present pub sign incorporates both men.

A statue of Edward, the Black Prince, on horseback, stands proudly in Leeds City Square. And the white rose of Yorkshire remains part of the Leeds United crest. So that clears that one up.

One sad fact that later emerged was that many Yorkists had, since the wars began in 1455, fought on the side of the Lancastrians. It can safely be assumed that their descendants are among the many

Yorkshire people who attend Old Trafford every week, such as the famous Yorkshire traitor Geoffrey Boycott. I follow Yorkshire County Cricket and felt absolutely disgusted when I was told by David 'Ghandi' Sutcliffe that Boycott was a manchester united fan. I was so incensed that the following week I gave my two books on Boycott, one of which was autographed, to the dustbin men.

But never mind the Yorkist traitors – they're a sad minority. And the good news is, the love of Yorkshire or Leeds United is not restricted to men or women born within God's own country.

I have a friend called Geir (pronounced 'Guy') Jensen from Norway – not to be confused with Geir Magne Fjellseth, another big Leeds fan from Norway – who has been a Leeds United supporter since the mid-'70s. Geir regularly travels to England to watch his team. He's a Viking with a difference – one who would rather be an Englishman than slaughter one. He often stays with me and in March 1998 he came to see Leeds play West Ham away and against Barnsley at Elland Road. To do this meant he stayed all week and Lesley wasn't that chuffed with the idea, but she hid it really well.

The day after the Barnsley game (an unsatisfying 2–2 draw) was Palm Sunday and I explained to Geir that on this day every year I go to the War of the Roses service at Towton. Geir was instantly very excited and, showing commitment that would put Geoffrey Boycott to shame, he explained: 'It's Yorkshire, Gary. I must come.' And so he did.

Every year the Towton Historical Society holds a special service to commemorate the Yorkists victory at the battle of Towton Dale in 1461. Prayers are read at the cross of Lord Dacre and a number of walking tours culminate in a quiet service in Saxton church. We chose one of the walks and set off with our group. After the walk, at the church, the vicar discussed the battle at great length as everyone sat listening intently.

'It was a total defeat for the Lancastrians,' said the vicar, solemnly. 'Cock Beck ran red with the blood of the Lancastrian army.'

Geir couldn't contain himself and began to laugh out loud. 'Ha, ha, ha! Good old Yorkshire!'

The rest of the congregation looked round in shock at this un-Christian sentiment and unusual accent.

I've known Geir for many years but he never ceases to surprise me. In 1992, when Leeds played a friendly against Stromsgodset in Norway and Lesley, Rob Who (that's his surname), Jeff and myself were his guests at his house. We were out in Oslo and came across a pub called Churchill's. Winston is one of my heroes so I suggested calling in there but Geir said it wasn't very good. But I insisted, so in we went, whereupon the barman, an Englishman, refused to serve me. I thought I began to understand what Geir had meant. I tried again, 'Look, we're with him, he's Norwegian!' I looked round and Geir had his back to everyone trying not to be noticed. As I turned back the barman replied, 'He's the reason I ain't serving you! He's a nutter!'

A visit to Geir's home would appear to support that theory. He and his brother live in the top half of a wooden house in the hills. Their parents live downstairs. Geir's living room is full of English memorabilia. Silk Slade scarves decorate the walls along with newspapers reporting the death of John Lennon. There are 92 rosettes, one from every English football league side – although I removed one that offended me for the duration of my stay.

When Geir next came to England we once again went to watch Leeds play. After many beers we returned home hungry and, looking in my fridge, I spied the perfect food for a Viking – a pair of large turkey drumsticks. I gave them both to Geir and went back to the fridge for more beers. When I came back, my two dogs, Jack and Cybil, sat drooling either side of Geir, who was sharing his food, bite for bite, with the hounds. In the morning, when he finally noticed that Cybil was missing a leg (it had been amputated months earlier), he wasn't at all sure if I was kidding when I told him he'd eaten it.

A few days after he'd gone home we received a parcel. It was a metal model of a Viking longboat. With it was a letter from Geir to Wub, thanking her for her 'Yorkshire hospitality'. I swear there was a tear in her eye.

So if a Viking can be so passionate, can I help it if I love the county of my birth? The only place in the world that I love almost as much is Key West in Florida. I went there with Lesley in 1992 and promptly decided it was an absolutely brilliant town. In fact, I've been back many times since and love it so much that I even admitted to her that it was the only place apart from Kippax I could ever consider living in. However, my musings quickly led me to the conclusion that it would be extremely difficult to get to Leeds matches. If I ever slept in on a match day and missed the one and only tram out of Key West, I would have to hitch-hike all along the Florida Keys to Orlando Airport. Up through the Everglades, keeping an eye out for any hungry alligators, through Kissimmee and all the rough ghettos surrounding it. From Orlando I would then have to fly to England and on to wherever Leeds were playing. So I decided to stay in Leeds. It's a shame, though, because the people in Key West are so laid back it's untrue and you never see a manchester united shirt.

Moored just off the beach is a famous buoy that declares: 'This is the southernmost point in the USA.' Walking back to our hotel at around five o'clock one morning I realised it would look even better with the words: 'Leeds United, League Champions, 1992'. I vowed to myself that before I left, I would carry out this assignment. Unfortunately I never got another chance and I regretted it even more a couple of months later. I was at Old Trafford watching Leeds and was flicking through their programme when I came to their fans page. There, was a photograph of two of their fans (from Yorkshire), stood posing in front of the very buoy that I had planned to decorate. The photo had been taken the very week after I was there. I've never got over the sense of disappointment.

So as you can tell, I hate Yorkshiremen who support manchester united and I hate to see people in Yorkshire wearing manchester united shirts. To me this is repulsive. I once even spotted one while driving into Kippax. At first I couldn't believe my eyes, but when I was certain I turned round and drove back. Gathering speed as I approached the offender I had to swerve to the other side of the road at the last moment . . . in order to drench him from a huge muddy puddle.

Towards the end of Leeds' title-winning 1991–92 season I was on a job decorating a hotel in Harrogate. At this stage the destination of the Championship was far from certain with Leeds and manchester united the two hot favourites. After we had been in Harrogate several weeks we noticed that we were on the route that the coach carrying

Yorkshire manchester united fans took. One particular Wednesday, when they were away at West Ham, we decided to wave them off. I had a word with one of the joiners on site who made me a board, eight-feet square, on which we would paint our message. At lunchtime, right on cue, a Yorkshire European coach came up the hill. Almost everyone on our job had turned out and as the coach passed with the sad Yorkshire outcasts on board, they saw our sign: 'Up the Hammers!' When they returned back late that night our sign was still displayed prominently on the wall of the hotel. They must have winced. West Ham had beaten manchester united 1–0 and seriously dented their title hopes.

On the day of the penultimate fixtures, Leeds were playing Sheffield United at Bramall Lane at noon, while manchester united took on Liverpool at Anfield at three o'clock. Leeds won their match 3–2, which meant that if Liverpool won, the title was Leeds United's. Thousands of Leeds fans scrambled into their favourite watering holes to see the Anfield encounter on television. I went back to The Lion at Castleford with some of the lads; the rest of our lot opted for The Waterloo in Leeds. After a 2–0 win to Liverpool, I received a telephone call; it was big John Martin calling from The Waterloo. 'We are the champions! We are the champions!' he chanted down the phone.

Everyone was leaping about, car horns were being sounded, I even saw two dogs shagging in the pub car park – everyone was having a great time! The party went on well into the night and through to the following day. The following Saturday Leeds beat Norwich at Elland Road in the final game of the season, winning the Championship by four points. I loved that. Our 1992 Championship was something special indeed. It was almost as good as when, in 1974, Leeds won the Championship and the same season manchester united were relegated. It doesn't get any better than that.

I hated the way that manchester united fans had taken that title for granted . . . In the '60s and '70s Leeds had beaten manchester united on a regular basis, but during the '90s these victories became rather rare. In 1992 I even read that one of their fans was so convinced his team would win the title that he had 'manchester united League Champions 1992' tattooed on his leg well before the season had finished.

My friend John Carey celebrated in impressive fashion. Delivering goods near Old Trafford, he parked up and walked into the Souvenir Shop.

'Good morning, love,' he said to the girl behind the counter. 'Have you got a scarf with "Champions 92" on it, please?'

She looked at him rather perplexed and said, 'Er, no. Sorry.'

John put on a brave face. 'Oh, never mind. I'll have a cap with "Champions 92" on it instead then, please!'

'I'm sorry, sir,' explained the girl, 'we haven't got one of those, either.'

John wasn't about to give up.

'Then I'll have pennant with "Champions 92" on it – surely you've got one of those?'

The girl was close to losing her temper. John thought for a moment and looked around the shop. 'So you haven't got anything with "Champions 92" on it?'

'No sir.'

'Why not?'

'Because,' the girl sighed, 'we didn't win the League!'

With that John bent down in front of the counter, out of sight of the girl. He then sprang up, wearing his Leeds hat.

'No, love – we did!'

The girl was almost in tears as John left the shop empty-handed.

So now you see what I meant when I said supporting Leeds United is a full-time occupation. And that hating manchester united keeps me just as busy. Now we've got that straight, let me tell you how it all started . . .

- 2 -

Leeds Seeds Sown

It sounds a bit crap, but just watching the floodlights go on sent a shiver down my spine. I was hooked . . . I never actually thought I had to go to every game. But I always knew I had to go to the next one.

I was born on 28 March 1956 and have loved football for as long as I can remember. I always wanted to be a goalkeeper (yes, you have to be a bit mad etc.) and at the age of nine I played in goal for my school, Kippax Infants. My first game wasn't exactly a dream debut, but I can remember it as though it was yesterday. We played Garforth Parochial School, who were a pretty decent side. In the first five minutes an innocuous-looking ball was sent into our penalty area, it passed straight through my defence, gathered up speed to what must have been all of three miles an hour and passed straight through my legs and into the back of my net. We lost the game 3–0. It wasn't the best of starts to my ambitions of being England goalkeeper, but I must have done something right because I kept my place all that season and the following season, before I moved on to a 'big' school.

As with most kids my dad, Arthur Edward Edwards, was my biggest fan and critic. We spent hours in our back garden with a big leather football soaked in dubbin, complete with laces. I was in goal and my dad would just keep pumping the ball at me.

It was about this time that I discovered my dad leads a double life. He is both Arthur Edward Edwards and Eddie Stevens. I first remember seeing him as Eddie Stevens in 1964. He was on stage singing in front of a couple of hundred people at a talent competition at Butlins in Filey. We used to go there every year. I can still smell the bacon as we queued with 300 others to get into the dining room.

I was only eight and quite surprised to see him up there on the stage. I recall that my sister Julie and I laughed and giggled throughout his turn. This wasn't because he wasn't good – he actually won – it was simply the unexpected sight of our dad, looking a little like Cliff Richard in his *Summer Holiday* period, singing and winking to the audience, while tapping his shiny shoe to the beat.

As Eddie Stevens (although I still think Arthur Edward Edwards is a better stage name), he went on to make an alternative career out of singing and even now, in his mid-60s, he is getting very regular bookings organised by his partner, Barbara, who doubles as his manager. The Cliff Richard look has gone, though, and these days he is most frequently compared – favourably, I might add – to Kenny Rogers.

When I watched Eddie Stevens performing at Flamingo Land a year or so back, the camp's mascot, a large furry bear, approached the stage, dancing. Dad immediately launched into the old Alan Price hit, 'Simon Smith And His Amazing Dancing Bear'. The bear continued wiggling about but it was very difficult for Eddie Stevens to get through the song because of huge fits of laughter. He regularly has these laugh attacks, especially when the older end of the female audience try rushing the stage, waving their knickers and other things at him. I once took 'Mad' Mick Poulter, a mate of mine from the Leeds games, to see him and a couple of Eddie's fans began approaching the stage. Mick volunteered to act as Dad's minder to prevent them getting any nearer but I was laughing so much that I was no assistance to Mick whatsoever. Dad regularly has groups of groupies turning up to his act, especially in the Barnsley and Dewsbury areas. In Dewsbury, regulars include a couple of well-built sisters called Alison and Kath. Quite frankly, they're both barmy and always turn up with a large bag of goodies, ranging from wigs and masks to more adult things.

Eddie Stevens isn't just a friend to mad women, though. When Frazer Pickard injured himself with a lawn mower and almost severed his foot my dad offered to play a charity concert in one of my locals, The Moorgate, the very pub in whose gardens Frazer had hurt himself. Three Kippax celebrity look-a-likes – Bruce Forsyth (Matthew Standish), Harry Potter (Rob Hirst) and Gareth Gates (Paul Abraham) – all volunteered to compere, but Eddie Stevens politely declined. Each of them was booked to turn on one of the three Kippax Christmas lights instead.

Another local, Hamish Boyle, offered catering facilities. He runs the La Venta restaurant in Boston Spa and can these days count Ian Harte, Mark Viduka and David Batty among his star customers. Sadly none of them could make it to The Moorgate, but the concert was still a brilliant success, raising quite a sum of money for Frazer and cementing the reputation and good name of Eddie Stevens.

Meanwhile, back in my back garden, Dad – as I shall once more call him – was proving to be a very good coach; he went on to get a coaching badge and also qualified as a referee. And he was also very clever. My 'goal' in the back garden was my dad's treasured aviary, where he kept his collection of British and foreign birds. Knowing how precious they were to him I did my best to stop every shot. And whenever the ball got past me and hit the aviary, Dad would frown and say through gritted teeth, 'Let's go again!' The combination of fear and persistence was steadily paying off, but I was facing a major distraction. It was about this time that my love for Leeds United Football Club began and so my playing aspirations began to take second place to watching Leeds United.

Dad used to work in Leeds city centre for a clothing firm called Stembridge's. He was the factory caretaker and odd-job man. He would clean all four floors of the factory at weekends and throughout the night. During 1966 I would help him there whenever I could.

Stembridge's was on Sovereign Street and from its windows I would look down at Leeds United fans boarding the special buses going to and from Elland Road. There were Leeds United pictures all over the factory. Photographs of young Eddie Gray or Mike

O'Grady decorated many of the women's sewing machines. In the men's areas, such as the cutting and pattern rooms, Billy Bremner, Jack Charlton and Norman Hunter were more commonplace. And everywhere I looked were photos of Albert Johanneson who, the previous year, had become the first black player ever to play in an FA Cup final. Everyone, including the managing director, Malcolm Bartliffe, seemed to be a Leeds United fan.

My father's business partner, John Hamilton, was a Leeds fan too. John was a Geordie who lived in nearby Garforth and used to watch most Leeds United games, home and away. John would leave me the programme from the previous game under the telephone in the canteen, and there I would read it from cover to cover. And then read it all again.

For my tenth birthday, Dad said I could go to watch a Leeds match. I couldn't believe my luck. They were playing Blackpool on my actual birthday, but it was away, so instead he said I could go to the home game, also against Blackpool, two days earlier on Saturday 26 March. Later that day I sat on the green, the patch of grass where my mates and I would play football for hours on end, and told everyone I was going to Elland Road in one and a half weeks' time. They didn't show it, but they were jealous to death.

Walking down Elland Road with my dad and John to the Blackpool game was absolutely fantastic. I was carrying a very large empty bean tin from the factory's canteen that I was going to stand on so I could see the game. At later games this was replaced by a wooden buffet (stool). My dad stopped and bought me a Leeds scarf. This was it, I was officially a Leeds fan! At the turnstile I squeezed through the same one as my dad (imagine that happening these days) and we took up our position on a bank of terracing I thought was called the 'spy and cock'. Later I found out it was the Spion Kop. I drank my soup as I looked round the ground from my perch on the bean tin. My dad handed me a programme but I put it in my pocket – there was too much going on to read it. Actually there wasn't, but I was totally fascinated by the steady build-up to the game. Already everyone was discussing who would play and where. Vendors were walking round the pitch throwing bags of peanuts and sweets into the crowd and then waiting while the money for them was thrown back.

Only two and a half hours later, the Blackpool players emerged from the tunnel on my right. They were in bright tangerine shirts and went over to the other end that Dad had told me was called the Scratching Shed. I am unable to describe how I felt when Leeds United came onto the pitch. Around me men were throwing their hats in the air and dozens of toilet rolls were slung towards Gary Sprake's goal. It took five minutes to clear them up and he did this himself. He then began gathering all the packets of chewing gum that had been thrown his way. There were rattles clacking away all round the ground. I was just staring at these players in brilliant white shirts, white shorts and white socks. They looked incredible.

When the game kicked off the noise was deafening. The crowd swayed forward and Dad had to hold me as I was almost knocked off my tin. I was in heaven!

'Go on, Jackie lad!' shouted John in his unmistakable Geordie accent, as big Jack Charlton charged forward with the ball. The crowd swayed forward again, but this time I rode it. I was getting used to this. Half-time and another soup came far too quickly. The second half kicked off and the crowd were chanting 'Leeds! Leeds! Leeds!' This was the famous Yelland Roar that I'd often heard about. Then they began laughing as an overweight St John's Ambulance Man, running towards a potential patient, tripped and fell flat on his face. He got up and straightened his glasses, looking a tad embarrassed. I felt sorry for him at that point. 'United! United! United!' My attention was back on the game, Leeds won a corner. 'YES!' everyone shouted. Jack Charlton had sent an unstoppable header into the back of the net. The place went crackers. Now the singing really started and the game was over in no time at all.

As we were leaving the ground, I said, 'That was superb! Thanks. When can I come again?'

My dad looked at me. 'Whoa, slow down. We'll have to wait and see,' he replied. 'I didn't think you'd want to come again, seeing as we lost.' He noticed my puzzled look and asked, 'What score do you think it was?'

'We won 1–0, didn't we?'

He smiled. 'We would have done if Blackpool hadn't scored two.'

It had been so quiet when they scored that I hadn't even noticed.

I was a little bit upset now. Once we were in the car I settled down in the back to read the programme as my dad and John fiddled with the wireless to get the other results. That didn't interest me at all. 'Dad,' I said, 'how can Leeds players play for other clubs?'

He looked at me through his mirror. 'How do you mean?' he said.

'Well, it says here, Jack Charlton of Leeds United and England and Billy Bremner of Leeds United and Scotland.'

They both laughed aloud, explained my mistake and I sat in silence all the way home.

The impact of my trip to the ground had an instant effect on me. When I got a pet tortoise I proudly named it Gelderd after the Gelderd End. Although when Dad sat me on his knee and explained to me what gelded meant, I changed its name to Tommy.

It was almost four weeks after the Blackpool match before I went to another match but I was well and truly under the spell. Whenever I didn't go to Elland Road but helped my dad, I would look enviously out of the factory window at the fans getting on the buses and going to the match. My dad gave me money when I helped him and I'd started saving almost all of this to buy souvenirs and get to games. Being an artistic lad, I also earned a few bob designing and painting posters for businesses around where we lived.

At my second game Leeds definitely did win – 4–1 against Everton at Elland Road. Again the atmosphere impressed me enormously. My dad began trying to temper my fanaticism by alternating a Leeds home game with a trip the following week to watch Huddersfield Town. I saw just one Huddersfield game. Dad's plan was never going to work. I preferred to watch Leeds. When they were away, I dragged my poor old dad down to Elland Road to watch Leeds United reserves. And while watching the reserves I would have the wireless with me, listening to every ball being played by the first team.

My dad had realised by now that his son's passion for Leeds United was growing stronger and stronger. He took me to my first away match, Burnley, at the start of the following season, on 3 September 1966. Eddie Gray scored for Leeds in a 1–1 draw, but once again it was the atmosphere more than the score that stuck with me. Thousands of Leeds fans massed down one side and one end of

Turf Moor. After the game as we walked back to the car I realised that watching Leeds United was all I ever wanted to do.

My uncle John used to take me to matches whenever my dad, or John Hamilton, couldn't. On Christmas Eve, 1966, I travelled up to Newcastle to watch Leeds win 2–1. Uncle John drove us up in his lime green Ford Anglia, Dad in the front and me in the back. My uncle was a big pipe smoker and I remember cringing in the back whenever I heard him making a loud noise with his mouth. He would clear his throat of phlegm, wind down the window and spit it out. I ducked in fear of the phlegm coming back into the car and hitting my face. Usually it would stick to the outside of my window and for the rest of the journey I would have to watch it slide slowly down the glass. All this with Tom Jones crackling away on the old wireless. When we arrived at our destination, Uncle John would casually wipe the phlegm from the window with his newspaper. A couple of years later when my cousin, Uncle John's son Graham, travelled with us, I'd make sure he sat behind his dad and I would look out of the opposite window.

Watching Leeds United has been a huge part of my life and luckily I have been on hand to witness some of their most historic matches. I was at Elland Road in March 1967 for the FA Cup fifth-round replay with Sunderland. It was the record attendance at Elland Road, packing in 57,892 people. It was 5s 6d to stand in the West Stand Paddock and opposite, in the Lowfields Road, a barrier gave way and hundreds of fans spilled over onto the pitch. No one was seriously injured and the game ended 1–1. It took a second replay and two goals, by Rod Belfitt and Johnny Giles, to beat Sunderland 2–1 at Boothferry Park, Hull. A 1–0 win over Manchester City at Elland Road in the next round set up a semi-final with Chelsea.

This FA Cup semi-final against Chelsea was the first time I saw Leeds fall victim to dubious refereeing decisions. I had travelled to the game at Villa Park in a minibus along with my dad and a dozen of his mates. Among them were big Jim King, who sadly died a couple of years back, and Keith Cook. On previous trips I had sat and listened to their recollections of how Leeds had been unfairly treated by the footballing authorities ever since winning promotion in

1964. I used to think some of the tales were exaggerated. How wrong I was. The semi-final against Chelsea was a prime example of precisely what I had been hearing about.

Trailing 1–0 to a Charlie Cooke goal, Leeds were awarded a free-kick on the edge of the Chelsea penalty area in the last minute. Johnny Giles squared the ball to Peter Lorimer, who fired an unstoppable rocket past Chelsea keeper, Peter Bonetti. The Leeds fans went mad. So too did the referee, Ken Burns. He immediately disallowed the free-kick, claiming that the Chelsea defence weren't ready. Unbelievable.

Leeds played Chelsea at Elland Road early the following season, in October 1967, and destroyed them 7–0. In doing so, Leeds established a new record, becoming the only team in the Football League to score seven goals from seven different players.

Because we had relatives in Newcastle we almost always went to the game, there and I would look forward eagerly to trips to St James' Park. In March 1968 I was standing with my Uncle John and my dad in the Leazes End of the ground, where the majority of the Newcastle hooligans stood. I was totally oblivious to any trouble that might occur or why my dad had discreetly removed my scarf as we entered the ground. Leeds were trailing 1–0 for most of the game, when Norman Hunter scored the equaliser with almost the last kick. Naturally I started jumping up and down and waving my arms about. Immediately, both my dad and Uncle John put their arms round my neck, arms and mouth leaving me unable to make even a muffled squeak. I was then bundled out, mingling with the crowd that were starting to leave.

The following season in October, after the previous season's close call, Dad had taken us into Newcastle's 'Popular Side' where most of the older generation of Newcastle fans stood. Throughout the game, a Newcastle fan a few yards in front of us was constantly barracking Jack Charlton. 'Mind your boils, Jack!' he kept shouting, referring to a couple of zits Jack was sporting on his face. It was obviously annoying my dad, but he kept quiet. Then, midway through the second half, Charlton scored with a header. My dad immediately shouted, 'Well done, Jack!' and clearly feeling a little braver than last season, added in a voice loud enough for the Newcastle fan to hear,

'That came off one of your boils, Jackie lad!' The bizarre chant did the trick and we never heard another word from Jack's tormentor. I was proud of my dad. And Charlton's goal, the only one of the game, meant we won.

Meanwhile my playing career had taken a positive step forward. In 1967 I had been one of the first pupils to go to the newly opened Garforth Comprehensive School. My support for Leeds United was as strong as ever, but my PE teacher, Mr Bradbury, didn't share my passion. He wanted me to play for the school team and this obviously clashed with Leeds' games on more than one occasion. On the days when I had gone to watch Leeds, I would tell Mr Bradbury that I had been working with my dad. He knew otherwise and threatened not to pick me for the school side until I could prove that I really wanted to play for the team. I could not do this and told him so. Shortly afterwards, the two other goalkeepers in the squad were injured and unable to play, so he took me to one side and said he was giving me one last chance. Leeds' fixture list in the coming weeks enabled me to play for the school for the next four weeks. During this time Huddersfield Town had watched me and had invited myself and another lad, John McEwan, along for a trial at Leeds Road. Mr Bradbury again had a chat with me, pointing out in no uncertain terms that this could be my big chance – I was now 12 years old, and should start to think seriously about what I wanted to do as a career. My dad fully supported me and he too told me to think long and hard about my decision. I'm not proud to say that I let both my dad and my teacher down. I went to the trial. It went very well indeed and Huddersfield invited me back for a second trial the following week. But the day of the second trial was 30 September 1967 and so I told Mr Bradbury and my dad that Huddersfield hadn't seemed too interested. I'm not suggesting for one minute that I would have made it as a professional footballer, but I had made up my mind that I wanted to watch Leeds United and play football when they didn't have a fixture.

A week later, though, the shit hit the fan. Huddersfield Town rang the school and spoke to the head of the PE department, Mr Diball. They asked if I had been injured and why I hadn't attended the trial, at Leeds Road, the previous week. After passing the message on to

Mr Bradbury, my days in the school team were over once and for all. For one game, when we were again short of keepers, a lad who normally played in midfield went in goal in preference to me. I couldn't complain but I felt I had let my dad down. West Ham and Leeds drew 0–0, by the way.

About this time a local Sunday league team emerged – Kippax Rangers. The manager was Dad and I must admit there was a bit of favouritism when I was named as goalkeeper. However, if I missed a midweek training session to watch Leeds, Dad would pick the other keeper, Brian Munroe, for the following Sunday.

On 2 March 1968 I saw Leeds win their first major trophy. It was at Wembley in the League Cup final against Arsenal. Ironically, a game I remember even better was the semi-final first leg against Derby County. Johnny Giles scored the winner from the spot as Leeds earned a 1–0 first-leg advantage at Elland Road. A 3–2 win away meant the 4–2 aggregate win that set up the Wembley triumph. I clearly remember celebrating in my classroom at Garforth Comprehensive with my school-mate, Graham 'Tab' Hunter when we both got our Cup final tickets. Almost all articles written about this game describe it as a poor encounter. I don't remember it that way. I had travelled down with my dad and John Hamilton in John's Mini van. From setting off to returning home I was totally transfixed by the day's events. The only goal of the game, scored by Terry Cooper, meant Billy Bremner going up the famous Wembley stairs to lift the Cup. On our way out I was so excited at what I had just seen that I didn't see this tiny man wearing glasses. I knocked him straight onto the floor. We helped him up and dusted him down before he muttered something and went on his way with a companion. Everyone about me was laughing, which I thought was a bit naughty. It was only when my dad told me that I had just knocked over Ronnie Corbett that I too saw the funny side.

In April 1968 Leeds played Everton, at Old Trafford, in the semi-final of the FA Cup, hoping for a second visit to Wembley. I, and 12 other hopeful Leeds fans, travelled across the Pennines with my dad in his 18 cwt Thames Dormobile. Despite being on top for most of the game, and Terry Cooper shooting against the crossbar, a mis-kick by Gary Sprake forced Jack Charlton to handle on the line.

Morrissey converted the ensuing penalty which gave Everton a 1–0 victory.

When I went back to school on the Monday I sat discussing the game with 'Tab' Hunter during a maths lesson. We agreed there and then that we would skip the next lesson to go see one of Leeds United's most famous players. Paul Reaney lived virtually across the road from the school. When he answered the door, we asked him to sign our bus passes and after he'd done that, we were stunned when he asked us if we wanted a cup of tea. Over our tea and a biscuit we talked about the semi-final at the weekend and then we went back to school with stars in our eyes.

He wasn't the only footballer I met back then. Jack Charlton had a sports/fashion shop in Garforth, and Tab and I were regular visitors there too. Jack was often in the shop, called 'His', and would chat away as long as you bought a small item before you left. Jack also presented the trophies on school sports day and one particular day I said to him, 'You're a lot better than your Bobby.' He winked at me and said, 'Oh, I know that, son, I know that.'

The 1967–68 season saw Leeds going well in Europe in the Inter-Cities Fairs Cup (the predecessor of the UEFA Cup). Between the League Cup final and the FA Cup semi, I was at Ibrox with Dad for the quarter-final tie with Glasgow Rangers. The score was 0–0 and to say the atmosphere was hostile would be an understatement. However, this was nothing compared to the return leg at Elland Road a fortnight later.

We went to Elland Road on one of the special buses from Leeds city centre. It was absolutely jam-packed with Rangers fans, shouting and hitting the bus ceiling in time to their chanting of 'We shall not be moved!' My dad looked a bit nervous as I sat there in a Leeds scarf and hat, along with a rosette the size of the Isle of Wight. There had been running battles in the city centre between Leeds and Rangers fans. One pub, The Hope and Anchor (now called The New Penny, a favourite with the gay community) had been completely wrecked. We were sat at the back of the bus and this huge Rangers fan spotted my hat and scarf. I gulped as he came over. He went into his pocket and brought out a bar of chocolate. Dad sighed. 'Ere, wee man,' the Scot said as he broke the chocolate in half and handed it to me. He then looked at my dad. 'Want a dram, pal?' Dad politely declined. 'Och, sure ya do!' The Rangers fan opened his coat to reveal a dozen pockets, each holding a bottle of whisky. Dad decided it best to take a drink. At Elland Road everyone piled off the bus. I hadn't seen the conductor take a single fare.

Inside the ground, as I stood in the Paddock (the price had gone up a shilling since last month to 6s 6d), I noticed countless empty bottles nestled in the back of David Harvey's goal. The game itself didn't seem to last two minutes, and once it was over Leeds had won 2–0. There were one or two scuffles after the match, but by and large, Rangers fans seemed to accept that a better side had beaten them.

The round before Rangers, Leeds had beaten Hibernian and after Rangers, Leeds were drawn against another Scottish side, Dundee, in the two-legged semi-final. On our way to Elland Road for the Dundee game I was in the front seat of the van with Dad and my mate, Melvin King. We found ourselves following a coach full of Dundee fans. Melvin, a great lad but not always the sharpest tool in the box, was on form today. Seeing the flag in the back window of the coach with 'Dundee' embroidered on it he leant over and nodded sagely towards the flag. 'I'll bet they've come from Scotland, them.' I'm not sure if he noticed that the ticket price to see the Dundee game had gone up another shilling to 7s 6d. Leeds won 1–0 on the night, which, added to the 1–1 draw in Dundee a fortnight earlier, saw them through to the final with Ferencvaros of Hungary.

Ferencvaros were one of the best sides in Europe at the time. They stood in the way of Leeds United becoming the first British club to lift the Fairs Cup. Strangely, the final, also played over two legs, would be held over until August and September of 1968 – at the start of the following season. The first, home leg, was a fairly drab game, due mainly to the defensive tactics of Ferencvaros, but was settled with a goal by Mick Jones. It was a very slender lead to take to the Nep Stadium in Budapest for the second leg. I have to admit that, as a young schoolboy supporter, I used to think Gary Sprake was brilliant and that night he produced probably one of the best goalkeeping displays ever seen. He pulled off a string of magnificent saves as Ferencvaros relentlessly bombarded the Leeds goal, looking for that vital equaliser. Sprake and the rest of the Leeds team held firm and carved out a 0–0 draw that enabled them to lift the Cup.

I went to Budapest – there and back in the same day – with John Hamilton and a total of perhaps only three or four hundred supporters. We flew from Yeadon – or Leeds–Bradford Airport as it is now known. On the plane I was excited that we were sitting near Phil Brown, who used to report on Leeds games for the *Yorkshire Evening Post*. Also nearby was Arthur Dunhill, an oldish chap who was regarded in those days as United's number one fan. I would write more on my first overseas trip, but the truth is I was too excited to remember most of it. As 1968 drew to a close I looked back on a year that was one of the most memorable I had ever known. Little did I know that there were plenty more to come – or that the League Cup semi in Derby was the last Leeds United game anywhere in Great Britain or Europe that I would miss.

We Shall Not be Moved: 1969–72

I've tried not to use the word obsessive because I don't like it.
I think this is normal.

In 1969 man landed on the Moon, but that year I witnessed a far greater achievement: I saw Leeds United win their first-ever League Championship. One point was needed in the penultimate game, which just happened to be against their nearest rivals, Liverpool, at Anfield. For previous midweek away games, I had just skipped school and then gone in with a note from my ma the day after claiming that I had suffered from an extremely bad attack of flu or pleurisy. But because of the importance of this game at Anfield, it seemed like every boy in school was going. I asked Ma to write me a note asking for the afternoon off to go to the match. I gave the letter to my teacher, Miss Yates, and stood back. I nearly fainted when she took me to one side and told me she couldn't allow me time off, but I recovered when she added, 'Just have one of your flu attacks and I'll see you bright and early on Tuesday morning.'

So at around three o'clock in the afternoon on Monday, 28 April 1969, I began queuing outside the Anfield Road End with thousands of other Leeds fans, my dad and my mate, Andy Robinson. The gates opened at about 5 p.m.; only two and a half hours to kick-off. At quarter past seven, 10,000 Leeds fans cheered as their team came out onto the pitch. I remember being that nervous I was almost sick. Leeds got the point they needed with a 0–0 draw. After the game the Liverpool Kop were generously chanting 'Champions! Champions! Champions!' to the Leeds team after Billy Bremner, at Revie's insistence, had led them to that end. He then led his side back to the Leeds fans at the opposite end of the ground. Andy and I ran on to the pitch and grabbed a handful of turf, which we stuffed in our pockets. I still have my bit of turf, although these days it looks more like grass of the smoking kind.

Two days later Leeds played their final League game. Already crowned Champions, a win over Nottingham Forest at Elland Road would give Leeds the record number of points ever (on the old two-points-for-a-win basis). A Johnny Giles goal ensured a 1–0 victory over Forest and the record of 67 points. At the end Andy and I were on the pitch again.

It was around this time that I acquired a nickname that has stuck with me ever since: 'Snake'. I had a grass snake, which I named Sid. I kept it in an old fish aquarium, without water of course, and it would escape on a regular basis. One day I searched the house and the garden but still couldn't find Sid anywhere and so I placed an advert in Eastwood's, the local newsagents. 'Lost. Snake. Reward etc.' It wasn't a good idea. I was inundated with frantic phone calls. 'Is it poisonous?' 'Does it bite?' I even had one woman call who told me her young son had been missing for over an hour – 'Does it eat children?' I have kept and protected animals of all shapes and sizes ever since. It's a passion almost as strong as my love of Leeds United. Sadly, Sid was still missing as the 1969–70 season started with a Charity Shield match – at Elland Road – against Manchester City. In fact, he hasn't been seen since.

Even his loss took a back seat in my mind in my fevered anticipation of the Man City game – which I nearly missed. The week before it I was larking around with some of the lads on my push-bike. The previous week we had all been to the circus and witnessed three clowns all riding on one tricycle. After a week training and practising we decided that we could go one better on one less wheel. With me on the seat, Andy sat on the handlebars, Stan 'Rastus' Richardson balanced on the crossbar and Kevin Spencer clinging on for dear life over the back wheel mudguard, we set off down Butt Hill, the steepest hill in Kippax. We sped off and soon reached what must have been 40 mph. We carried on zooming down this main road. At the bottom of the hill there is a sharp right-hand bend. As we approached the bend I turned the handlebars but, because Andy was sat on them, they didn't respond. We left the road, shot through a small wooden fence, across a lawn and smashed straight into a greenhouse. With the wheels still spinning, one by one we got up, dusting ourselves down, gingerly removing the mess of glass and tomatoes. Much to our surprise, the owner appeared and stood there with his hands on his head stuttering in disbelief. Then his shock turned to anger.

'Look at my greenhouse!' he shouted.

One of the wheels stopped spinning as I picked up part of the smashed greenhouse door and said, 'Sorry, mate. We'll mend it.' The four of us then watched as the man began to change colour. Nervously, Andy stepped back and put his foot through one of the few hitherto unbroken glass panes. The man's eyes had now disappeared into his head. 'You little bastards!' he screamed. 'You little bastards!' Stan was busily picking up whole tomatoes, which had escaped unhurt, and placing them in a small plastic bowl that was lying near the wreckage. The second wheel finally stopped turning so we could clearly hear the sound of glass crunching under his feet as he walked over to the man and offered him the bowl. 'These are all right,' said Stan.

That was the final straw. The man took a massive swing at the bowl, knocking it clean out of Stan's hands. Just then, as if we were back in the circus, two of the tomatoes left the bowl and flew straight into the face of the local copper, Irish Mick, who had heard the crash too and was striding towards us over the broken fence and taking out his notebook. A small crowd had now gathered and began laughing. This laughter had a disastrous effect on the four of us and we started giggling. This angered Irish Mick and he demanded all our names and addresses. I tried to pull my bike out of the carnage and it caught on the corner of the frame and two more glass panes crashed to the floor.

'I'll start with you. Name?'

I gave the officer my name and address and stood with my head bowed as he took the details from the other three. The owner was now sat on a chair with his head in his hands, being consoled by his wife. Irish Mick ushered the audience away with the familiar words, 'Go on home now, the show's over.' Unfortunately it wasn't over for us. The next day, as the same four of us sat in my front garden, we watched as Irish Mick pulled up on his push-bike. I had managed to sneak my bike into our garage and not seen the need to mention the incident to my parents. Now Irish Mick opened the gate and asked to see my dad. I explained, truthfully, that he was at work but added that my mother was in. As soon as he had gone round the corner to the back door, all four of us legged it. It was dark when I got home. Both my parents sat there at the table as I walked in and casually said hello. Dad didn't get angry much. But when he did, he did so in style.

'I'll give you hello, you little bleeder. What happened yesterday? Why didn't you say 'owt?' he raged.

I muttered something about being scared and how it was only an accident. They both looked at each other and then Dad said, 'Well, you won't be going anywhere for the next two weeks, and you'd all better get some money together to pay for the greenhouse.' I used to chop firewood and sell it at four shillings a bag, so paying towards the greenhouse wasn't going to be a problem. So I was just feeling OK about the punishment when he added: 'And don't even think about going to Elland Road next week.' That was the one I had secretly been dreading.

'But . . .' I started.

'No buts. That's it, you're finished.'

I tried the old 'Ma . . .' option but that was never going to work. She said, 'You should have thought about that before you started clowning around on your bike.' I felt like crying. And pledged to kill the next clown I saw. I had to stay in every night when I came home from school and I grew more and more worried as match day approached. How could I miss the Charity Shield match against Man City?

On the morning of the game, I had all but given up hope of going to Elland Road, when Dad came downstairs and said, 'Are you going to get ready then?'

Sensing a glimmer of hope I replied, 'Ready for what?'

'Well, I'm off to Elland Road. You please yourself.'

I ran upstairs and grabbed my scarf.

Our new signing, Allan Clarke, made his debut and goals by Jack Charlton and Eddie Gray rounded off a 2–1 win over City. Leeds had won another trophy. The following week, with me firmly back in Dad's good books, I was at Elland Road to see Allan Clarke score in his league debut in a 3–1 win over Tottenham. In fact, I saw every goal Clarke scored in his Leeds career.

I have a lot to thank my dad for. Another thing was later that 1969–70 season when he organised a Kippax Rangers charity game against our mothers. Two Leeds players had been invited to attend, and to play in, the game. These were Nigel Davey and John Faulkner – both fringe players in Don Revie's squad at the time. There were some real tackles flying about, and nearly all done by the mothers.

After the game Davey and Faulkner came back to our house for tea and to look at my ever-growing shrine to Leeds United. Davey, who still lives in Leeds, could have played for most sides in the first division, but preferred to remain part of Revie's squad and deputise for Paul Reaney when required. He might also have taken over when Terry Cooper broke his leg in 1972, but Davey did the same thing in a reserves match the very same day. He eventually moved on to Rotherham United. Faulkner had impressed Don Revie so much while playing for Sutton against Leeds in the 1970 FA Cup, that after the match he signed him. Although he only made two first-team appearances for Leeds, Faulkner went on to play over 200 games for Luton and helped them win promotion to the First Division in 1974. He later played in the North American League. I went on to have a fairly successful career, playing amateur football for Sunday League sides for over 28 years and winning 42 medals and awards on my way. My dad – and Eddie Stevens – got over it.

Meanwhile, back in 1970, Leeds reached the semi-final of the FA Cup, against manchester united. The first match at Hillsborough ended in a 0–0 draw. Just before the replay at Villa Park, which also ended 0–0, it was announced that Billy Bremner had been voted

Footballer of the Year. Then it was off to Burnden Park, Bolton, for a second replay.

Two days before the game I got flu, bad flu. My dad had always suffered badly with it, but up to now I'd always managed to avoid it. Now it had got me. I went to school, purely because I wanted to go to the semi-final on Wednesday, but after an hour I was forced to come home. I was so ill my teacher Miss Yates brought me home in her car. This was the same Miss Yates who the previous season had given me time off to go to the match at Anfield and she mentioned the forthcoming match at Bolton. She could tell I wasn't faking and as she dropped me off, she said, 'I hope you're fit for Wednesday.' I told her I did, too, and went inside. When Wednesday finally came around, I was still bad, but I was determined to go to the game. Dad, bless him, had managed to swap our standing tickets for two seats in the main stand. At the game I sat there shivering but within ten minutes I forgot all about it as Billy Bremner fired Leeds in front. The Leeds fans went wild. It proved to be the decisive goal and during the last five minutes the stands were ringing with the chant of 'We shall not, we shall not be moved!' I'll never forget that five minutes as long as I live.

Ironically, Dad had to go into hospital for an operation and missed the final at Wembley. This sparked off a major discussion between two of his brothers, my uncle John (the one with the pipe) and my uncle Ernie as to who would go with me. On the Wednesday before the final, Leeds had been beaten 1–0 at Elland Road by Celtic in the European Cup semi-final, first leg. I tried to forget that result as I left Leeds Railway Station at seven o'clock in the morning with my uncle Ernie, bound for Wembley. As everyone in the world knows, Leeds 'murdered' Chelsea but could only draw 2–2, the first time ever that an FA Cup final at Wembley had been drawn.

Come the European return leg at Celtic, four days later, Dad was still in hospital and neither of my uncles were able to travel to Scotland. Up stepped my grandma's boyfriend, George Dean, to make good use of Dad's ticket. George was a lovely man, who adored my grandma, and despite being in his senior years, was still an exceptional drummer who taught music in colleges throughout the region. The tie at Glasgow had been switched from Celtic Park to Hampden Park to accommodate as many fans as possible. The switch ensured a European record attendance of 136,505. George and I were standing in the large open end and when Billy Bremner levelled the tie with a magnificent strike after a quarter of an hour, I, along with the other Leeds fans, went berserk. Unfortunately for George, we weren't standing with the rest of the travelling Leeds fans; instead we were stood among the home fans. Luckily – and almost certainly because of our respective ages – we didn't get our heads kicked in. But following on from the disappointment of Chelsea's late equaliser at Wembley, Leeds' bad luck continued when an injury to Gary Sprake helped Celtic draw level. It got worse. The first time David Harvey, his replacement, touched the ball was when he went to pick it out of the net. Jimmy Johnstone had scored to put Celtic through 3–1 on aggregate.

For the FA Cup final replay two weeks after that, with my dad still out of the picture, Uncle John got the honour of escorting me to Old Trafford. Again, Leeds totally dominated Chelsea, but again Leeds' bad luck travelled with them. After leading through a Mick Jones goal Leeds' season finally ended trophyless when Chelsea won 2–1 in extra time. Travelling back across the Pennines in Uncle John's green Ford Anglia, I wondered how the Leeds players, and also Don Revie, must have felt. Leeds had fought on three fronts – the Championship, FA Cup and European Cup – and ended up with nothing. They had played a total of 62 matches plus two friendlies. I was 14 and had only watched every game, and I was knackered! Paul Madeley, who appeared in ten different positions for Leeds, had played in 60 of those games. One wintry night in 1999 I was on my way into The Old Tree pub in Kippax when a Mercedes pulled alongside and a tracksuited man got out and called me over. 'Excuse me,' he said, 'I'm looking for a place that makes snooker cues.'

I walked over and said, 'It's just up . . .' I then noticed it was Paul Madeley. 'I'll show you where it is, if you sign my hat,' I said. He laughed, obliged and I sent him on his way. I had completely forgotten to ask him how he felt back in 1970.

In 1971 Leeds won the Inter-Cities Fairs Cup for the second time, beating Juventus in the final. I had travelled to Turin in a party organised by Camkin Sports who regularly looked after members of the Leeds United Travellers Club. Arriving in Turin, we faced a thunderstorm from hell. We were only staying one night and then leaving the day after the game, but this was just as well given that we wouldn't be able to see anything of the city in such horrendous weather. Once the game got underway it was obvious that it wasn't going to last long. It was much worse than the Rugby Challenge Cup final at Wembley had been in 1968 when Leeds RL and Wakefield Trinity played on what can only be described as a lake. With about half an hour remaining, the Dutch referee abandoned the game. The following morning after breakfast, representatives from Camkin Sports said that although the game had been abandoned we still had to return to Leeds that day as planned. Almost everyone in the party said they weren't leaving. The entire day was spent trying to persuade the company to extend the stay until the final had been played, which we had now been told was the day after next.

Eventually Camkin Sports told us that they could organise a flight for just after the re-arranged final but we could only have one more night in this hotel and nowhere else in the city could take a party of our size. We could all split up and try different places, but it could mean that the night before the final would be spent on the street. I was only 15 years old, and although I did look much older I was a little worried that if the police saw me they would arrest me, or even worse deport me. A friend, Paul Smith, was a bit older than I was and if the worst came to the worst we decided to say he was my dad. Our main aim, however, was to stay out of the way. In the end we needn't have worried; we found a small hotel, not far from where we had been staying. It wasn't exactly The Ritz but once we got used to the wildlife scurrying around the room and the dirty bedsheets it began to seem almost cosy. Almost – I woke up next morning on the floor at the side of my bed. Paul had done the same at his side. Both of us had slept under our coats.

We skipped breakfast and met up with the rest of our party at our chosen rendezvous. During the match Leeds twice came from behind, with goals from Paul Madeley and Mick Bates, to draw 2–2. These away goals would turn out to be enough to win the trophy, following a 1–1 draw in the return leg at Elland Road. At last Leeds had been blessed with a little bit of good luck for a change.

During the next two weeks I had a very important decision to make. I had been blessed with a good right hand – by which I mean that I am a fairly good artist and have gained a couple of diplomas over the years. I had been sending my work to a popular football magazine, but had been told: 'Your work is very good, but unfortunately we cannot use it at this time.' Weeks later, however, my cartoons were appearing in this publication under another name. Letters and phone calls from my dad were met with denials. There didn't seem to be a thing I could do about it.

After a few months of sending examples of my work to other publishers, one of them, D.C. Thompsons in Dundee, offered me a job as cartoonist for *The Beano* and *The Dandy*. It felt like the ultimate prize and I was floating. This could finally be the break I was looking for.

Then I re-read my two-page letter from Thompsons and my heart sank. Along with the job was accommodation, which would be provided by the company for the first eight weeks of my contract. From then on, apparently, I would have to find my own place to live. I didn't want to live in Scotland; how would I possibly get to the Leeds games? I made a couple of attempts to persuade them to let me work from home but, as I expected, they again stipulated that I had to live in Dundee or the surrounding area. So for the sake of Leeds United Football Club, I had to say goodbye to Dennis the Menace and Desperate Dan.

My last and most memorable year at school was 1972. I had stayed on an extra year in order to take my art O level and decided to take English and history, too. I had studied for a geography O level as well, but missed my final exam on Friday, 31 March because I went to watch Leeds draw 2–2 at West Ham. The school would not allow me to re-sit the exam because they knew where I had been. I passed my other three O levels with flying colours.

Leeds' form in both the League Championship and the FA Cup was electrifying. In the League a 5–1 victory over manchester united was followed the weekend after with a 7–0 thrashing of Southampton. In the Cup, a 0–0 draw at Anfield set the scene for a replay at Elland Road. Meanwhile, Britain was in the grip of a recession, and believing that the country was behind him Prime Minister Ted Heath called an early election in order to strengthen his position against the country's striking miners. His confidence was misplaced and Labour, under Harold Wilson, regained power. Three-day working weeks continued and depleted coal reserves eventually led to nationwide power-cuts. This inevitably led to midweek football matches being played during the afternoon. The Leeds–Liverpool replay was one such game.

The teachers at Garforth Comprehensive were fully aware that pupils would be seeking to leave school en masse in order to attend the match. At lunchtime around 15 teachers linked arms across the front school entrance to deter any would-be escapees. Just then the fire alarm went off. Plan B had been put into operation.

A small fire had mysteriously started in the school library, and was threatening to rage out of control. Half of the teachers 'on guard' had to rush into the library to offer their assistance. With the line depleted, around 50 pupils made their escape. The small train station at Garforth was swarming with pupils as the train arrived for Leeds city centre. Later that afternoon, a 2–0 win over Liverpool made all the risks worthwhile.

The following day back at school saw long queues outside the headmaster's office as members of the escape committee awaited their punishment. Detentions and extra homework had little effect, as most of the pupils would be leaving school over the next few weeks. The library fire had been brought under control fairly quickly and no extensive damage had been reported. However, the cause of the fire was never discovered.

Leeds went on win the FA Cup, beating Arsenal at Wembley. Dad and I travelled down the night before in his Ford Transit van. We parked in a car park on Edgware Road and after a supper of fish 'n' chips, settled down in home-made beds in the back of the van. I awoke next morning to the mouth-watering smell of bacon being fried. 'Good morning. One egg or two?' said Dad. He was cooking our breakfast over a Calor gas stove. This was living.

The atmosphere walking up Wembley Way was electric. Dad bought me a rosette with the FA Cup on it and pinned it to my Leeds hat. Once inside the stadium we were entertained by the international singing sensation, Tommy Steele. Dressed in an all-white suit, he belted out, 'Once upon a time there was a little white bull'. The Leeds fans made a better job, joining in with 'Abide With Me' before the teams strode out onto the pitch.

Arsenal were playing at Wembley for the second year running, but their hopes of retaining the trophy were foiled by a spectacular Allan Clarke header. As David Coleman famously said in his commentary, 'Clarke – one–nil!' Leeds had won the FA Cup – and in its Centenary year, too. The guest of honour to mark the occasion was, therefore, Her Majesty the Queen, who presented Billy Bremner with the Cup. Later, amid huge cheers, she was on hand again as Norman Hunter helped the injured Mick Jones up the famous Wembley steps to receive a winner's medal he'd almost missed out on.

After the match we went to see the Harlem Globetrotters at Wembley Arena before returning home. These had been two of the best days of my life. But the elation didn't last. Leeds were forced to play their final league match at Wolverhampton Wanderers the following Monday night – just 48 hours after the Cup final. They needed only a point to secure the League Championship and win the celebrated double. Well over 20,000 Leeds fans filled the South Bank and an entire side of Molineux. Leeds were again cursed by some diabolical refereeing decisions. This time Welsh official, Alan Gow, was the culprit. He failed to see that Allan Clarke was brought down in the area by Wolves keeper Phil Parkes or that their full-back, Bernard Shaw, clearly handled in the box. And so the game continued and Leeds eventually went down 2–1. Derby County, who were on holiday in Majorca, were handed the title without kicking another ball.

My school days were over but following Leeds United had taught me an important lesson. Football could be a cruel mistress.

– 4 –

Done Up Like a Kippax

It started as just mates from the village. But soon we were hugely outnumbered – people from all over joined the Kippax Branch. We must have been doing something right.

Some people organise trips to matches with their mates. Others go with a branch. I do both at the same time. Most people I know are in a branch. In the '70s, when clubs were nervous of hooligans, belonging to a branch gave you an identity and credibility. These days it's simply a lot less hassle to obtain away tickets if they are booked through a branch.

Around the 1971–72 season, when I turned 16, I used to travel to Leeds United matches – home and away – with half-a-dozen mates on the Wallace Arnold coaches that ran from different locations all over Yorkshire. I would get on three miles down the road from Kippax in Castleford. But the numbers dwindled and eventually there were only two or three of us and we would have to go all the way into Leeds. There we would queue with hundreds of other fans who, initially, we didn't know, but who over the weeks and months formed into regular groups.

We travelled in this way for a couple of seasons but the flasks and sandwiches weren't quite what I had in mind. So we formed our own branch at The Viaduct pub in Leeds – and although we did from time to time base ourselves at other pubs, the current Viaduct landlord, Les Hince, is delighted that after 26 years we still return to that very pub.

One of the other pubs we moved to, and the one where we made our first stab at forming a branch, gave its name to the official Three Legs Branch. A committee was formed, including myself, and the branch grew. Tony Frith was larger than life and therefore the man we chose to run our new branch. Tony hailed from the Gipton area of Leeds, a tough neighbourhood where I too spent much of my childhood whilst my grandma was alive. He lived behind a pub called The Courtiers where in those days it was quite easy to purchase the firearm of your choice. Finally, Tony always wore a suit (the same one) and he always carried a briefcase; he was the original 'Del Boy' Trotter. He was definitely our man.

While with the Three Legs it dawned on us at that if we had 50 to 60 regulars and around two thirds of them came from Kippax, we could form our own Kippax Branch. We applied to the Leeds United Supporters Club, and the LUSC secretary Eric Carlile and the chairman John Redmond were both on hand to attend its inaugural meeting in The Royal Oak pub in Kippax. And so the Kippax Branch of the LUSC was formed on 31 May 1978 by myself, Gordon 'Gord' Findlay and Malcolm 'Mally' King. We were chairman, secretary and treasurer respectively and our membership was all around us – 50 super-keen Leeds fans pretending to be wallflowers but straining at the leash to hear what we were talking about.

While Tony Frith continued with the Three Legs (he later became secretary of the Leeds City Transport Club and eventually took on a pub in Bridlington), we spent that summer opening a bank account, getting letterheads printed and finding a reliable and affordable coach company. We gathered loads of quotes and decided on Wallace Arnold. The fact that I later received a bottle of whisky every year from them was immaterial.

We ended up running two full coaches to every game, paid on account, but still leaving many members disappointed. Although we were called the Kippax Branch, members joined from all over Leeds and the surrounding areas and our buses would pick them up at various points. Our motto '*et lege et multi*' – Latin for 'call us legion, we are many' – could not have been more apt. The Kippax soon became 'terrace famous' and membership grew to the point where we were taking four coaches on many occasions. Even supporters from other clubs knew of us. I have to say, though, that some of the stories about us were grossly exaggerated. But everything in this book is true.

The first coach we ever ran was for the opening game of the 1978–79 season at Arsenal. Leeds were without a manager after the dismissal of Jimmy Armfield, and although Jock Stein was waiting in the wings, I was against his appointment simply because I felt certain he was only using Leeds to get the Scotland job. Which he did, 44 days after he joined Leeds.

All 54 seats in our coach were sold weeks in advance and we could have easily filled another bus, but decided to hold off. I paid around £200 up front, got my money back, and made a small profit for the Kippax bank account at the very first attempt.

The 54 of us were stood on the Clock End terracing when a bit of a fight broke out between Leeds and Arsenal fans. It wasn't much of a brawl but it was enough for Tony Brown. Tony was attending his first ever game and after the scuffle he said, 'Fuck this, you're all mad!' He's never been to another game since. Others took a different view. In fact, Neil 'Butter' Butterfield saw it as the perfect opportunity to get acquainted with rival football fans and he was nicked for wrestling with one of them up the side of our coach as the rest of us got back on it after the game.

The Kippax Branch was only one game old and already one of its members had had his collar felt. Ah, well, he wouldn't be the last.

We've had members come and go over the years, some lasting longer than others. Two that certainly didn't last long were a couple of right thickos, Ibbo and Stoggy. They were both only 19 and eager to impress the older members of the branch. They thought their case would be strengthened if they both got tattoos. So off they went to Blackpool and came back with their 'works of art'. Ibbo's was a Yorkshire rose. Underneath it were two green petals shaped into the letters S and Y, which he proudly explained stood for South Yorkshire.

'I thought you were from Sherburn?' I said.

'Yes, I am,' Ibbo replied.

'But your Sherburn isn't in South Yorkshire, it's in North Yorkshire.'

'I know, but this is the only Yorkshire rose they had on display.'

I couldn't believe it. Stoggy started laughing and Ibbo looked cross.

'I don't know what you're laughing at! Show him yours.'

And so sheepishly Stoggy pulled up his shirtsleeve to reveal a red rose.

'What the fuck is that?' I said.

'I was a bit nervous when I went in and just asked for a rose. I thought the bloke knew I was talking about a Yorkshire rose. As he was doing it I kept thinking, that's bleeding a lot. When he'd finished it, he wiped it and I asked him how long it would be before it turned white.'

We didn't see much of those two again.

Another member was Eddie Lowther. During one trip to Southampton we were all congregated in a pub en route. A drinking competition was about to start and Eddie was up against Ian 'Robbo' Robinson. The ashtray in the middle was overflowing with betting money. Eddie and Robbo each picked up their pints and put them to their lips. Eddie was beaten, but only narrowly. In fact, it was all over in seconds. I'd never seen anything like it, but over the years I've seen it many times since.

In those early days the coaches we booked didn't have toilets on board and this made it quite uncomfortable for anyone who'd had had a pint or two, never mind those who could down them in seconds. We overcame this problem with the famous Kippax Piss Pot. It was a plastic five-gallon drum. With a lid. It was positioned in the well near the front door and only had to be emptied a couple of times per trip. Well, a Midlands trip. London trips required further stops. On our return the pot would be left beside the public toilet in Kippax and would still be there for our next journey. We were very hygiene conscious and occasionally a member would take the pot home to be disinfected.

As the years went by the pot was retired and we progressed to a funnel. This was secured onto the inside of the door and a rubber pipe connected to it and ran under the door through the draft-excluding brushes. Ingenious. This option did, however, prove a little difficult if you were really desperate as the funnel would fill up very quickly, often resulting in wet jeans.

Most of us preferred another routine which was less messy but equally risky in other ways. The driver, who in those early days was a smashing fella from Wallace Arnold called Brian Greaves, would simply open the door. Whoever had to pee would then stand on the bottom step and unzip his fly. This being the Kippax Branch, he was not alone. We drink together, we pee together. And so a second person would stand behind holding him steady by the back of his belt. Obviously this method required a strong belt and an even stronger buckle. If you didn't have a belt or were wearing one of those elastic snake-buckle efforts, it was a definite no-no.

Some people vividly remember the Kennedy assassination. I remember the first time we had a coach with a toilet on it. It was for the trip to Ipswich Town in 1981.

Suddenly everything was different. Ah, the relief. Literally. The new bus seemed to us like The Ritz on wheels. The lads were queuing constantly for the toilet throughout the journey. I swear only half actually wanted to use it. The rest were just curious.

But the Kippax Branch being what it is, it soon became the 'in thing' for those outside to put their foot against the door so the occupant couldn't get out. I'm embarrassed to say the novelty of this wheeze still hasn't worn off even today. A couple of seasons ago, when we were travelling to the home game with manchester united, Andy 'Rolf' Rollinson had gone into the toilet and the giant we call 'Tico', but whose parents christened Mark Randles, thought it would be funny to put his foot up against the door. The toilet was situated towards the rear and I was sat on the back seat with a very good friend of mine, Alan Osborne, who lived in Kippax for 18 years, but has since moved back down to London. Al is a big West Ham fan and encouraged me tremendously to write this book. I heard Rolf try the handle. Now Rolf's a big guy, too, and not one to cross so I told Tico that it was probably not a good idea. To underline my point

Rolf shouted through the door, 'I'm coming out. Take your bloody foot off the door!'

Tico wasn't scared. His foot remained on the handle. I told Alan to assume the crash position. Seconds later there was an almighty bang, and all three walls of the toilet collapsed and the door was left leaning over Tico. Rolf merely laughed and walked back to his seat. Luckily, we have many tradesmen members and the toilet was soon reconstructed, good as new.

As the years have rolled on the Kippax branch has unfortunately received some unfair criticism from the committee of the official LUSC. At times the criticism was warranted but more often than not, it was our so-called 'reputation' that rose above anything else. With the benefit of hindsight I'd admit our logo of the Jolly Roger probably isn't the most sensible emblem, but it is only a joke.

Once, though, we devised a plan for about a hundred of us to stay in Whitby the night before a match in Middlesbrough and sail there aboard a hired trawler. Whitby John found a suitable boat with willing pilot. But there was a snag – the voyage would have taken over a day. And the insurance we would have needed was astronomical.

So let me make this perfectly clear: we're not real pirates, just pretend ones. We travel by bus, not galleon. Not everyone understands this. The police once confiscated our Jolly Roger. At Millwall. Claiming it could cause a riot. Get a grip, please!

On 11 May 1985, the tragic fire at Bradford City, in which 56 people lost their lives, overshadowed the riot at St Andrews on the same day. Leeds were playing Birmingham in the final game of the season and the game had to be held up because of fighting between Leeds and Birmingham fans. The disturbance continued long after the game had finished, with police and both sets of fans involved in a pitched battle. A 12-year-old Leeds fan from the Midlands was killed outside the ground when a wall collapsed. He was attending his first football match. In the case of the Heysel Stadium disaster, many Liverpool fans were charged with manslaughter when they rushed at Juventus fans, who died when a wall collapsed. At Birmingham the wall collapsed due to pressure inside the ground from Leeds fans who were being crushed against the wall by surging West Midlands Police officers. I firmly believe that certain officers should have faced the same charge of manslaughter.

All these events led to the Popplewell Inquiry (1986). The Department of Sociology at Leicester University held an investigation and, headed by John Williams, submitted a major report to Justice Popplewell as part of a government inquiry. Williams referred to an occasion when he watched a match at Elland Road from The Kop terrace with a number of Kippax members.

He noted that during the first half, a group of Leeds fans from Brighouse began throwing objects at the opposing goalkeeper as he began his run-up for goalkicks. Despite a number of warnings from within the crowd, the throwing persisted and many Kippax members surged down to the area where the objects were being thrown from and, in Williams's words, 'dealt out some summary "justice" to those involved'. The injured party left and the throwing stopped.

The report appeared to defend the Kippax's use of violence in this manner in order to stop a potentially damaging episode for Leeds United. Other Leeds fans he spoke to told him that similar intervention had once prevented the destruction of a television gantry at Oxford United when some Leeds fans tried to force a match to be abandoned.

The report also cited Collar and myself for attempts to restore peace in a match at St Andrews. 'On this occasion,' the report reads,

> with the pitch littered with missiles and the occasional brick and lumps of wood still flying from the Leeds terrace at Birmingham fans and the police, 'Collar', a miner now in his 30s, but still acknowledged and recognised as a respected leader, in their travelling end, by the Leeds fans, walked down onto the pitch between the lines of police officers and the Leeds terraces and began clearing the pitch of missiles. Other members of the 'Kippax' crew followed and within a matter of seconds around 50 Leeds fans were involved in the clearance. 'Snake' and other members of the 'Kippax' manned the open gates at the fence at the Leeds end of the ground to see that others did not misinterpret this peaceful

gesture as the signal for an aggressive pitch invasion. 'Scouse', another Kippax fan involved, shook hands with a police officer who thanked him and told him that Leeds fans had 'done their best' but that they should now leave the pitch before they were arrested.

It should be noted that, after the publication of this report, one of the authors, John Williams, arrived at Leeds to find out what the reaction would be from the Kippax. Many members took exception to the branch being cited and certain members who were named confronted him. He was asked, in no uncertain terms, to leave.

But despite the credit – or otherwise – afforded to Kippax by the Taylor Report, one major incident on 13 May 1989 was, I believe, the opportunity the LUSC authorities were waiting for. We had been to watch Leeds play the final game of the season at Shrewsbury Town. We had settled in Stafford for a drink, when we were approached by some policemen.

'I'm sorry, lads, we'll have to ask you to move on. Wolves fans are on their way back from Preston, we don't want any trouble.'

Neither did we. We moved out with out any argument.

'Where can we go at this time of night for a drink?' someone asked a policeman as we boarded our coach.

'I don't really care, mate,' he replied. 'Just get out of our jurisdiction.'

We headed up the M6 and turned off onto the A6. 'Alsager six miles' read the sign. It was dark as we arrived, and as I headed into the nearest pub with a few others, some opted to walk down the road in search of another.

About an hour later our coach driver Dave Walker, my brother-in-law at the time, was sat playing cards with myself, Gord, Tico and Mally King. Then Andy Bell ran in.

'Quick, it's kicked off at the other pub!' he said and disappeared.

We didn't take much notice to be honest. How much trouble can there be in a sleepy place like Alsager? Ten minutes later Andy came running back in.

'Come on!' he insisted. 'It's really kicking off, big style!'

And so, reluctantly we left the pub. Coming up the hill were about

50 local lads who didn't look like they were about to buy us a drink. Our coach was parked further down the hill in the 100 yards or so between us. It didn't take a genius to work out that if they got to it before we did, they would surely smash it to bits. We had no choice. Mally led the charge. We ran past our bus, which Dave hopped on to, while the rest of us continued on to meet them face-to-face. Some more of our lads appeared and joined in. A right old rumble took place. And lasted fully half an hour. I had never witnessed anything like it before – or since.

At one stage a single police car arrived with four officers inside. They drove into the middle of the melee but chose discretion over valour and sat there awaiting reinforcements. When three or four police cars and vans arrived they waded into the fray and, finally, peace broke out in Alsager. It was about eleven o'clock.

As we were ushered back onto our bus we realised that Tico was missing. We were told that he had been attacked further down the road and was on his way to hospital. Having established where, we opted to go by taxi to visit him immediately. But as Jack Pratt, Gary Sharp and I prepared to set off, a policeman blocked our exit.

'Can I have your attention gentlemen, please?' he said, addressing the whole coach. 'I'm afraid your friend in the hospital is in a coma and is in a bad way.'

His comments were met with stunned silence. Our taxi plan was cancelled. Within half an hour we were all in custody, including our driver, and were interviewed well into the night before being allowed to go to sleep. The following morning we all received a cooked breakfast in our cells, indicating the day ahead would be a long one. An hour later we were allowed out into the yard to play football. At lunchtime another meal arrived and then it was back out to play football. At around five o'clock we were called in for our tea. At about ten o'clock I was just about to ask for a menu and the wine list, when we were told we were about to be released. Sadly for the Kippax Branch every one of us had been charged with the very serious matter of violent disorder. Even sadder was that we still had no news of Tico.

Driving home it turned out that we had all been interviewed very thoroughly, even as far as being asked which school we had gone to.

Mark 'Jaws' Dunn, never the sharpest tool in the shed, had apparently replied: 'Oh, the one at the end of our street.' The detectives sighed and he went to have his photograph taken. After a full-face shot had been taken he responded to the command of 'Turn left please' by innocently doing a half turn to face the wall, revealing the back of his head. He was released almost immediately. Maybe he wasn't so thick after all.

Tico came out of his coma the following Monday afternoon, 48 hours after the incident. Mally, Gord, Stevie Priestley and I went down to see him that night. Even today Tico doesn't fully recollect what happened and occasionally suffers from loss of memory.

We all waited anxiously through the summer, expecting to hear from the police. Finally we each received a letter requesting our presence at Crewe Police Station one weekend in August. Some would be seen on the Saturday and the rest on Sunday, but we would not be notified until a couple of days beforehand of which.

On the Sunday in question Leeds were due to play Anderlecht at home in a friendly. I hatched a plan in case I was called on that day. I was going to take a 'fall' down some stairs and go to casualty, instead of the police station. Luckily this far from flawless plan was never put to the test and I was able to go to Elland Road without any bandages on. It transpired that the ones called on the Sunday were the ones who would be charged.

Out of the forty-five lads on the coach, five or six were charged and each fined £400. About the same number of Alsager lads were also charged and fined. It appeared that the 'sleepy little town' we had driven into was actually the Dodge City of Cheshire.

Word soon got around about our little adventure after it appeared on the television news and in newspapers. Ray Fell and Eric Carlile from the LUSC went to Alsager to investigate the incident and interview local people. There was insufficient evidence to lay the blame firmly at our door. But by now the committee was firmly on our case. Our copybook was indelibly blotted.

But that incident wasn't what the Kippax Branch was about. Far more typical is something that happened just a few months later, at the start of the following season when we were travelling to an evening fixture at Stoke City in August 1985 and we drove into a small town for a pint. I'm certain we were travelling *to* the fixture because Leeds were about to lose 6–2 so on the way back we'd have been looking for more than one pint . . .

One of the lads discovered a skip full of old junk and looking through it he came across dozens of old school caps. He gathered them all up and came into the pub to begin distributing them. Before very long we were all sat there wearing these caps. When the time came to board the coach again Dave the driver collapsed in laughter as nearly 60 lads – most over six-foot tall with large beer bellies, all wearing these brown school caps – filed past him.

As we drove away we became aware of a massive police escort, including a police helicopter. Surely they weren't about to nick us for lifting caps out a skip? Not exactly . . . We found out from them later that they thought the caps were part of our 'hooligan outfit' and we were a large gang looking for trouble with City fans. I still wonder, even today, what the police must have thought when they saw this crew of lads sporting brown school caps, easily four sizes too small on most of us. Most of us – I still see little Greg Sturrock wearing his now and it's a perfect fit.

Unfortunately, nobody from the LUSC was there that day and rarely have they recognised that as well as having more than a few laughs, we have also showed some real community spirit.

Throughout the existence of the Kippax Branch we always contributed to collections by the LUSC, took part in inter-branch quizzes, always supported the annual dinner dance and were ever present at the fortnightly meetings. Since 1983 we have had a very good relationship with Manchester City Supporters Club, in particular their Denton & Gorton Branch, who we still play annually in the Kippax Versus Kippax football game – of which much more later. The official LUSC, however, never recognised this event and never mentioned it at meetings and other gatherings. This despite the fact that any similar activities by other branches never fail to be well publicised. We also had – and still have – a very good ongoing relationship with many overseas supporters from Belgium, Holland and Scandinavia. And the Kippax Branch was mentioned favourably by Justice Popplewell in the Taylor Report.

Before my halo slips and chokes me, I'll admit again that some Lurpak did melt in our mouths, but at times we were most certainly unfairly treated.

It was a sad day for me when the Kippax Branch was voted from the official LUSC in 1995, six years after the incident in Alsager. Even that seemed to be done unfairly as we had received many proxy votes in our favour, but they weren't accepted on the grounds that: 'The branches should have made personal appearances, if they felt so strongly.' This despite the fact that many of the branches were from hundreds of miles away and the meeting was held on a Thursday evening. The vote margin on the night was very narrow and would not normally have been enough to carry through our expulsion – but it did.

Naturally we appealed, but that was a bigger farce than the first meeting. Two 'independent' supporters were handpicked to act as adjudicators. When I saw who the supporters were, I was encouraged. I knew them both and they had both been good friends with me over the years. Our other representatives and I were asked to leave the room while our friends were 'briefed'. When we came back in the room, they were both a bag of nerves and had obviously been warned against supporting us. The meeting was over in less than 15 minutes and, even then, I walked out before the end. We will always be eternally grateful to the branches that gave us their support, as well as Eric Carlile who remains a good friend to us all.

After the demise of the Kippax Branch we went underground. Initially, we were told that we couldn't join any other branch en masse but should split up and join other branches in small numbers if we chose to. Some did briefly form other unofficial groups before almost 60 of us, rather cheekily, regrouped under the banner of the existing Holbeck Branch. Holbeck only had about six travelling members, one of whom was Ray Fell. Ray, as expected, promptly resigned and joined another branch. Ray and I have crossed swords on many an occasion. But during recent events at Elland Road, notably the sales of Woodgate and other top players, Ray stood up to the club and Peter Ridsdale on behalf of the Supporters Club and let them know of the fans' feelings. For that he must be commended. Holbeck, under the leadership of Ralph Benson and Paul 'Robbo' Robinson, became one of the largest branches in the country with nearly 200 members.

But the spirit of Kippax lives on and in September 2002 we formed a splinter group, the Hunslet Branch, officially recognised and run by Tony Pritchard and John 'Bremner' Greenhill. John we call Bremner because he looks like him – or like Jerry Springer, take your pick. We have one or two other celebrity lookalike members such as Paul 'George Clooney' Trueman and Mick 'Danny Mills' Halliday. Less famous looking but far noisier is Collar's brother Laurence Coles who – despite not being able to speak or hear – can, along with his buddy Marie Muter, make more din that the rest of us put together.

We now have a bizarre situation where there are three different branches drinking together in The Viaduct before every home game. But there is no animosity and when the coaches arrive we split up and head for the game separately!

For our London trips we invariably end up in the nick! A good friend of ours, Mick Tomlinson, is a prison warder and regularly arranges visits for us to the officers clubs inside Wormwood Scrubs, Pentonville and Holloway. Tommo then travels with us to the game along with other 'Leeds-Supporting Screws'.

I look back over the Kippax days with great fondness. They were, without doubt, the best years I have travelled. During the '80s it was simply a laugh a minute. The LUSC thinks differently, but the Kippax lives on.

- 5 -

Marriage Made in Seven (Days)

At least with football I know where he is.

Lesley Edwards

I think she has something else lined up.

Gary Edwards

To be perfectly honest, I don't think I was suited to normal married life. But then my marriage to Bev was a less than significant part of my life, as it only lasted a matter of weeks. In fact, it took longer to arrange the wedding than it did to separate afterwards. She and I initially planned to get married in the summer of 1978. But when I bought and moved into a house in Kippax in the spring of that year, Bev suggested bringing the wedding forward. I pointed out that this would mean getting married midweek, but she insisted. We chose 1 March. It was chaos from the start.

The very day we were to wed, Leeds United, in the middle of a fixture pile-up caused by heavy snow in February, rearranged an away game against manchester united. The snow had started falling one Thursday evening as people were making their way home from work. Mine became one more of several vehicles abandoned for a couple of days up the hill into Kippax. All over the district, people were stranded in the towns or cities where they worked. This caused havoc with the football – as well as my wedding. I took Bev down to the registry office in Park Square to cancel our big day and book another. The man at reception drew a line through our names and sighed. He was full of the joys of spring. So was I, when a few days later, Allan Clarke scored at the Stretford End and Leeds won 1–0.

Meanwhile, back in Park Square, I had an idea.

'Let's get married on my birthday,' I suggested, trying to raise Bev's spirits a bit.

The man at reception booked us in again, this time for March 28th – when I'd turn 22. But once again, Leeds United intervened. Despite the fact that they played at Everton on the 25th and were at home to Wolves on the 27th, they brought a home fixture with Leicester City forward a day to the 28th. I didn't realise at the time but fate was surely trying to tell me something.

The man at the registry office was delighted to see me again. He looked at me over his glasses, with a smug smile.

'Ah, Mr Edwards . . .' He opened his book. 'Shall I scrub this date as well?'

I nodded and apologised for the inconvenience.

'Shall I make it for April Fools' Day?' he suggested sarcastically.

'I can't,' I replied. 'That's Norwich away.'

He wasn't at all amused.

In the end, Leeds beat Leicester 5–1 – an extra birthday treat – and we postponed the ceremony until the end of the season, around the time the World Cup finals in Argentina started. We would be divorced before the competition had ended.

The ceremony, too, was what could only be described as brief. We were to be married at 1.30 p.m. and at 12.45 p.m. I was still playing darts with my best man Gordon in The Royal Oak. The landlord, Harry Britten, came through to the bar.

'Your sister Julie's on the phone again, Gary,' he said.

It was the third time she had rung, each time telling me with increasing urgency to hurry up or we were going to be late. This time she sounded a little concerned, demanding I tell her exactly what I was up to.

'I'm not sure about this,' I replied, in all honesty. But Julie wasn't amused.

'I've bought a new frock for this,' she said. 'I'll pick you up in ten minutes. Be ready!'

She arrived outside the Oak as promised, ten minutes later, driving her purple Morris Marina decorated with white ribbons. She drove Gordon and I straight to the registry office where we were greeted with icy stares from Bev and her family. I liked Bev's family, especially her two brothers, Andy and Michael, and I hoped they liked me, but they didn't seem too impressed at the moment.

'Hello, dear,' I said, innocently. 'You look nice.'

She said nothing. Julie's husband at the time, Dave, worked on the buses. He would later become our branch's regular coach driver for away games. Today he'd taken half an hour off work and was dressed for the occasion in his rather fetching, dark green Leeds City Transport uniform. I winked at him and laughed, keen to get the ordeal over with. In minutes it was and we were back at the Oak for the reception. I'll never forget the first words I awoke to the next morning.

'You won't be going to Queens Park Rangers on Saturday, will you?' said Bev. 'Now that we're married and all that?'

For the first two years I had known her, Bev had been great, but she changed with married life. Selfishly, perhaps, I didn't. A number of conflicts developed, not least over my devotion to following Leeds. The final straw came one day when she came home from shopping, smiling mischievously. She struggled through the door with a large box, put it down and encouraged me to open it. I slid a knife through the seal and lifted the lid. It was a full set of saucepans. Red saucepans.

'What do you think?' she asked. By way of an answer I picked up the box, opened the front door and threw the pans, one by one, all the way down Helena Street. It was the only time either of us heard anything like the sound of church bells ringing.

A couple of weeks after my marriage to Bev, I decided to have a Christmas party. In fact, I had an unofficial party every week, but I thought a proper Christmas party would be just the ticket. It was

July, but people might not notice, I thought. So 100 invitations were sent out and the following week 100 people turned up. Everyone brought small gifts, which were placed under the tree. Small pine trees being difficult to come by in July, I made do with an artificial one.

Many of my guests had been taken by surprise, so not all of them brought a card. No matter, I'd made a few of my own. One was from Stevie Wonder. I remember some of his words seemed to continue off the edge of the card.

Paul Matthews and his wife Hilary were among the first to arrive. Like everyone else, they were still there the next day when the pub opened for lunchtime. It must have meant that people had enjoyed themselves. I certainly had. And so my July Christmas parties became an annual event. And everyone buys an extra card in December.

The first one I held after moving into my present house, in 1986, must have given the neighbours quite a shock. The house is in a quiet, respectable cul-de-sac. And so they probably cringe at the large Leeds United flag I have flying from a mast on the roof. It was the Christmas parties, though, that initially got the tongues wagging. I do actually get on well with the neighbours, but one particular festive gathering did strain relations with Brian and Geraldine, the couple next door. Things were in full flow and although I tried, I apparently had no success in minimising the noise levels.

Brian knocked on my door and pointed this out. In fact, he returned to do this several times throughout the night. But apart from Big John and Eddie having a friendly wrestle over the bonnet of my van on the drive, everything went off peacefully, if not quietly. Music was one thing, but what really raised the decibel levels was when someone found my videotape of Leeds United 5 manchester united 1 from 1972. The stereo was rested but every time Leeds scored, the roof nearly came off. When the tape finished, it was rewound and the whole ritual was repeated.

The Southampton 7–0 video didn't help any either and at half past six in the morning the police came. Brian, quite understandably, had had enough.

I met the two police officers at the front door. 'Happy Christmas!'

I said. Fortunately they took it in good spirit, but they left me in no doubt that the noise levels would have to fall dramatically. 'Just try and keep it down a bit,' said one. 'It's late, er . . . early . . . er . . . whatever. Anyway, just keep it down!' The other officer was looking at the Christmas tree in the bay window. The lights were flashing on and off merrily. He looked back at me, then at the lights, then at me again. He didn't say a word. Just as they were about to leave one of the lads, Fish, made his way to the door and asked them which way they were going. 'Back to the station at Garforth,' said the first officer. Fish seized his chance. 'Do us a favour, old mate, take a left and drop us up t'hill will ya?' The police obliged.

I returned to the party and stumbled upon a crowd gathered around John Sutcliffe. John had fallen asleep. This was the cue for someone to Sellotape his eyes and mouth closed and stuff a cigarette butt up each of his nostrils. It seemed only a matter of time before John woke up and the crowd were eager to see his reaction. Ah, the joys of Christmas.

Although Brian and Geraldine moved out many years ago, I'm happy to say I'm still on their Christmas card list. Although it arrives in December.

It takes a special kind of woman to put up with me. And Christmas parties in July. That woman's name is Lesley. We met around this time in 1978.

I didn't plan to get re-hitched quite so soon but we met in the romantic setting of the Kippax Oak's pool room – the same pub where I'd had my wedding reception – and it was love at first break.

I don't mean to be sloppy, but Lesley is a special breed. I don't think there is another female on the planet who would tolerate my exploits. In 2003 we celebrated our 25th anniversary together and she probably deserved some kind of medal.

Actually, although we call it an anniversary, we aren't married. She took my surname by deed poll because we were about to take a pub in 1979 and in those days prospective hosts had to be married. However, the same surname was sufficient for us to be awarded a pub. We were all set to move in when Lesley looked at me a little puzzled.

'You're being very calm about all this,' she said.

'Er, what do you mean?' I replied.

'Well, you know that for the first 12 months of our tenancy the brewery expects total commitment – without holidays or bringing in relief staff . . . You'll have to give up Leeds United.'

I pulled the plug on the plan and got my paint brushes back out.

Lesley and I are the same age – but only for two weeks every year. Then I become older. Every week and day of the year I call her 'Wub'. It's a bit soppy but it comes from my childhood. When I lived at home with my parents and sister, Julie, we took in a foster child for a short while. Her name was Annette Morris. She was about nine and she had a slight speech impediment. Unable to pronounce 'love', she said 'wub' instead. Annette's brother Trevor, who was taken in by our neighbours, the Booths, nurtured my cartooning and painting skills. I still keep in contact with him almost 40 years later. His third and eldest child, Norman, is now married to my sister Julie.

Notwithstanding her devotion to me, Wub is highly intelligent. She has successfully completed a seven-year Open University course in psychology and is a member of Mensa. She works in Leeds and holds down a good job at Tetley's brewery. We were clearly made for each other.

She does suffer, however, from one mental deficiency, of a geographical nature. She is not very good at finding places. Show her an atlas and she comes over all faint. It might be some kind of chemical imbalance that plagues her sisters, too. Her younger sister, Julie, a lecturer and children's nursery inspector, once turned down a lunch invitation to Park Lane College in Leeds because all the doors and corridors in the college were painted the same orange colour and she knew she would not be able to find her way back to her designated classroom if she left it.

Wub's affliction is particularly noticeable when she is driving but certainly isn't confined to those terrifying moments while at the wheel of car. She has worked at Tetley's since the early '70s, but even after three decades got lost on her way to a board meeting when she strode purposefully into a cleaning cupboard instead. The cleaner inside it, skiving off work for a quick smoke, got the fright of his life. It is on the road, though, where she is at her most useless and her powers of navigation are almost totally flawed. Wub firmly believes – as does her other sister, Gina – that there are two M1 motorways: one heading north, the other going south. All three sisters hold down successful jobs, Gina in hotel management. Her career has taken her to some of the world's top hotels and she somehow found her way to all of them, even one as far away as San Diego, California. It must have been a fluke. On her way up the ladder she fluffed an interview at Green Flag Breakdown when she was directed to a map of Great Britain and asked to show where certain places were. It was the end of the road for Gina and Green Flag. She just put her face in her test paper and cried.

As someone who finds his way to football grounds all over the world I can do nothing but offer sympathy. Then laugh. I must add however, that I always sit at the back of a coach.

The gene for this chemical deficiency has also been passed to my daughter Vicky, aka Spoon, but she is in denial. She too holds down a good job in the hotel trade. On her very first day as a hotel receptionist in Leeds city centre, Spoon took a call from an Irish customer. He wanted to book in a party for a forthcoming Leeds game. After checking the book she said: 'I'm very sorry, sir, we're bully fucked.'

I'm happy to report that she has since moved well up the ladder in her hotel career.

Once upon a time, though, she sold mortgage finance. As a reward for her supreme performances, she was given the use of a brand new BMW Z3 to drive for two weeks. But aiming to drive to the NEC in Birmingham, she joined the M1 and travelled north. In those days, it only went as far as Leeds but she stuck at it until the road ran out. A few years ago she was travelling with friends to a cinema between Leeds and Huddersfield, a few miles to the west. She rang me, and I gave her very clear directions, but three hours later as the car was moving slowly in traffic, she noticed an ambulance draw alongside, bearing the words Humberside Ambulance Service. They had found the M62 without any problems, but had headed east and were in Hull, 70 miles in the wrong direction. It could have been worse. If there had been a ferry in the port with its doors down they could still have been driving round Europe today. If it had been summer time,

I could have gone to find her, but if Leeds were playing it would have been down to Wub. On second thoughts, that doesn't bear thinking about.

Back in the mid-'80s Wub used some of her spare time to throw 'parties' and sell goods for Ann Summers. That's the company that markets marital aids and lingerie among many other items designed for adult fun. She was so successful at her part-time venture that Ann Summers offered her a full-time position with a new car and a great salary. After much thought she opted to stay at Tetley's, but she continued do three or four parties a week. Once the orders were taken I liked nothing better than to accompany her on her rounds delivering the goods. It was great fun to wave at the girls from the car as they came to receive their 12-inch vibrators and handcuffs. They would snatch the bags (plain brown paper, of course) then run back indoors blushing like virgins. Wub threatened me every trip that if I didn't stop doing this, she wouldn't let me come anymore. I promised each time that this had been the last, but it never was.

I used to chuckle, too, when she was getting ready to go to her parties. She took her job very seriously and her sales pitch involved taking a large bottle of wine, which she would open if she reached a certain target; it worked every time. The funny bit was that she used to take a large male blow-up rubber doll with her. I christened the doll Rupert and got quite attached to him myself. But not in the way you're thinking.

Poor old Rupert had a few tiny punctures and no matter how hard she tried she could not stop him, er, going down. In an attempt to locate where the air leaked out of him she would fill the bath with water, throw Rupert in it, push his head and body under the surface and wait for bubbles to appear. It was an alarming sight, very reminiscent of Britain's notorious 1940s serial killer John George Haigh – except he used to immerse his victims in a bath full of acid. She would push Rupert's torso under but his leg would stick up; then she pushed the leg down, an arm would stick up. But she persevered and having located any leaks she would towel Rupert dry and apply special glue to his damaged areas. She would then bundle him into two black dustbin liners, one over the top half of the body and the other over the lower half and walk briskly to the car and place him in the back. I used to watch out of the front window and every time, without fail, I would count at least four windows down the street with the net curtains twitching.

Many of Wub's friends were regular customers and I knew most of their partners. One of them, Gordon, drinks with me in The Royal Oak in Kippax. The landlord there, Noel Axall, we used to call 'Dormouse' because he was nearly always asleep and we hardly ever saw him. In fact, he usually only woke up just before closing time and would then want us to stay a little longer because he hadn't seen us all evening. Whenever we can we like to help a friend out. As well as dozy, Noel was very unobservant. After one of Wub's parties Gordon placed one of his wife's latest purchases, a 14-inch black rubber dildo, on one of the shelves of bric-a-brac, between a dusty teapot and a pile of old books. Four days later Noel still hadn't spotted it while all his customers grinned, winked and pointed. Then Gordon brought his wife in for a drink. She spotted it the moment she sat down and brought the house down by shouting, 'Gordon, that's my dildo up there! I wondered where that had gone.'

In the Oak on Saturday, 19 August 1987, the bell rang for last orders. I was sat there with some of the lads. We were in high spirits as we had returned from Elland Road after seeing Leeds United slaughter Leicester City. The score was only 1–0 but we had still slaughtered them. A brilliant solo effort by John Sheridan separated the two sides. Actually it was a penalty, but a bloody good one nonetheless.

This particular day Rupert had spent the whole day in the pub – he didn't have a ticket. He was still dressed in a Leeds shirt and was wearing some rather fetching black lace knickers inside which, for added realism, was a large vibrator. It was nearly time to take him home. Looking around I spied Rupert stood at the bar in the tap-room. He liked it there. After yet more talking with the lads singing John Sheridan's praises, Rupert and I finally prepared to leave in my American car.

As I left the Oak's car park I checked my rear-view mirror and noticed a police car. When I looked again I saw it was following me. Now I'm not saying I was over the limit, but I thought I'd better play it safe so I pulled over and stopped the car. As I did the coppers overtook and pulled up in front of me. They then began reversing back towards me. Thinking fast, and bearing in mind that because it's an American car I'm on the pavement side, I took the keys from the ignition and got out. As the police car crept towards mine, I bent down and shouted back: 'Cheers for the lift, goodnight.'

I then made my way round the back of the house I had parked outside. Once there, I couldn't resist peeping back through the hedge and watching the two officers walk towards my car. I saw one tap on the window and then shine his torch into what he thought was the driver's side. Rupert just sat there with a blank expression, mouth wide open and both his arms stretched out. I thought it best to leave. Not surprisingly, I was never contacted by the police and never heard anything about the incident. But I often imagine the two officers entering into a pact right there on the spot: 'You say nowt, I say nowt.'

The next day I returned for the car and realised that in my haste I had parked it not far from a school. As I approached, a group of children were pointing at it and peering inside, some sniggering among themselves about the 'funny man in the car' while another asked its mother about the 'big tube of smarties' he had in his knickers. I walked straight past the car and returned under the cover of darkness.

That American car, and many others since, were a result of the influence of Wub's dad, Harry. He is an amazing character, a former diver and firearms expert who is as fit as a fiddle even in his 60s. He wears his hair in a tight crew-cut, drives only American cars and always has a stogie clamped between his teeth. Harry used to buy and sell shipwrecks, and when the coastguard informed him that someone had been spotted 'working' a wreck of his off the north-east coast near Amble, he asked if I would go up with him to investigate. As it turns out nothing untoward happened but I did by chance stumble across an ancient-looking sports shop that contained a set of very rare metal Leeds United badges. I'm an avid collector and once took Wub on a five-day 'holiday' round England scouring sports shops looking for just such badges. Like I said, she's a very special breed of woman.

Spoon got married during the summer of 2002 to Steven. His father, Mick, suffers from the common disease of being a fan of manchester united. In his defence, I have to say that Mick is above average intelligence. He is also very brave and I am sure that in time to come, and with the continued help and support from family and friends, he will overcome this nagging illness, and will soon be able to live a normal life. Thankfully the disease is not hereditary and Steven is a happy and healthy Leeds fan.

I went on Steven's stag day and night out. During the evening we trawled the countless bars in Leeds city centre and during the day, about 20 of us went go-karting at Tockwith near York. As we all sat there being briefed on the rules and safety aspects, I noticed that all the overalls were red. I looked around desperately to find overalls of a different colour. I spied a pair of bright-orange ones under a table – they looked as though they belonged to one of the instructors, but I was having them. I shuffled my chair along the floor until I reached the table. As the briefing went on I ducked under the table and snaffled the orange overalls. When the talk was over, everyone scrambled to get their helmets and overalls and I ran out of the room with my orange ones under my arm. The helmets all seemed to have red stripes on them as well, so I scoured the pile until I found a black-and-yellow one. I then retired to a quiet corner to get ready. Now, I am easily 15 stone and my overalls would have been a tight fit for a Gerry Anderson puppet, as would the helmet. With the sleeves halfway up my arms and almost my entire shins showing, I tried to pull up my front zip – not a chance! My beer belly prevented the zip moving more than a couple of inches. Putting the helmet on was another major operation. I squeezed it over my head, but it was so tight it must have looked as though I had turned Japanese. I struggled to the kart with my legs wide apart and both my arms sticking out. Paul Naylor was my teammate and he laughed as I slowly lowered myself into the seat. Despite being relatively slow at our changeovers, due to my movement restriction, we finished a creditable third. Gina's boyfriend Steve had to help me out of my overalls afterwards.

The wedding itself took place at Gretna Green and it was a splendid affair. Our party arrived the day before and headed for the nearest pub to watch the World Cup game between England and

Argentina. The favourable result got our weekend off to a great start, and, of course, our Scottish friends were also delighted with England's win. Me, I was already thinking about Leeds United's next pre-season tour.

6

Big in the '70s

I'm not in it for the glory. I'd have changed teams long before now. I know we will never ever win the FA Cup again while I'm alive. We just won't.

Gary Noble was my constant travelling companion during the 1970s. He's a fellow Kippax resident and Gaz and I became inseparable during our trips the length and breadth of Britain and Europe.

Gaz was not blessed with the best luck in the world. He was once hitch-hiking to a match in Ipswich when a van hit his outstretched thumb and broke his hand. Another time, in Blackpool, he became separated from Albert Woodhead and myself and found himself at the fairground. This we learned a few hours later when he arrived back at the hotel with a broken jaw sustained in a fight with some fairground workers. His jaw was wired up for three months. All he could eat was soup. On the bright side, however, he became a very accomplished ventriloquist.

In Leeds' 1973–74 UEFA Cup campaign, sandwiched between trips to Norway and Portugal was a November journey to an away match against Hibernian in Edinburgh. The first leg at Elland Road had been a goalless draw. As Gaz and myself set off on a full Wallace

Arnold coach we hoped for better in the second leg. Once in Edinburgh, the two of us went into the Hibs Supporters Club.

Over the years I've had some good slurps in opposition supporters club bars. Contrary to what you might expect, most are OK if you behave yourself. Liverpool, for example, is a particularly good one. But it has to be said that the Hibs fans there weren't the friendliest I had encountered, so we didn't stay long. Perhaps it was because in those days I wore a denim jacket with Leeds patches sewn all over it. Gaz had jeans with Leeds patches on them. I guess you could say that we stood out a little. But we weren't the only ones, as the Hibs fans seemed to be having no trouble identifying people they fancied thumping. As we entered Easter Road, where the ground stands, quite a few minor scuffles were breaking out between the two sets of supporters.

Inside the ground, the main mobs of Hibs fans were congregated on the halfway line, directly opposite Gaz and me. Leeds fans were split into small bunches all around the ground. Some English squaddies were stood near us and were shouting for Leeds – sometimes a little too loudly for our liking. Inevitably they attracted attention and pretty soon there were aggressive-looking Hibs fans dotted all around us. As the chant of 'Hi-bees! Hi-bees!' echoed all over the ground, the game remained tense and goalless. In fact, after both periods of extra time it was still 0–0, which meant that the tie would have to be decided on penalties.

Lorimer scored one for Leeds and a bottle hit one of the squaddies on the head. Come Leeds' fifth penalty all we needed to do was score to go through. Billy Bremner stepped up to take it. As if things weren't bad enough on the terraces, Bremner, unbelievably, began teasing the Hibs fans and taunting them as he prepared to take the kick. The catcalls and boos were deafening as he slowly deliberated over placing the ball on the spot. The referee told him to get a move on. I was doing the same thing under my breath, eager to escape the increasingly hostile atmosphere. Suddenly and unexpectedly Bremner took just one step back and tucked the ball confidently into the corner of the net, sending the keeper the wrong way in the process. It was one of the cheekiest penalty kicks I've ever seen.

As the Leeds players celebrated, we braced ourselves for the onslaught. 'Here we go, Lar,' Gaz said. For some reason he always called me 'Lar'. 'Get ready!' There was fighting all around us as Gaz and I slipped out of the ground, mingling in with the older, non-fighting, home supporters. I had slipped off my denim jacket and was holding it as low down as I could. Our biggest fear was ending up in an open space where our sew-on Leeds badges would stand out like flashing beacons. We got lucky and arrived unharmed at our bus and clambered on board. But we were not yet safe. As they filed past the coach, the Scots banged on the windows, scowling and gesturing. As the last passenger got aboard and the driver moved off we breathed more easily. Then we arrived at some traffic lights and I gulped as they turned red. Seconds later a brick came flying through the window of the seat directly behind Gaz and me. The driver decided to take the law into his own hands. On a crazy impulse he leapt off the bus and was followed off by . . . nobody. He'd been sat in the bus all evening. We'd met these guys at close quarters. And so we watched as he disappeared down a side street chasing about 20 Hibs fans and wondered who should drive us home. But about ten seconds later he reappeared, blood all over his face, and ran back onto the bus. Closing the door behind him he quickly sped off. He was minus his watch but had our total respect.

Nineteen seventy-four was a brilliant year. Leeds won the League and manchester united were relegated. Also, in 1974, the Kippax Scooter Club was formed. Almost all the Scooter Club were avid Leeds followers. Some of the lads even went to the games on their scooters, but I never bothered.

My first scooter was a Lambretta SX 200. I had about 40 mirrors on it and a beautiful Ancellotti seat. I wasn't what you would call an archetypal Mod. In fact, I was soon known as the scruffiest Mod in the area. My hair was way past collar length, I wore a tattered old Levi jacket that was falling apart and although I did (and still do) have a large collection of northern soul music, most of my record collection was heavy metal. It really was a bit weird.

Gaz and I had been for a pint one evening and as we came out of the pub, we both climbed onto my scooter. I started it up and rode off. As I did two large Dr Marten boots appeared briefly in the corners of my eyes. Some bastard had taken all the bolts out of my seat rest and, as we pulled away, Gaz leant back onto the rest and fell off the back.

A couple of years later the Kippax Scooter Club met at The Royal Oak pub and then 97 scooters headed for the Sherburn Coffee Bar. The police followed us all the way to Sherburn and then disappeared as we arrived at the coffee bar, a regular haunt for bikers and Hell's Angels. I don't think anyone quite knew why we had gone there in the first place. We were all young and reckless and obviously had a death wish.

The bikers looked stunned when we all pulled up and went inside for a coffee. We had been there about half an hour and although things were a bit tense, no trouble occurred and gradually the scooter boys drifted away – until there were just six of us. Like I said, we obviously had a death wish. Out in the car park, with a rising sense of foreboding, I just had time to say to Gaz, 'Here we go!', before I was hit straight between the eyes by a full-face crash helmet. The six of us stood our ground and I still recall Gord Findlay standing on his scooter wielding a large piece of lead pipe until the police arrived. Unfortunately, they arrived too late to save my scooter, which had been smashed to smithereens. I managed to ride it home, but that was its last outing. As I nursed a black eye the following night, I watched the full story of our adventure replayed on Yorkshire Television's *Calendar* programme. The fighting apparently didn't stop at Sherburn, but continued in nearby Garforth. Eddie Rollinson subsequently received a six-month jail sentence for his part in the ensuing fracas.

Various members of the scooter club were in a downstairs Gelderd End bar one Saturday afternoon before a match with manchester united.

Shortly after one o'clock our ales were interrupted by someone running down the steps. 'Quick!' he shouted. 'The bastards are coming over the pitch!' Their fans had indeed scaled the low wall at the front of the Scratching Shed and were running across the pitch aiming to 'take' the Gelderd. The stand was suddenly like a huge fire station at red alert as everyone ran upstairs to head them off. Some were already in the lower terracing and were heading up the steps towards the back. There used to be two rear stairways from the bars into the back of the Gelderd, and hundreds of Leeds fans used these to race up and repel the invaders from above. Leeds fans were also still piling up from the front stairs, so this left the manchester united fans caught in the middle. Those at the top and us at the bottom, thousands of Leeds fans in all, began singing in unison –– to the tune of 'Wandering Star' – 'I was born under the Gelderd End/Boots are made for kicking/Guns are made to shoot/If you come in the Gelderd End we'll all stick in the boot!'

Our uninvited guests didn't appear to want to sing along but seemed happy to fill us in on the chorus. They were, however, despite the advantage of surprise, hopelessly outnumbered and had no chance in the battle that ensued before hundreds of police intervened and escorted those still standing back to the Scratching Shed. Medical staff from St John's Ambulance tended to the others. The manchester united fans got what they deserved. After all, such warnings as 'Uri Gelderd, we bend limbs' had been painted very clearly on countless walls around Elland Road.

That's the only time any visiting fans came in from the other end. Although there were some who tried when the roof first went on. Many went in mistakenly thinking it was still the away end.

Neil Butterfield was there that day. He was one crazy son of a bitch in the '70s and '80s. Butter has mellowed over the years, but in those days he used to wallow in the action. He too was a member of the Kippax Scooter Club and became a regular in the South Stand that replaced the old Scratching Shed in the 1974–75 season. He liked to be as close as possible to his tormentors. Then again, he was easily tormented.

One Saturday after a home game I was in the city centre with Butter, walking from The Three Legs to The Nag's Head. A man came up to Butter and asked him for some loose change. The man was black, quite well dressed and was wearing a tan-coloured camel-haired coat. Butter took hold of him by the scruff of the neck, called him a 'cheeky bastard' and threw him up against the wall. I quickly intervened. Butter had been about to kick seven bells out of Albert Johanneson, the former Leeds United winger.

Butter continued his antics when we were outside Wembley for England's World Cup qualifier with Hungary in 1981. Match tickets were rarer than the proverbial rocking-horse shit and we still needed one more – for Butter. We encountered a ticket tout who had one, but at a price. Butter agreed to pay. They gingerly exchanged ticket for money, but Butter snatched the money back. The tout wasn't pleased when Butter decided to give him only half of the original cash back.

'Come on, mate,' said the tout. 'I've got a living to make. I'm cutting my own throat.'

Butter replied, 'Well, allow me!' and produced a flick knife. The tout held his hands up and disappeared into the night. Butter then calmly flicked the 'blade' out and combed his hair. It was only a flick comb.

At the end of the 1973–74 season I travelled down with a group of Leeds fans to watch Leeds United clinch the League Championship at Queens Park Rangers. A goal from Allan Clarke ensured United's second title under Don Revie.

Among that group was a good friend of mine and a top Leeds fan, Stuart Hayward. Ten years later Stuart was involved in a horrific car accident which left him disabled. Stuart uses a wheelchair, but very often can get about on crutches. He very rarely misses a Leeds game. He is a member of the Leeds United Disabled Organisation (LUDO), set up in 1992 to assist all disabled Leeds fans, where a very nice lady named Sam Riley keeps a watchful eye over her 'flock'. All sorts of fundraising takes place with regular contributions from all over, but in particular at the Stag in Queensbury, thanks to the landlord, Pete. Stuart attends matches with his mate, Steve Hall, who was also injured in 1984 in a bike accident. Stuart's brother, Rob, and good mate, Paul 'GG' Gee are the happy helpers, making sure everything runs smoothly – in theory.

Surprisingly, Stuart and his chums have encountered real animosity at many grounds up and down the country. On one such occasion, however, they had the last laugh over their able-bodied enemies. I remember leaving Old Trafford pushing Stuart – as usual he was dressed up in his colours – across a bridge back towards the coaches. I heard a voice shout: 'These are Leeds fans here – let's have 'em!' I then heard another voice say, 'Give over. He's in a wheelchair.'

I felt slightly relieved until the first voice shouted again, 'That bastard pushing him isn't!' Fortunately, his mates had the last say and we crossed the bridge safely.

At another game there, Stuart also had hassle trying to get a beer. It was about an hour and a half before kick-off and GG asked a steward where they could get a drink. The steward looked at the four of them and then at the two wheelchairs.

'I'll send someone round with a trolley of tea and coffee.'

'I don't think you understand . . .' said Stuart.

'We mean a drink drink!' interrupted GG.

The steward went onto his walkie-talkie and then informed them that the only place they could get a 'drink drink' would be in the home supporters' bar. Stuart and GG said they were fine with that and were duly shown the way. As they entered the bar, Stuart said it was like walking (and wheeling) into the gunfight at the OK Coral. Everything went quiet and everyone stared.

'Four pints of lager, love,' GG shouted as everyone looked on in disbelief and the barmaid began pulling a pint.

'Whoa, hold on, love,' said GG, 'not in that!'

Inside Old Trafford beer glasses carry the manchester united emblem on the side. Stuart was prepared and produced four clear glasses from his bag and handed them to GG.

'Here y'are – in these please!'

The barmaid laughed and leant across: 'I'm a City fan. I have to serve these wankers, this is great.'

As the '70s progressed, the Kippax Branch held Sunday-evening meetings in The Viaduct, although nothing was ever discussed until we had finished watching the current episode of *Fawlty Towers* on the bar television. After that it was open season on everything from the imminent departure of Duncan McKenzie to Gary Noble's recent sexual exploits in Chesterfield. These were legendary.

Travelling back from a match down south we would regularly stop off for a Saturday evening in Chesterfield. The city with its famous cathedral and crooked spire was a favourite haunt for us because with its many pubs and willing ladies of all shapes and sizes, there was something for everyone. After a match at West Ham and a night in Chesterfield we were doing a quick headcount back on the bus when Dave Walker spotted that the reason Gaz was missing was because he was behind the back of the bus 'involved' with a girl of more than ample proportions. When Gaz had finished he joined us, once again grinning from ear to ear, to a huge round of applause.

At that time I regularly drove a van for my dad's firm, Stembridge's, between Durham and Chester-le-Street. Gaz had told us that this girl, Beryl, was from the north-east and had been on a night out with friends in Chesterfield on the evening they had met. As I drove up the A1 one day I hatched a fiendish plan. Beryl hadn't revealed her surname but she and Gaz had swapped addresses. After I had dropped off my delivery I stopped at a telephone box in Chester-le-Street. I flicked through the directory looking for a random surname for Beryl. In the end I invented one – Paterson. I wrote down the telephone number of the telephone box and noted the address of the first Paterson in the phone book. I then scribbled a quick letter, cunningly with my left hand, and posted it from a post box a few yards from the telephone box. 'Dear Gary,' the letter said, 'I am writing to thank you for a great time in Chesterfield last Saturday night. I really would like to see you again. If this is OK please ring me next Monday night at 8.15. Love Beryl.' I added the phone box number and the address I had plucked from the directory in the top right-hand corner. Gaz told me of his letter and even showed me it. The agony of trying not to laugh there and then was unbearable. He asked me not to say anything to any of the lads. As if I would. Gaz and Beryl's secret was safe with me. Well, me, Alan Thursfield, Albert Woodhead, Mick Jones, Kenny Smith – in fact all The Royal Oak football team, with whom I trained every Monday night before a few beers back at the Oak.

On the appointed Monday, right on time, Gaz moved over to the public phone on the wall near the back door of the Oak – in sight of where we sat but a fair distance away. Convinced I was the only one who knew what he was doing, he kept looking over at me and shaking his head. The rest of the lads were trying to act normal, but Liam White had tears running down his face. Gaz returned to the table and normal conversation resumed. It wasn't long before Gaz leant over to me and said quietly, 'She wasn't there. I'll try tomorrow.'

Over the next couple of days he tried, unsuccessfully, to speak with Beryl. If anyone had answered the call box, the joke would have been over. Cruelly, I wrote another couple of letters and every Monday we would all sit there watching him on the telephone in The Royal Oak. I felt sure that someone would slip up, but no one did.

A couple of weeks later Leeds were playing at St James' Park, Newcastle. We were travelling up in the Stembridge's van. The van was a Luton-type Ford Transit, with no windows in the back and a metal roll shutter at the back that couldn't be opened from the inside. I arranged it so that Gaz was in the back with a couple of others and Dave Walker was in front with me. There was a small window connecting the cab with the back so it was possible to see where we were going from inside the back. Shortly before we arrived at Newcastle's ground, I pulled up outside a house. I saw a man cutting his hedge and went over to him and began talking to him. Gaz watched through the small window. Dave knew what I was doing and watched the man point over some houses and into the distance. I had actually asked him where the ground was but turned round to Gaz and said, 'See that bloke there, Gaz? That's Beryl's dad. I got the address from one of your letters. I think it's only right that you sort it out with her. He's just showed me where she works. I'm taking you there.'

With that I pulled the flap down over the window so that Gaz was completely in the dark and couldn't see where we were going. He went absolutely berserk! He was banging and kicking at the side of the van so hard it was difficult to keep driving. 'You bastard, Edwards!' he kept yelling. I definitely preferred 'Lar'. In the front beside me Dave was crying with laughter. We pulled up in a car park near the ground and I opened the back door. Gaz jumped out and ran off in the opposite direction to the ground. In his panic he hadn't even seen it. He was at the van when we returned after the match. Thankfully he had calmed down. And I told him all about the joke and the letters.

7

Glory and Disappointment in Europe

Obviously we got robbed left, right and centre. As far as I'm
concerned we won the Cup-Winners' Cup in 1973 and we
won the European Cup in '75. Both refs were then banned.
Alex Ferguson would have had the games replayed.

When what we now know as the UEFA Cup was born in 1958, it
was known as the Inter-Cities Fairs Cup. Barcelona of Spain were its
first ever winners. Leeds United became the first British team to win
the trophy, in 1968, and became the last ever team to win it before it
was re-christened by UEFA in 1971. Fittingly, with a new trophy
freshly cast, Leeds were to play Barcelona, in Barcelona, on 22
September 1971 in a play-off game to decide which team would retain
the old Fairs Cup trophy for all time. I flew out to this game with a
friend called John Walker from Middleton in Leeds.

To my eyes, the crowd in Barca's Nou Camp Stadium looked
rather small, not much over 35,000. I was disappointed because I
expected a much bigger turnout for what seemed to me a very
important game. But in the magnificent setting of the Nou Camp, a
huge bowl of a stadium that could accommodate over 100,000 fans,
just a third of that number seemed to rattle around – sadly for those

among them supporting Leeds, although Joe Jordan scored for the men in white to give us some pleasure, we went down 2–1.

After the game a few buses were on hand to take Leeds fans back to the airport and on to the flight home. By three o'clock in the morning we were touching down at Leeds Airport.

The one thing that helped me through the disappointment following Leeds United's disastrous 1973 FA Cup final defeat by Sunderland was the up-and-coming European Cup-Winners' Cup final against AC Milan in Thessalonika, Greece. I flew out on a trip organised by a firm called 4S Sports with Coleen Johnson (who later got engaged to my mate Gaz Noble), Christine Harrison (now married to Phil Beeton, a prominent member of the LUSC committee), Mick Collins, John Walker and Ralph, a small pervert from Thornton Le Dale.

As I'll say on numerous occasions in these pages, UEFA have never done Leeds United any favours, and this final was certainly no exception. I had been to Greece the previous summer when Leeds drew 2–2 with Olympiakos in a friendly. The locals had been really friendly and once again in Thessalonika, the Greeks really took Leeds United to their hearts and made us feel very welcome. Well, all of them apart from a couple of police officers when a few of us were playing football in a car park near our hotel. The officers shouted at us. We ignored them. The officers shouted at us again. We ignored them once more. Rather foolishly as it turned out. Our game was suddenly disrupted by a high-pitched scream seemingly just above my head.

'What the fuck was that?' gasped Mick Collins.

We turned to look at the police and got a sizeable clue. One of them was down on one knee, with a rifle pointed at us. The screaming noise had been a bullet whistling over our heads. We immediately put our hands up and forgot all about the ball.

It quickly became apparent that we weren't in a car park at all, but some high-security, top-secret area that was part of a military base. We were as puzzled as they were as to how we had managed to get past two security gates manned by four armed guards. We could see them now, but hadn't noticed them earlier. Then again, they hadn't noticed us either. We were allowed to leave after about ten minutes of questioning, but they kept our football. The arrest and trial of some British plane spotters in 2002 made me realise just how lucky we had been all those years ago.

On the day of the game we were all invited to a banquet laid on especially for Leeds fans. The food on our plate looked like a burger and lots of chips. Word quickly spread that the 'burger' was in fact horsemeat. When I looked up our table afterwards, all the chips had gone, but on each plate the horsemeat remained virtually untouched.

We boarded dozens of coaches and headed for the stadium. We were greeted by thousands of Greek supporters who swarmed round us, wanting souvenirs of Leeds United. I didn't want to part with my Leeds scarf, so I handed a young Greek my match programme, that I had been presented with at the hotel. This programme would today fetch well over £50, but I've still got my old silk scarf.

Paul Reaney led Leeds onto the pitch as the captain in place of the injured Billy Bremner. Within only a few minutes of the start, the Greek referee, Christos Michas, awarded AC Milan a very dubious free-kick on the edge of the Leeds penalty area. To add to our frustration at the award of the kick, Milan scored from it – the ball going in off the post after ricocheting off Trevor Cherry, Terry Yorath and an Italian forward. The referee might have been Greek but every other Greek in the stadium vented their anger towards their fellow countryman as throughout the game he denied Leeds dozens of free-kicks and penalties. This referee was determined that AC Milan were going to win the Cup-Winners' Cup and so they did, 1–0. A month later, amid allegations of bribery, Michas was banned by UEFA and never refereed a match again, but it was too late for Leeds – and the locals in the crowd.

As the Italians attempted to do a lap of honour with the trophy the angry crowd pelted them so much they retreated down the tunnel. Leeds players sat in the middle of the pitch thoroughly dejected and obviously very angry. Then with the Leeds fans and Greeks chanting together, the players did a lap of honour.

Outside, as we made our way back to our coaches we were again mobbed by the locals. We also saw a car leaving at high speed surrounded by police. It was the referee.

Back at our hotel the mood was despondent. That was until a

group of American tourists joined us. Unlike most Americans they understood football and said they had watched the game on the television and couldn't believe the decisions made by the referee. They said that the hotel staff had been apologising for these decisions all evening. In the hotel lift, the attendant spoke sorrowfully to Mick and myself: 'I am truly ashamed to be Greek this evening.'

The next morning at breakfast one of the waiters translated newspaper reports to us: the Greeks had reacted very strongly and even prominent ministers were calling for an enquiry. As we left the hotel for the airport one of the staff ran over to me and gave me the Greek flag.

As if two defeats in two finals weren't enough, news began filtering through that Don Revie was about to leave the club. Apparently, he had spoken with the players at great length before the game against Milan and informed them of his decision to move on. What a disaster 1972–73 was!

But fortunately for everyone connected with Leeds, the Don stayed on for another season and Leeds took the league apart and won the Championship. In doing so they stayed at the top of the league for the entire season, and went 29 games – almost until the end of February – before they lost a league game. And at the end of that campaign, manchester united were relegated. What a triumph 1973–74 was!

I returned to Barcelona the following season, in April 1975, to watch the second leg of the European Cup semi-final. Leeds had narrowly beaten Barcelona 2–1 in the first leg at Elland Road, with goals from Billy Bremner and Allan Clarke.

At this time I was working for a painting company, JF Meehan Ltd. For three years I had managed to keep my love for Leeds United quiet, so that I could sneak off to midweek away matches in England without anyone knowing I'd gone. However, my workmate at the time, Clive Richardson, told me that Meehan's managing director, Dick Coates, knew I was a Leeds fan and suspected I'd been taking paid leave to watch them. He was going to keep an eye on me.

For previous away European games I had split my holiday allowance up and taken it a couple of days at a time, but without saying where I had been. Camkin Sports were running a day trip for the Barcelona semi-final so I booked myself onto that.

My job at the time involved painting on building sites, working outdoors priming skirting boards, frames and doors prior to their being fixed into new houses. I did not mix with the other painters on site and instead ate my lunch with the labourers and other tradesmen in their large hut. None of them could understand why I wasn't working inside the houses with the other painters, and why I had volunteered to do the job that the other painters hated. It was really quite simple: I could leave and go to a match without anyone missing me. One building site was at Garforth, and for the home matches I'd jump on the Wimpey workers bus that dropped workers off in Leeds city centre.

The flight to Barcelona was scheduled to fly from Leeds Airport at half past eleven in the morning, but I had to show up for work first. I had arranged with Kevin Stoker, an apprentice painter who worked for another company, to pick me up at the site at half past nine in the morning. He was going to Barcelona, too. I had met Kevin at Jacob Kramer College in Leeds, while studying for my City & Guilds, along with two other Leeds fans, Steve Pattison and Tim Turner. Nine-thirty was the time for the first break of the day. As the workmen entered their hut to get at their sandwiches, I made my way to the rear site entrance into Kev's waiting car. As we drove to the airport, I changed into the clothes that he had brought me – the old denim jacket and jeans and my white silk Leeds United scarf. Most of the workers in the hut knew about me and my dedication to football and on the odd occasion that someone came looking for me they would cover for me, saying that they had just seen me going to paint a door in some street. That would do the trick and I made sure I looked after my allies, regularly supplying them with tins of paint for their DIY projects. Kev and I arrived in good time at the airport, that was by now filling up with Leeds fans.

Although the Nou Camp Stadium held 100,000 there were only 1,500 tickets made available to Leeds fans – and even then they split us up and put us into separate corners of the ground. It's a policy that many Spanish clubs still adopt today when English fans visit their stadiums.

But despite the authorities' apparent fear of the Leeds fans, the Barcelona team were supremely confident of overturning their 2–1 deficit and making it to the final. As we arrived at the stadium, there were hundreds of cars, buses, vans and bikes all painted in the blue and red stripes of Barcelona. Flags and horns were abundant and John and I agreed the Catalan supporters seemed to think the game and Barcelona's progression to the final in Paris in a month's time was a mere formality. As we entered the stadium our Leeds chants were drowned out by the overwhelming noise from the Spanish fans. We took our seats and watched in surprise as countless Barca fans were allowed to parade round the pitch with huge flags and banners. The flags were so big each one needed two or three people to hold the pole at either end of it. The poles looked big enough to hang telegraph wires between.

One banner had a cartoon painted on it showing Barcelona's Johan Cruyff driving a tank towards a kneeling Leeds player, apparently begging for mercy. The Eiffel Tower was drawn in the background. Other banners proclaimed '*Advanca Barca!*' The noise was deafening as the game got under way. Midway through the first half, Peter Lorimer put Leeds ahead. Apart from the Leeds fans, the stadium fell silent. One man had silenced over 90,000 people. Leeds led 3–1 on aggregate and still did at half-time.

During the interval, sulking that their red-and-blue-striped heroes had been unable to muster a goal in response, the Spanish fans began to get restless. Kev was hit on the back of the head by a 'missile'. Further investigation revealed that the missile was in fact a cabbage. Strangely, there were more to come. In fact, a group of Spaniards sitting ten rows behind us began hurling dozens of these green vegetables in our direction. It was one the most bizarre acts of revenge I've ever seen at a football ground. But we got quite good at dodging or catching them and it passed the time until the second half got under way.

Leeds' goalkeeper, Dave Stewart, a Scot who until three months earlier normally played for Leeds reserves, had what must have been the best game of his career to protect Leeds' lead as Barcelona sent wave after wave of attacks towards his goal. Eventually, however, one attempt did beat him and with Leeds leading by just one goal on aggregate, the home side redoubled their efforts. We feared the worst when centre-half Gordon McQueen was sent off but Leeds continued to defend brilliantly. The Barcelona fans became ever more frustrated and those in the main stand began hurling their cushions onto the pitch. This didn't bother Leeds, though, and our remaining ten men held firm to the end and as Barcelona trooped off the pitch with their heads bowed, Billy Bremner led his players to all four corners of the ground to salute the pockets of jubilant Leeds fans. Outside the ground it was almost impossible to believe it was the same place as before the game. The streets were fast becoming deserted and there was no sign of any blue and red flags anywhere. Instead Leeds fans danced about in the streets and all that could be seen was the white, blue and yellow flags of the travelling army.

Our joy was made complete when back at the airport we met and talked to the racing driver James Hunt, then driving for the English privateer Lord Hesketh. He said he was a big Leeds fan and had managed to get a ticket for the game. He was now on the look-out for a ticket for the Paris final. He certainly wasn't the only one . . .

Thursday, 8 May 1975. Seven o'clock in the morning. I was 19 years old and still living at home with ma, my dad and sister, Julie. I was sitting at the bottom of the stairs, just like I had done for the previous four days. I was waiting for the postman to deliver my ticket for the 1975 European Cup final to be held in Paris between Leeds United and Bayern Munich. Somewhere, a blond-haired racing driver might have been doing the same.

I'm not sure about James, but I had been to every Leeds game in the competition, including a trip through the Iron Curtain for the match with Ujpesti Dozsa in Hungary. This, I was informed by Leeds United, still did not guarantee me a ticket. The letterbox rattled at about quarter past seven and a bunch of letters landed on the carpet. I grabbed them and quickly discarded any that didn't have my name on them. Then I found one that did. Could this be it? Some of the other lads had received tickets, some had got letters saying they weren't going to get one. I was shaking like a dog as I tore the envelope open. I noticed immediately the Leeds United crest at the top of the letter, and, as I unfolded it, what looked like an orange ticket fell to the floor. I left it for a moment and read the letter. 'Dear Mr Edwards, we are pleased to inform you . . .' I didn't read the rest. I bent down and snatched the ticket. It read: 'FINALE – de la Coupe des Clubs Champions Européens – TRIBUNE BOULOGNE'. I started shouting and jumping about; our dog Sam was barking excitedly – he was pleased too.

'Ma, I've got one!' I shouted upstairs.

'Good lad,' she shouted back.

Then I stopped celebrating. Julie and my dad were also waiting for tickets. Dad had already gone to work and I heard nothing from our Julie's room. She appeared at the top of the stairs. 'Is there anything for me and Dad?' she asked.

'No, but they'll be on their way, I know it.'

Julie said nothing and went back into her bedroom.

Just then I heard someone outside shouting my name. I opened the back door and over the small fence that separated our two houses I saw Haggis – Graham Hargraves – beaming from ear to ear. He was clutching an orange ticket, too. 'Yessss!!' I shouted to him, waving my ticket. We began jumping about like idiots.

The next day, two tickets arrived for Dad and Julie and I felt brilliant. My ticket was for behind the goal, theirs were down the side, but it didn't matter – we all had tickets for the final.

I was going to Paris with Karen, my girlfriend at the time. Her mother Coral and father Geoff weren't particularly happy when I asked them if I could take her with me. She didn't have a ticket, but wanted to come along for the trip. After a bit of persuasion from her brother Des, they eventually agreed to let her travel. She was laughing at me through the coach window as I had my picture taken by the *Yorkshire Evening Post* just before we left Elland Road to go to Leeds Airport. I was dressed in a big white coat with Leeds painted all over it and a big white bowler hat. On top of the hat was a small replica European Cup. Karen and I were flying with the Leeds United Travellers Club and Camkin Sports. Dad and Julie were going independently and got a train from Leeds to Gatwick and then a flight onto Paris. We met them there and soon managed to get Karen a ticket from another Leeds fan in a bar, so we were all set. There were 28,000 Leeds fans in the French capital for the match, to be held at the recently built Parc des Princes Stadium. I don't know if James Hunt was among them – I looked but didn't see him there. Neutrals and Bayern fans would complete the 48,374 attendance figure.

Much has been reported on the European Cup final over the years, but much has not. Leeds United were without doubt the superior side on the night and only diabolical refereeing by Marcel Kitabdjian from France prevented them winning the trophy. Two blatant penalties were turned down and then, with about 20 minutes left, Peter Lorimer hit a perfect volley past the Bayern keeper, Sepp Maier. Leeds had been plagued with awful refereeing displays over the years, so much so that I always used to look at the referee before celebrating. This time, he signalled a goal and clearly pointed back to the centre circle. The 28,000 Leeds fans went wild. But amid the celebrations I noticed Bayern's captain, Franz Beckenbauer, run over to the linesman, who had returned to the halfway line and was recording the goal in his notebook. Leeds fans were still celebrating when the referee was called over by the linesman. Some of the celebrating stopped, then it all stopped as, unbelievably the referee ran back to the spot where Lorimer had scored from and pointed to the ground. Everyone was totally confused and this confusion turned to anger with the realisation that the goal had been disallowed. We discovered afterwards that, in effect, Beckenbauer had disallowed Lorimer's goal because he said that Billy Bremner had been offside. The mere fact that Bremner had tried to step back on-side and was impeded by German defenders didn't come into the equation. The Leeds players and fans could not believe what was happening. I clearly remember crying with anger as around me Leeds fans began to vent their anger.

Leeds fans have often been criticised for the riot that followed, but mostly by people who weren't there and who never mention some important points of provocation. Immediately after the goal had been ruled out, small numbers of Leeds fans were demonstrating their anger. It began with angry chanting – 'Cheat!', 'Gelderd aggro!' and 'There's gonna be a riot!' – of that there is no doubt. But the catalyst for the full-blown riot – in which the scoreboard in the upper tier was completely smashed, bottles and stones were thrown and hundreds of wooden seats were torn up and thrown onto the pitch – was the violence employed by about a thousand riot police. These men were armed with batons, shields and gasmasks and took over when a few hundred tracksuited French policemen backed off.

Mainly after Bayern had scored, the riot police began goading the Leeds fans with 'Come on then!' gestures. Leeds fans surged forward, waving poles from their banners, but the police over-reacted. Many leapt up and pulled Leeds fans over the wall and onto the stadium's perimeter track. Once there they would punch and kick the hapless fan. This happened many times, sending tempers through the roof. Terry Yorath, who had been subbed, came to the Leeds end and appealed in vain for calm.

The Leeds crowd, already incensed at having just witnessed a total injustice on the pitch, would not be pacified. They, just like the team themselves, had waited years for European Cup glory. They had overcome a Barcelona side featuring Dutch legends Johan Cruyff and Johan Neeskens in the semis. They had earned the right, after decades of dominating English football, to be crowned kings of Europe. But now, just when everyone thought that moment had arrived, it was cruelly and unlawfully snatched away from them. Things became worse when, minutes later, Franz Roth scored for Bayern Munich. A second goal by Gerd Muller seven minutes after that was the end for a very unlucky and brave Leeds team. Thousands of Leeds fans, many men in their 50s, couldn't take any more heartache and the place erupted with their frustration. The French riot police could do nothing as hundreds of seats were hurled at them. In the background Bayern Munich received the trophy almost unnoticed. Then, as if he hadn't caused enough resentment, Beckenbauer led his team, with the European Cup over to the Leeds end – what a despicable act of arrogance. A barrage of missiles followed by police intervention prevented them from coming any nearer. Leeds players were sat around the pitch just staring in disbelief at the events that unfurled before them. This would be their last ever chance of the European Cup. The subsequent ban imposed on the referee following allegations of bribery, did nothing to ease the pain.

All these events were captured on my dad's Super 8 Cine Camera as he observed from the side stand with my sister Julie. He tells me that even today he doesn't need his projector – he can still picture me stood there afterwards, dejected and motionless in my white bowler hat and white coat.

I have spoken to many Leeds United players from that era and several have stated that, although not condoning the violent scenes, they could fully understand the anger and resentment. Outside the Parc des Princes the rioting continued. I saw a mate of mine, Kenny Bowers, just sitting there crying. Many of the Kippax lads – Gord, Jim and Frosty – sat down in the middle of the road numb with disbelief. The realisation that this chance would not come our way again for many, many years began to dawn on people. Under the guidance of Don Revie, Leeds had reached a peak, but now Revie had moved on to manage England and many of his great team were coming towards the end of their careers. New boss Jimmy Armfield was rebuilding but in those days only one club, the reigning Champions, entered the European Cup, and Leeds were unlikely to qualify.

Downstairs on the Paris Metro we boarded a train and waited. One Leeds fan shouted abuse at some Germans on the platform. As the train doors closed, they trapped his head, but rather than re-opening, the train began to pull away. People around him tried frantically to prise the doors open. As the train approached the tunnel wall, the doors were forced apart enough for him to pull his head in, just in time. Mostly with relief the rest of the Leeds fans started laughing. I laughed so much, I started crying again. I realised then that I wasn't crying at this Leeds fan at all, I was still thinking of events that had just occurred.

The following evening we were back in Kippax. I saw Dave Walker and Polly. They were just going into The Moorgate pub, but I decided to go straight home. I had never been so depressed. On my way home I bumped into Dennis Ruddick and Stevie Griffiths. They could see I was upset and persuaded me to go for a pint in The Royal Oak; I had one pint but could not be consoled so I went home. Near home I felt my eyes filling up and instead of going straight into the house I went up the garden and sat inside my dad's aviary and told the two golden pheasants what had happened in Paris. They listened intently but I could see they were tired so I too settled down, pulled my bowler hat over my eyes and slept for an hour. When I awoke I noticed that the lights were turned off in the house. I slipped into my bedroom and went to sleep.

- 8 -

Satanic Hearses

Maybe driving to matches in a hearse was what started it. Leeds were never the same after I started doing that.

In 1978, probably due to my failed attempt at marriage, I acquired a fascination for hearses. It seemed a natural progression from my previous fascination – a worm.

I had walked out of my local pet shop the year before armed with accessories for the worm. In my bag I had a ladder, a bell and a mirror. Looking after any pet is a huge responsibility, so I was determined to gather all the information I could before coming home with my pet. I learned that worms are asexual invertebrates. So prepared I introduced Willie to his new home – a top-of-the-range cardboard box full of muck, complete with under-soil heating (courtesy of a berth in the airing cupboard). Willie looked so cosy after I had neatly arranged his furniture. As I hung the mirror on the wall opposite the bell, Willie surfaced briefly and gave a nod of approval before burrowing back beneath the soil. I had saved the best till last and next time Willie appeared he smiled at the huge 'I hate man utd' badge pinned to his feature wall. As a special treat, I let Willie have a box-warming party. It was so sweet watching about a dozen worms all having a good time listening to 'Leeds United's Greatest Hits'. And then I got into hearses.

My first one was an old 1966 Austin. It was plenty big enough in the back to get a dozen of the lads in and so off I'd take it down to Elland Road on match days. As I turned into Lowfields Road, or into Wesley Croft, where my cousin Ian would let me park outside his house, the police would remove their helmets. The car park attendant, older and wiser, would simply laugh as I handed over my ten bob. I would then open the back and the lads would all pile out, dust themselves down and head for the Gelderd End. I became really attached to my 'Doombuggy' and was therefore extremely sad when told by my garage that she should be laid to rest.

Looking back I suppose it was inevitable. Hearses are, after all, only built for one in the back. Nevertheless I was devastated. Doombuggy had been a dear friend and we'd had some great times together. I decided to do what anyone else would under the circumstances: buy another one.

After all, my hearse saw service not only on match days. At that time there was a brilliant Leeds band called The Sneakers playing all over Yorkshire. A dozen of us would arrive in the hearse and the band's lead singer Russ Elias would announce: 'Ladies and gentlemen, the "hearse mob" are here. Let's party!' The Sneakers would promptly break into the song 'Dead On Arrival'. This would lead to everyone leaping about like crazy, with their own version of the pogo.

There was no doubt I'd be lost without my hearse and I was determined to get the right replacement. I found it in an old barn in Ripon. It was a 1964 Zodiac and was being used as a chicken coop. It looked very sad, but my heart raced. Could this be the one? The chassis seemed solid enough, but the body was somewhat decomposed. The owner was very surprised that I wanted to buy it. He was even more surprised when I thrust £80 into his hand and drove it away. I got as far as the gates of the farm and had to return immediately – I had driven away with two dozen hens.

Some brilliant mechanical work by my father-in-law Harry Hemsley soon had the hearse running like a dream. The bodywork was fully restored and re-sprayed in a beautiful shade of black, and the name 'Rehearsel' sign-written on in lurid dripping green script. Gleaming Phantom side pipes were added, along with white-walled tyres. It looked perfect.

My daughter Vicky, however, then four years old, seemed totally unimpressed by the beautiful monster parked outside. So I took her for a spin. I smiled to myself as I pressed the button which opened the glove compartment and activated a mechanical, skeleton hand which moved eerily towards the front-seat passenger. Vicky was chatting away about what she had been doing with her friends. Without pausing, she simply hung her toy handbag on the hand and continued with her story. I took the handbag, placed it back on her knee and pressed the close button. Feeling very miffed I took her home.

Apart from Vicky's apathy, the only other drawback of the new hearse was that the bar and coffin took up so much room it could only carry two passengers, both in the front, to Leeds games. Nevertheless, the vehicle became quite a celebrity in the area. Once I was driving home when flashing blue lights appeared from everywhere. One police car pulled up behind me, another in front and a third at the side. I wondered what the hell was going on. Then I recognised one of the officers walking towards me as a friend of mine, Gary Crossley, who had been in the force for a number of years. He had spotted me a couple of miles back and after a few calls to his colleagues, decided to ambush me. Laughing, they spent 20 minutes admiring the hearse, particularly the bar. Apart from one speeding ticket, in another area, I was never hassled by the police. In fact, when the hearse's electrics failed one night as I drove my mate Brod home from Halifax, and I was being given a tow home by a van driven by Lesley, we were even met by a police van and given an escort, with lights flashing, to the garage at Kippax.

I received an invitation to join the prestigious Leeds & District Cruisers, a club for top custom cars. The car appeared in countless car shows, winning several trophies along the way. One car show in 1979 was held at the old Greyhound Stadium and was a huge success and a great day out. I took with me Paul Booth, and we both dressed for the occasion in full undertaker's outfits with top hats and black gloves. We looked the business. From the speakers under the car David Bowie's *Low* album (mainly the B-side – macabre and eerie, just right for a hearse), blasted out, creating an awesome atmosphere.

The kids, encouraged by the skull-and-crossbones black balloons we were handing out, loved it too. The judges may have been encouraged by something else. They kept returning to the car to 'check something again' but each time collected another drink from the bar. We won the 'Visitors' Choice' along with 'Most Unusual Custom' and then 'Most Imaginative Interior'. As we drove out of the stadium at the end of the day, I gave everyone a large blast of 'The Death March' on the horn to huge cheers.

One evening, I took Lesley in the hearse for a meal at the exclusive Bingley Arms restaurant near Leeds, reputedly the oldest inn in Great Britain. We arrived with green spotlights shining on the coffin and the Jolly Roger flying high. As we pulled up among all the Bentleys and Rolls-Royces in the car park, I swear I could hear the sound of eye-glasses dropping into gin and tonics.

I was even invited to race the hearse down the drag strip at Melbourne, near York. That was indeed a great honour. Paul and I donned our undertaker outfits again and lapped it up as we roared down the strip at 120 mph, receiving a brilliant write-up in the *York Evening Press* as we went. The car was also subsequently featured in *Custom Car* magazine when Paul and I took a team of journalists to Killingbeck Cemetery for a photo-shoot before retiring to the pub on the journalists' expenses. Another time, at the Birmingham NEC Custom Car Show, Alice Cooper – as I'm sure he'll recall – had the privilege of having his '57 Chevrolet parked next to Rehearsel.

My fascination for hearses continued well after Rehearsel and still lingers today (I intend to get another very soon). Even eight years after Rehearsel, Lesley and I were invited to the annual dinner dance of a local undertaking firm. The sight of 60-year-old funeral directors dancing to 'The Monster Mash' is one I will remember for ever. I took away my menu as a souvenir. At that time I only had one decent jacket and the undertakers' menu was still in its pocket when I wore it next, at a Kippax Branch dinner. Gary Speed and David Batty came along, as they always did, and in a fit of inspiration I asked them to autograph it. They knew about the hearse and so laughed like hell as they signed. After that I displayed the menu on the dashboard at car shows.

One day in the middle of summer Paul and I, fully kitted out, went cruising round Leeds in the hearse. We were talking about football and other things and thought little of it when we came upon a queue of traffic. Assuming there were road works ahead we continued chatting as the traffic crawled forward at walking pace. I noticed that the people in the back of the car in front of us were staring but I had got used to such attention. A young boy in the car, who was pointing at our Jolly Roger, was made to face forward by the man next to him. Then Paul looked behind us. The people in the car behind were watching us, too. As he said so, I looked beyond the car in front and saw a large black limousine. My heart sank when I looked further forward – in front of the limo was a hearse. We were in the middle of a funeral procession. I immediately pulled out, drove over the central reservation and headed the other way. I prayed to God that the rest of the procession behind didn't follow me. Luckily, too, I didn't need to blast the horn.

In 1979, on my way to the UEFA Cup game against Valletta at Elland Road, I pulled up in the hearse outside The Nag's Head in Leeds to pick up Brod. As I left, I noticed over my shoulder that the coffin wasn't there. I removed it sometimes but I doubted this was one of those times.

'I'm sure it was in the back when I set off,' I said to Brod.

'It can't have been,' he replied. 'Who is gonna nick a coffin?!'

A fair point. But it was still on my mind as the game kicked off. After the 3–0 win, I raced home and confirmed my worst fears. The coffin had been nicked. I was mystified. The next day the news bulletin on Radio One ended with the traditional 'And finally . . .' tale. This day it was about a coffin that had been 'left last night in a pub in Leeds . . .'

I couldn't believe my ears. It turned out that for a prank while I met Brod, some of the lads had nipped out of the pub, taken the coffin from the hearse and moved it to another pub, The Grange. There they had a pint and left, leaving the coffin behind. The landlord had gone berserk and called the police, who had taken the unusual lost property away with them.

The next day Paul and I donned our undertaker suits and headed for Millgarth Police Station, in Leeds city centre.

'Good morning, officer,' I said. 'We've come for our coffin.'

The desk sergeant looked up and saw us both standing there in top hat and tails, black gloves, white faces and dark sunglasses. He wasn't at all impressed.

'Can you describe it?' he said.

'Of course – it's round,' I replied, sarcastically. 'How many coffins do you have?!'

A few minutes later, we signed for our coffin as two officers came in carrying it, laughing at every step. At least they could see the funny side. Thanking them, we returned the coffin to its rightful place where it remained until 1981 at least, when £2,000 offered by a garage owner in London who wanted to display Rehearsel in his showroom proved an offer I couldn't resist.

After five years driving funeral cars, during which I'd gone from driving around in an old battered hearse for a giggle to customising another into a top-quality show-car hearse that won countless trophies all over the country, I thought it was finally time to hang up my top hat.

Three years before, in 1978, it had begun getting pretty morbid at Leeds United too. In their infinite wisdom, the Leeds United directors appointed Jimmy Adamson as manager. He was brought in to replace Jock Stein who, although without doubt a brilliant manager, had used the club as a stepping stone before taking the Scotland manager's job. In the short period before Stein took over, Maurice Lindley had been caretaker manager and many Leeds fans felt he was the man for the job at the time. Adamson was totally the wrong man. Leeds fans did give him a chance, but after two years they became impatient at the lack of direction of the club and anti-Adamson protests became a regular occurrence both at home and away matches.

Butter and I were stood on a barrier at Villa Park with a huge 'Adamson Out' banner. Two police officers came and told us to get down, which we did – for five minutes. Ten minutes before the end, we were both ejected. But they allowed us to keep our flag. Despite protests from the vast majority of fans, the board, led by chairman Manny Cussins, refused to budge.

Undeterred, we were gathered in The Nag's Head before an evening game at Elland Road. Peter Sutcliffe, aka The Yorkshire Ripper, was still at large and the police were trawling the pubs with a huge tape-recorder containing the voice of a man with a north-eastern accent who had telephoned them claiming to be the Ripper. As the officer played the tape, everyone in the bar shouted: 'That's Adamson – nick him!'

I wasn't too upset when the season ended in May 1979 – although Adamson was still there, Leeds had finished fifth – and I flew off to Benidorm with Gordon Findlay, Willie Stevenson and our respective girlfriends. It was one of the best holidays I've ever had and just what I needed to recharge my batteries for next season. One night in Benidorm, Gord, Willie and myself went to watch Nottingham Forest on television in a bar. They were playing in the European Cup final. In those days whenever I went on holiday I used to take my 12-by-18-foot Union Jack with me (these days I take a St George's flag) and Benidorm was no exception. I had taken my Union Jack to the bar, displaying it as I had on the way over as we drank our last cans of Samuel Smith's Old Brewery Strong Pale Ale, brought with us from Yorkshire. I don't let go of home easily.

We watched Forest win 1–0. As we left the bar and walked back towards our hotel, waving my Union Jack on the end of a large bamboo cane that I had found earlier, Willie noticed that we were being followed by a car containing half-a-dozen apparently local boys. It pulled up a side street then reappeared ahead, speeding towards us. Gord was stood near a litter bin looking for something to throw at the car and pulled out an empty can of Sam Smith's Pale Ale. 'Well, would you believe that?' He was being very casual but this wasn't the time or place. By now the car had screeched to a halt and a couple of them were opening the doors. Then, with a silly rush of blood that could only have come from watching all those episodes of *Fawlty Towers* in The Viaduct, I raced over to the car and began belting it Basil Fawlty-style with my bamboo cane and flag. Willie and Gord came racing over and our actions so surprised the locals that they jumped back into their car and sped off.

Adamson's unexpected success had seen Leeds qualify for the UEFA Cup and in the first round, first leg we were drawn away against Valletta in Malta. The game went well and Leeds won 4–0, thanks to a hat-trick by Arthur Graham and a goal by Paul Hart. After the match around 250 Leeds fans who had been invited to a special dinner gathered to celebrate the victory. We arrived at a banqueting hall and began enjoying the hospitality laid on by the locals. Malta has a large contingent of Leeds fans and both teams were also in attendance. Shortly after our meal, Adamson stood up to give a small speech. He thanked the Maltese people for their generosity, in particular the island's Leeds fans. He thanked both teams for a 'splendid encounter' and finished off by thanking the catering staff for a 'tremendous meal' and sat down.

Brod immediately leapt to his feet and shouted, 'What about us daft bastards who've travelled over from Leeds?'

Adamson stood up again and added, 'Oh, and of course, thanks to the Leeds fans from England too.'

Adamson was still at the helm when Leeds played Universitatea Craiova, in Romania, in the next round.

We stayed over the border in Yugoslavia and travelled into Romania for the game. We travelled by coach with a driver, a Yugoslav named Stavros, who was mental. He drove through the Transylvanian mountains at 100 mph. He shouldn't have been in that much of a hurry to get there because Romania was in the grip of Communism and things around the town were very dismal. Hardly anyone could be seen with a smile on their face. We were having lunch in a small tavern when Manny Cussins came in. He spotted our Leeds shirts and came over. Noticing we were eating pork he joked in his best Jewish accent, 'Go easy on the meat, boys, it might not be kosher!' Well, he thought it was funny, anyway. Collar opened a can of beer and in the process, cut his finger. He asked the waiter for a bowl of water to bathe his injury. The waiter placed the bowl in the centre and within seconds it had turned red with Collar's blood. As we were paying the bill at the end of the meal I noticed we had been charged for a vodka which we hadn't ordered. When I queried this with our waiter, he pointed to Collar's bowl, which hadn't been water after all. Collar promptly drank it. Now that really was a 'Bloody Mary'.

A miserable performance by Leeds ended in a 2–0 defeat, and we encountered further misery as we prepared to leave Romania. We were told at the very last minute that we would not be allowed to take any Romanian currency (leu) out of the country. As the place had been so dismal we hadn't found much to spend our money on and most of us had quite a bit left. So after our race back through the Transylvanian Mountains, as we approached the checkpoint on the Romanian–Yugoslav border, we stopped at a shop by the side of the road. After stashing a few bottles of beer on the bus we spent the rest of our money on sweets and cakes which we gave to the dozens of Romanian children that had gathered outside the shop. It became obvious that this must have been a regular occurrence as the children scoffed cream cakes and biscuits by the score and one or two adults arrived to join in the feast.

On arrival back at Heathrow it was straight to Southampton where we witnessed a 2–1 win with goals from Alan Curtis and the 'famous' Wayne Entwistle. At half-time I was queuing for a hotdog with Mally King. Some of the Leeds fans were tormenting the girl behind the counter – shouting and throwing plastic forks about, that sort of thing. Suddenly she lost her temper and grabbed a large bucket that stood on the counter. With a flick of her wrist, she threw the whole of its contents – tomato ketchup – towards the rowdies at the front. One more innocent fan, who had been stood patiently awaiting his burger, bore the full brunt of the gloopy deluge. As the girl slammed the shutter down he was left with a completely red head and sauce dripping down onto his clothes. As he made two eyeholes in the sauce with his fingers, the people round him began dabbing their hotdogs on his head and proceeding to eat them. He endured this for a few minutes before walking away without saying a word.

The catering at Elland Road was treated with rather more respect come the second leg of the tie with Craiova, but the 2–0 defeat meant that this would be our last competitive game in Europe for 13 years. One shining light from 1979–80 was Leeds' 2–0 home victory over manchester united. Gordon McQueen was making his first return to Elland Road since his move across the Pennines to the enemy. It was a handball by McQueen that enabled Kevin Hird's penalty to add to a previous effort by Derek Parlane and eventually a victory that prevented manchester united from winning the title. But the writing was on the wall for Adamson.

Things began coming to a head during the summer of 1980 after Leeds had finished 11th and exited both domestic cups early. His team were in Zurich for a pre-season friendly. An hour before kick-off, as the players were inspecting the pitch, Adamson joined them to chants of 'Adamson out!' from over 400 Leeds fans situated behind the goal. He looked defiant but as the 1980–81 season got underway, demonstrations continued at Elland Road and six games into the season the board relented, replacing him with Leeds legend Allan Clarke. But the decline had begun and Clarke too would struggle.

- 9 -

Going Down . . . Smiling

I did it all sober before I could drink – and in the days when
I drove the hearse. It was only in the '80s when the boozing
kicked in.

In the late 1970s, as memories of Revie's great Leeds team began to
fade, the fans cheered themselves up by beginning the tradition of
attending some of the final away games of the season in fancy dress.
And so it was that en route to a largely insignificant fixture at
Nottingham Forest's City Ground on 16 April 1979 almost everyone
on the Kippax bus was dressed in a stupid costume.

Gordon 'Gord' Findlay has occasionally gone to matches as a Russ
Abbot-style kilted and ginger-wigged Scotsman. Ian 'Jack' Frost likes
to dress as a woman (more Lily Savage than Liv Tyler, it has to be
said). Martin Barrett has been known to borrow an outfit similar to
Andy Pandy's from Gord's wife. And Terry Ford looked splendid in
his army combat uniform as 'Jack Knife Johnny' from Alice Cooper's
From The Inside album.

Predictably, given my interest in hearses, I went as an undertaker
complete with tape measure. Later I changed to Jesus Christ. I had
the robe specially made by Lesley's mum, Gloria, and donned a long

wig, a pair of sandals, and a crown of thorns made out of old twigs. It looked perfect. Well, almost. It wouldn't be complete without a cross. I made a ten-foot cross out of cardboard and for the final touch put a telephone inside it, so I could call my dad (God) if I was going to be late home. But the best costume I ever saw undoubtedly belonged to Mouse (aka Kevin Broadbent) who had come as the Invisible Man.

He was clad from head to toe in bandages, with just two peep-holes to look through, and a tiny hole to breath through. On arrival at the turnstile, however, the police didn't think much of Mouse's costume. They told him he must uncover his face. Unfortunately, just one bandage covered his entire body so to unmask himself he had to be completely unravelled and was left without any costume whatsoever. Nevertheless, his supreme effort has never been forgotten.

A few years later, poor Mouse was diagnosed with cancer of the throat. Discharging him from the hospital, his doctors stressed that he must avoid any sudden jolts to his neck. This he noted and resumed his trips to watch Leeds.

Early in the following season, returning from a game at Chelsea, our coach stopped at Loughborough for the evening. It was obvious as we moved from pub to pub that, even having split into small groups, the local lads weren't particularly happy to see us. This surprised us. We had stayed in Loughborough on many previous occasions and had never had any trouble with anyone. But tonight was different – people seemed hostile to us in every bar. Towards the end of the evening, Mouse, Gord, myself and half a dozen others were in a small pub as more and more locals began to arrive. The atmosphere was so tense that about half a dozen policemen came into the pub and had a good look round. They noticed our group in the corner and must also have noticed that almost everyone in the pub, including women, were glaring at us. But the police left without saying anything and when shortly afterwards the women began gathering glasses and bottles and handing them to their lads, I remember saying to Gord Findlay, 'We'd better get out of here, mate.' The idea seemed an even better one when the landlord looked away and went into another bar. There was a door behind us, but it was locked. We realised we would have to make for the main door – inconveniently situated behind the now advancing mob. Not waiting for them to get any closer, we charged.

Even outside, glasses and bottles rained down on us as the women continued to supply their men with ammunition. Just as we thought we had managed to escape with minor cuts and scrapes, we saw Mouse hit on the back of the head with a flying bottle. The impact knocked him face-down onto the pavement. We ran back and picked him up. Outside the pub doors were two police vans. Strange coincidence, that. The coppers did nothing to help us but one of them did get out and say: 'Now get back on your coach and get the fuck out of here.' We took our injured Mouse back to the bus in a Morrisons' shopping trolley. He was hurt, but not as seriously as we feared.

After talking to some of our other lads back at the coach, we learned the reason for the night's hostility towards us. A few weeks earlier, some of the Leeds Service Crew had also stopped at Loughborough on their way home from a Leeds game, and had trashed a few bars along with some of the locals. We had walked straight into a revenge attack. If only we'd known, we wouldn't have taken Mouse anywhere near the place.

At the next branch committee meeting, still feeling guilty, we reviewed what had happened. It was a delicate matter but we voted that, in view of Mouse's illness and uncertain future, he should travel free for the rest of the season. In the back of our minds was the sad thought that it was likely to be his last. He thanked us and humbly accepted.

Well into the following season Mouse was still well enough to travel with us. In fact, his condition seemed to have improved. We were delighted, but assuming this was the common period of remission that precedes a final decline, the committee decided to continue his 'free pass' indefinitely.

He was still able to take advantage of it all the way to the following May. And in August, the start of the next season, Mouse was still very much alive and with us. In November, the committee enquired, somewhat awkwardly, as to his condition.

'Oh,' said Mouse, 'didn't I tell you? The doctors have said I can have an operation on my throat. They could operate and remove the cancer, but it is a 70 to 30 chance against me surviving the operation. If I leave it and do nothing, the odds are much better. They think there's a good chance I'll live my life out normally.'

We were delighted to hear the news, which Mouse admitted he had been meaning to tell us ever since he learnt it, 18 months earlier. Mouse is still going to matches with us – and now pays whenever he travels. I'm convinced he will outlive the entire branch. In fact, those bandages he wrapped himself in back in 1978 seem to have preserved him better than any Egyptian Pharaoh's.

In 1980, I received a phonecall from a professor of psychology at York University. He was doing a study on travelling football supporters, had heard of the Kippax Branch and wanted to travel to an away game with us and make notes. I arranged for him to join us for the game at Sunderland on 27 September. Leeds had won only one game that season so I hoped he might bring us better luck. He got on the coach armed with folders and a tape recorder. The lads were intrigued. He looked like a fully paid-up member of Academics Anonymous: beard, long hair, green cords and one of those checked shirts that geography teachers seem to prefer.

Ten minutes into our journey the beer was flowing and some of the lads were passing a joint round. Pointing a microphone at each of us in turn the professor got us all to tell stories of past journeys. When one of the lads offered him a can of beer, he took it. Then he was offered another. And another. I then saw him take a draw of one of the joints being circulated. The next thing I knew, one of the lads had rolled the professor a whole joint to himself. By the time we stopped at a pub near the Sunderland ground for lunch, our guest was nicely relaxed. Or to put a less academic slant on it, he was absolutely shit-faced. He had begun by asking sensible questions about football and violence but then, sometimes giggling like a schoolgirl, he'd gone rapidly downhill.

Kick-off was approaching so we, and the professor, only had time for a couple of pints before heading for the ground. Two pints turned out to be more than enough for him. As we filed through our turnstile, we looked around in time to see him being led away by two policemen. He was so drunk he had been refused entry and arrested. We knew they'd only hold him until after the match so left him to sleep it off. But when we went to the police station after the game, they wouldn't release him. In fact, they kept him there until eight o'clock. So we had to leave him. We never did hear the results of his study.

Later that season, on 28 February 1981, the Kippax Branch was out in force for what turned out to be an historic occasion as Leeds travelled to Old Trafford and won 1–0, Brian Flynn getting the all-important goal that sent 16,000 Leeds fans into raptures.

Andy 'Rolf' Rollinson was stood next to the fence that separated Leeds fans from manchester united fans down the Cantilever side, when he spotted David 'Ghandi' Sutcliffe, who comes from Kippax, but had the disease of being a manchester united fan. He was stood at the other side of the fence with his manchester mates, when Rolf called over to him. 'Hey up, Ghandi, do you want a cig?'

Ghandi responded by coming over to the fence. 'Aye, cheers Rolf,' he replied. As he put the cigarette in his mouth he leant over to Rolf to get a light. Instead, Rolf snatched the cig out of Ghandi's mouth and poked him straight in the eye with his finger. 'You bastard!' Ghandi said, while everyone around him was rolling about laughing. A few years later Ghandi saw sense, and began to follow Leeds, claiming it was unnatural to support manchester united and that he'd finally seen the light. No pun intended.

Ghandi's assailant, Rolf, is quite a character. The following summer he, Martin Barrett and I went to Scarborough for the weekend. The three of us shared a room and next door there were two girls from York. At lunchtime we had a drink and a laugh with them and said we'd meet up later for another drink. That night, when we returned to our room, Rolf knocked on their door. There was no answer.

'They are in there,' said Rolf. 'I can hear them.'

He tried the door and although it was not locked, it was stuck. He barged it and it flew open. He was in high spirits and by way of breaking the ice he jumped onto their bed and started bouncing up and down singing the Adam and the Ants favourite 'Ant Music'. He got halfway through the chorus when the bedside light was turned on and there sat a petrified-looking man of about 70, hastily putting his glasses on as his wife beside him pulled the blankets up to her chin. The two girls had checked out.

Rolf apologised to the surprised couple and we quietly left their room, Martin and myself in hysterics. Rolf was good at getting things wrong. A couple of weeks later we were kicked off a Bridlington bowling green because the officials objected to his bowling style – over-arm.

Come the start of the 1981–82 season, when it never occurred to me that at the end of it Leeds would be relegated, I was getting my cans of ale out of the fridge ready for the journey to Swansea for the first game of the season. I noticed Lesley had left me a plastic box full of sandwiches. I shoved them in my bag and went on my way. The game didn't go well and Leeds got a 5–1 hammering. On the way back I decided to cheer myself up by opening my box of sandwiches. In with them Lesley had hidden a baby's bib. It had a lovely little bright-yellow duck on it. The lads insisted I put it on, so I fastened it around my neck and opened another can of lager. We were chatting away when all of a sudden there was a loud bang. A bad day got worse as our bus trundled onto the hard shoulder and ground to a halt. The driver took a quick look and said he'd have to phone for a replacement coach.

We soon got bored waiting for it and to pass the time began playing football with an old beer can in a nearby field. We were doing this when a police car pulled up. The officers got out and ordered us back onto the stricken coach. Sulkily, we agreed, and as we did so one of the coppers asked which one of us was in charge. I went over and introduced myself. He looked me in the eye and then down at my chest. I was still wearing my bib with the duck on it. He sighed and made me promise to get everyone back on the bus and not to leave it until the replacement arrived. I'm not sure he thought I looked like a responsible adult.

In September 1981, we were travelling to Maine Road, when our coach pulled up in the traffic. We drew alongside a bus stop that had half a dozen people standing at it. Rolf opened the skylight and lobbed out a foot-long dead rat that he had smuggled on board. It landed on the head of a man waiting for a bus. The look of horror that crossed his face when he realised what had hit him was unforgettable. So too was the speed with which he brushed it off – only to see it land on the shoulder of the woman standing beside him. She screamed, too, and – just as the man had – brushed it off herself onto the next person in the queue. The rat was still being thrown along the line as our bus pulled away.

Rolf has calmed down a lot over the years, but he still has a classic sense of humour. For the Champions League semi-final with Valencia in 2001, as did hundreds of Leeds fans, we stayed in Benidorm. The day before the game we were all sat outside a seafront bar. It was packed with Leeds fans all having a good laugh, catching some rays and of course enjoying a cool light ale. We were watching a street entertainer mimicking people walking by the bar. He was very good at it. An old lady walked past clutching her shopping bag and the man walked behind her imitating her every move. A man walked in their direction, hunched forward. Our man stopped following the old lady and turned to copy the walk of the hunched man superbly. Rolf stood up and said, 'Watch this!'

He slipped, unnoticed, behind the entertainer then walked passed him limping badly. Our man took the bait instantly. Rolf then upped the stakes by launching into a perfect cartwheel, followed by another. He then stood and looked back at the street entertainer: 'C'mon then, do that!' He couldn't, apparently, and stopped, gobsmacked, in his tracks, muttering in Spanish. He then quickly moved on to another bar amid howls of laughter from the Leeds fans who had been watching.

When the great Liverpool manager Bill Shankly died in 1981 the Kippax Branch decided to donate a cheque to the memorial fund that was set up at Anfield. In October, when Leeds met Liverpool at Anfield, Collar and I went to the Main Stand to hand over the cheque on behalf of the branch. A police officer took us into the stand and pointed into a small room where a number of people were counting money and cheques. A man with a suede coat and large white collars took our cheque, said thanks and continued counting the other monies. We turned to leave, when the police officer held us back. 'Hold on a minute,' he said, and turned his attention to the man in the coat. 'Listen, mate, these are Leeds fans here and this is a great gesture.'

We were a little embarrassed and said to the officer, 'It's all right, mate.'

'No, it's not all right!' he said and again spoke to the man in the coat. 'Look, can't you get them in to meet the players?'

Now we began to feel out of our depth. But the man in the coat responded to what the policeman had said: 'Yeah, c'mon, lads – I'll see what I can do.'

We followed him down the corridor. There were 15 minutes to kick-off and both dressing-room doors were locked. So we were led instead along the corridor. We had no idea where he was taking us but suddenly we passed down the players steps and under the famous 'This is Anfield' sign and then out onto the pitch. It was the last thing we had expected and we stood on the pitch looking like a right pair of lemons. There was nothing to do except wait for the teams to emerge from the tunnel. When they did, they seemed huge. But instead of running off to warm-up, Grobbelaar and Souness led the entire Liverpool team to us, each to shake our hands. We were then escorted around the pitch and into the Leeds end to huge cheers. We had even got in for free!

The only recollection I have of the 1981 FA Cup is the third round defeat at Spurs in January. Outside, before the match, a massive brawl occurred and Tim Thorpe emerged from the middle of the fracas on the back of a huge, spinning Tottenham fan, shouting 'It's all right, lads – I've got him,' while the brute he was clinging to spun round and round, like a dog chasing its tail. It was hard not to smile.

With just four games to go, a glance at the league table on 8 May 1982 would produce anything but a smile. But at quarter to eight in the morning I had other grim thoughts on my mind. The sun was up and we were driving down the M1 in an unmarked Ford Transit. We were heading for Tottenham again, but before reaching White Hart Lane, we had a very important task to carry out en route.

As we approached the signs for Worksop, the level of chatter among the lads began to lower and I admit myself, the nerves began to build up. This mission was not going to be easy. As we left the motorway, one by one we put on our black balaclavas, specially made with just two small eyeholes.

'ETA four minutes,' said Mick, the driver.

We went over the final plans; there was no room for error.

'Got everything, Mal?' I said.

'Yep, let's do it!' he replied.

'Let's not forget who we are and why we are here,' I reminded everyone as we pulled up at our destination.

The van was parked at the edge of a large forest. In the adjoining field was our target – a large group of men had gathered, every one of them possessing a high-velocity firearm.

'This is it, lads, let's go!' shouted Mick and we all leapt from the back of the van. We too were armed – with placards. We were the Clay Pigeon Preservation Society and we were sick and tired of this cruel activity taking place in our countryside. Our enemy looked round, obviously taken aback by our surprise attack. We started putting our many placards into the ground. 'Stop this senseless slaughter – now!' read one. 'How many more must die?' proclaimed another. Our enemy was totally confused. We ran round and between them, picking up any clay pigeons that were scattered around – they were dazed but as yet unhurt.

Kev blew his horn and we all looked up. 'Over here!' he shouted, pointing to a box of around 30 poor clay pigeons awaiting their cruel fate. Kev grabbed the box. 'These are the fortunate ones. Others aren't so lucky,' he said. 'Call this sport?' he snarled at our bemused enemies. 'They are flung out of a crude homemade device and then are either shot or plummet to their deaths.'

Kev was right; as we headed back to our van, still facing our gun-toting foes, we came across many clay pigeons who hadn't been so lucky. They were scattered around, smashed and ruined. There had been casualties, of that there could be no doubt, but it could have been a lot, lot worse.

The men with the shotguns were silent. So, fortunately, were the guns. It was obvious to all of us that they had no answer to our accusations. The stunned look on their faces told its own story. We all leapt back into the van and sped off down the M1 to London. The pigeons now in our care would be sent to good homes, awaiting their arrival, all over the country. Some were even sent abroad and all are doing well, most holding down good jobs as ashtrays. Unfortunately Leeds United didn't show quite the same fighting spirit as we had at Worksop, and despite a Frank Worthington goal, were beaten 2–1 by Tottenham. The drop loomed.

That drop became inevitable at The Hawthorns on 18 May, when Leeds United went down 2–0 to West Bromwich Albion in their final game of the campaign. It was a Tuesday night and we were left to await favourable results from elsewhere. The Leeds fans were in a predictably ugly mood and some began rioting. The riots continued after the game and I remember seeing afterwards on television the Leeds manager Allan Clarke being asked what he thought of the fans' reactions.

'I saw no rioting, what rioting?' replied Clarke.

The interviewer was taken aback by this response, and prompted: 'What about the policemen on horseback? That large white horse missed your foot by inches.'

Allan Clarke was brilliant: 'White horse? I never saw a white horse.'

The interviewer finally gave up.

The result meant that Stoke City only needed to beat West Brom that Thursday to avoid relegation and in doing so, send us down. Following the events at The Hawthorns it didn't need Einstein to determine that West Brom wouldn't exactly bust a gut to save Leeds United. On Thursday afternoon Gord Findlay, Mally King, Tony Denton and I set off in Tony's car to try to persuade them otherwise. The signs at Stoke's Victoria Ground were not good. Before the kick-off both sets of supporters sang 'We all hate Leeds and Leeds and Leeds'. By half-time the score was 3–0 to Stoke and we decided to leave.

As we turned to go we overheard a Stoke fan gloating: 'Fucking Leeds! I wish there was some of the bastards here tonight!'

He got the shock of his life, when Mally, who is 6 ft 4 in., leant over his shoulder and announced in a broad Yorkshire accent, 'We're here, old cock. What are you gonna do about it?' Nothing, as it happened.

We arrived back in Leeds at around half past nine knowing that Stoke had won and Leeds United had dropped out of the old First Division. It was a bitter pill to swallow and after a few pints we returned home.

In a Different League

We needed a change. We were getting stale.

Come the start of the 1982–83 season, Leeds United had sacked Allan Clarke. He was very dignified about it, never once slagging anyone off. The board appointed another of Don Revie's former players, Eddie Gray, as the new manager. Although we were hoping that Leeds under Gray would bounce straight back up into Division One, things were a bit hit and miss on the field. As the season wore on, the dream became increasingly unlikely. One big plus, however, was the phenomenal support that Leeds continued to receive, especially away from home, even though the fixtures were for the most part played in far less glamorous settings. The Kippax Branch alone used to take at least two coaches and most of the time, three and four. We had a good mixture of lads on our coaches. As well as people from Kippax and Garforth we had lads from Castleford, Bramley, Guiseley, Shipley and many other towns and villages around the city.

One of the first trips was a short one down the M1 to Hillsborough on 11 September. We didn't always have the same driver and a couple of those we did have were right miserable buggers. One of them was driving us back after a 3–2 win over Sheffield Wednesday and some of us were messing about at the back of the coach. Greg Gater was playing at being the wrestler Big Daddy and was throwing his weight around. He barged into one of the lads and knocked him towards a window. To everyone's amazement the window fell out and smashed onto the hard shoulder. The driver stopped and, chuntering away to himself, walked back up the hard shoulder to salvage the rubber seal that had fallen out along with the window. He wasn't a bit amused when just as he was getting back on the coach, Martin 'Slugger' Jackson shouted: 'Oh look, the driver's caught a snake!'

Slugger's best mate was Stevie Priestley. On our way back from a 3–2 win at Portsmouth in February 1984 (sealed with a Peter Lorimer penalty) our chemical toilet was beginning to stink a bit. Now, you're not supposed to empty these whilst in transit but I don't suppose we're the only people to have done it. On this occasion Stevie had been told what to do by the driver. It was simply a matter of the bus slowing down, moving onto the hard shoulder and then Stevie pulling the lever at the given instruction. Sure enough, the bus slowed and our driver shouted over his shoulder, and Stevie pulled the lever. Unfortunately, because the message got lost in translation via Carl Ryan, Stevie hadn't heard the driver properly – he was merely slowing because of traffic. Too late. We were still in the middle lane and were trailing a slick that spread across all three lanes. First in the firing line immediately behind us was a dear old couple driving an old Morris Minor who unfortunately bore the brunt of the avalanche. The vehicle's old wipers were no match for the battered turd that had nestled itself between the bonnet and the windscreen. The car swerved all over the road and after slowing down, eventually disappeared out of sight.

When we finally got back to Leeds, I went drinking in the city centre with some of the lads. Snow fell all night and by closing time it had settled almost six inches deep on the ground. All buses and trains were cancelled. Taxis were very hard to come by and even then, the drivers couldn't guarantee getting you home. So, instead of struggling for ten miles back to Kippax, I decided to walk the four or five to the Shadwell area of north-east Leeds and stay with Lesley – this was before we'd set up house together in Kippax. As I headed up the main Roundhay Road and past the landmark Fforde Greene pub it was impossible to tell where the road finished and the pavement began, but with no cars about it didn't make any difference. I passed by Roundhay Park and headed on towards Shadwell. Around the park are some really big houses, some of them have been owned by footballers over the years, and as I passed one particularly impressive mansion I decided to take a closer look. I sneaked up the drive and, realising the owners had gone to bed, tip-toed up to one of the windows and pushed my nose against the glass. It was dark but light reflected from the snow meant I could see into a very plush room. I smiled and thought how great it would be to be able to afford such a place of my own.

But I was only upsetting myself so I carried on my way. When I had reached Lesley's flat, she opened the door with a look of shock on her face. I was, by now, soaking wet and looking rather pathetic.

'What the hell have you been up to?' she said, adding, not at all sympathetically, 'come in and get dried, you daft git!'

An hour later I was dry, warm and sleepy in bed when there was a loud knock on her front door. She got up and went to answer it. I then heard her invite someone in and call me into the lounge to join them. Rubbing the sleep from my eyes, I walked into a reception party of herself, a policeman and a rather irate-looking gentleman. The copper was first to speak.

'Hello there, sir. Would you mind telling me where you've been this evening?'

I explained that after returning from the Leeds match I'd had a few drinks in town and then walked home. 'Why, is there a problem?'

'Which way did you walk home, sir?'

I realised then that the irate-looking gentleman in Lesley's lounge must have owned the house I peered into but omitted to mention my detour and simply described the route before asking: 'Why? What's the matter?'

The copper glanced at the other man and explained: 'Well, sir, this gentleman has reported seeing a prowler in his garden, and the footprints have led us to here.'

I'd done no damage so offered my trusted defence: 'I've a had little bit too much to drink, that's all.'

My interrogator obviously had better things to do and, after noting my name and address, he let me off with a gentle warning. 'That's fine sir. Well, no harm done. Take it easy with the drink next time, eh?' The two of them left.

I shrugged, received the stare from Lesley and we went back to bed. I lay there wondering what all the fuss had been about then thought back to my walk home.

'Oh God!' I said, sitting up.

'What now?' she moaned.

'Er, oh, nothing . . . It's all right, go to sleep.'

Suddenly I thought it best to keep what I'd remembered to myself. After peering through the irate gentleman's window I began to find the final leg of my journey boring. To pass the time I began hopping on one leg for as long as I could before stopping to turn and admire the trail of single footprints in the fresh snow. I then hopped some more, and just to make it interesting, I'd stopped and hopped back the other way for a while on the other foot, then turned and carried onward, hopping in the original footprints. The trail I left this time looked as though I'd been walking with one of my feet on the wrong way round. It was fun. I'd then continued on one foot for a while before jumping over a wall and covering my tracks for a bit – before resuming further up. I remembered thinking the large gap in between would make it difficult for anyone following my tracks to guess how it had been done. Lying there in bed I now realised that someone really had followed my ridiculous footsteps. The copper and irate gentleman would finally have seen where I had walked along like Charlie Chaplin before opting to roll full length like some manic winter gymnast.

But what was really bothering me was that on my way down one particular alleyway I had stopped to answer the most serious call of nature. I had squatted on a small wall then wiped my arse on a couple of snowballs. And left them on the wall. Thank goodness neither of my trackers had mistaken them for profiteroles.

The season of 1983–84 was when Paul Turnpenny joined the branch. He had been introduced by Collar, who had told him that we were a good bunch and didn't get into any trouble. Well, hardly ever.

A trouble-free trip, however, wasn't in the script for Paul's first game – at Crystal Palace. As we got near the ground, a Ford Transit van containing a few Palace fans hell-bent on goading the lads on our coach, came alongside us in traffic. To their credit, our lads responded by just laughing. But at the next traffic lights, the van pulled alongside and its driver leant out and smashed Brod's window with a hammer. The van then pulled away at high speed as we stopped our coach and pushed out the remaining glass. We shrugged and carried on our way.

At the next set of lights we encountered more trouble. As we approached them, we could see a mob of lads arming themselves with bricks and bottles. They were clearly going to pelt our bus – and weren't banking on any retaliation.

As the bus slowed we made our way to the front seat, where we each helped ourselves to a can or bottle from the stash of empties which had been mounting up during our journey south. We keep these at the front, planning to dump them at the first opportunity. That opportunity was about to arrive. As the mob prepared to attack us we got our retaliation in first, pelting them with empties through the gap left by our broken window. This was one thing our 'ambushers' weren't expecting and the looks on their faces was one of the funniest sights I've seen in South London.

Paul Turnpenny sat down and looked around at us. 'So much for no trouble,' he said. True – we had seen more trouble in the last 15 minutes than had occurred all the previous season.

Once in the ground, we stood on the terracing that has now been replaced by the Holmesdale Road stand. Collar prepared to climb onto one of the terrace's crush barriers to lead the Leeds chanting as usual. Paul Turnpenny was stood next to him.

'Here, hold my hand,' said Collar.

This was Paul's first ever football game and who was he to argue? Within a flash, he was stood by Collar's side holding his hand tightly.

'What the fuck are you doing?' shouted Collar.

'Holding your hand, like you told me to,' replied Paul, confused.

'I meant just to steady me as I'm climbing on the barrier, you idiot!' said Collar.

In those days we used to stop off and have a game of football in a field or anywhere we could whilst travelling to or from a game. It was during one of these games that Paul received his nickname. He had a style that cannot easily be defined. But it could be compared. One of the Leeds United defenders of a little before that era, Keith Parkinson, was not blessed with the greatest football skills seen over the years and he had a unique way of tackling that was best described as lunging. Paul and Keith Parkinson's playing techniques were almost identical. It came to pass then, that Paul became 'Lunge'. We even tried, on occasions, playing him in goal, but that didn't work either. Indeed, during one game, Gary Sharp was bearing down on Lunge in a one-to-one situation. We screamed at Lunge to come out to him. No such luck. Sharpy scored, unopposed, whilst Lunge was coughing and choking over one of the coats put down for goalposts. He had swallowed a fly! Realising we'd be more successful playing without a keeper we made Lunge sit on the bus.

That Sharpy is a quirky character, too. Once, after a night in The Royal Oak in Kippax, we stopped in at the Indian takeaway. Gary lives about four miles away in Swillington, and he ordered his food to be delivered to his home address. 'It will be about 20 minutes, sir,' he was told. 'No problem,' said Gary, 'I'll wait. You can drop me off with my supper.' They did just that for his cheek.

Barefaced cheek didn't work for Lunge when he was once stopped at the turnstile at Villa Park and refused entry for allegedly having had too much to drink. He was wearing one of those baseball caps with a ponytail hanging down the back – although he's actually as bald as a coot. Unfortunately he was arrested and kept in custody. As we returned to Leeds without him we wondered what the police – when they searched him – would have made of the application form to appear on *Blind Date* which someone had slipped into his jacket pocket on the way down.

Poor old Lunge. He likes a beer and he likes the ladies. And in the privacy of his own attic he likes to watch the odd top-shelf video. But he doesn't know as much as he thinks he does. At his local video shop the staff there know his tastes and so he should have listened when the young girl behind the counter told him he needn't bother to hire *Dirty Dancing*.

'Paul, it's not what you think,' she offered helpfully. But Lunge was defiant. She offered him a more suitable replacement, free of charge, when he returned shame-faced half an hour later.

Despite the tremendous following the team attracted, one of the downsides of this era was the dilapidation of some of the grounds the fans had to go to. When visiting Cambridge United, we had to walk a mile across a field and up and down banking between where our coaches were made to park and the actual stadium. On a visit to Cambridge it had been snowing and it had settled over the mud, making the trek very slippery. Halfway there a Cambridge fan appeared in the middle of our group and said to me, 'Hello Leeds, I'm Cambridge, what do you want to do about it?', then took a swipe at me. He missed and instinctively, I took a swing back at him, but I too missed and lost my footing. I slid all the way down some banking in the mud and snow. Cambridge laughed but Leeds were not amused. It then became like something out of a *Laurel and Hardy* movie as one by one our lads tried to catch this Cambridge fan and ended up slipping down the banking too. We were covered in mud and soaked in snow as we finally reached the ground.

Almost every time we played at The Den against Millwall trouble was anticipated. It was a hostile place and so the authorities ordered an early kick-off, before the pubs opened, to minimise the chances for fans to drink beforehand. We went there one Good Friday for an eleven o'clock in the morning start. After the game we got back on the bus and left with the other coaches in a Leeds convoy. We had only travelled about a quarter of a mile when our bus broke down. The front suspension had collapsed and a breakdown truck was called. A police van parked behind us to ensure we didn't leave the bus. A mechanic arrived and got to work underneath us. He was still there an hour later when a large mob of Millwall fans arrived. They surrounded our bus and I feared the worst.

It became a bit of a stand-off – there weren't enough police to move them on, they wouldn't come onto our bus and we certainly weren't getting off. The only thing that changed was that the mechanic threatened by the Millwall mob decided to bugger off.

To liven things up a bit we were showing some bravado by

gesticulating out of the window and inviting them onto our bus. We were only trying to show we weren't scared, and hoped that they'd get bored and leave. It didn't work as we planned and instead a police officer got on the coach. He was shaking like a leaf. 'Don't antagonise them,' he hissed, 'or they'll be on this coach in a flash!'

And so we continued our act and the stalemate continued. I then noticed someone I knew among the Millwall mob. It was Mark 'Belfast Bill' Cosgrove, a Leeds fan who had recently had to move down to London with his work. This made it awkward – if they knew that he knew us, he could be in for a right kicking. While I wondered what might happen, the police made a decision. The suspension might be damaged but it could still move, they reasoned. So they instructed our driver to start the engine and move the bus carefully away from the area. The coach creaked and groaned as we weaved our way down the road. The Millwall fans chased after us. But gradually we left them behind and, as we passed a pub with another group of Millwall fans stood at the door, we felt confident enough to raise two fingers to everyone looking on. Then we sat down and prepared for the long journey home – too soon.

To our horror, the road bent to the right and took us round and past the rear door of the pub. The Millwall fans we had just insulted simply ran through their pub, armed themselves with bottles and pool balls, and waited for us to approach. They were laughing as they threw the lot at us. Many windows were smashed and although we were able to keep moving, we realised it was going to be a drafty trip home.

Stevie Preistley did his best to make it fun, though. He put a carrier bag over his head for warmth and poked two eyeholes in it so he could see. He then grabbed the broom we swept the coach with and hung it out the side of the coach where a window used to be. Pretending the brush was an oar he rowed us up the M1, singing the theme to *Hawaii Five-0*. Brilliant.

A month or so later we came across Belfast Bill in The Vine in Leeds city centre. He explained that some of the Millwall lads were teammates from the pub he played football for and that he was totally embarrassed by what had happened. Stevie slapped him in the face and said, 'You deserved that, Bill.' He then bought him a pint and that was the end of the matter.

Another famous Kippax character from the Second Division days was Kenny. Kenny looked like a cross between Hugh Cornwell from the Stranglers and '70s singer Alvin Stardust. He relished his nickname of 'The Strangler'. Once, in the centre of Norwich before a match, he spotted a man wearing a manchester united shirt. The Strangler ran over to this complete stranger and in front of bewildered shoppers ripped the shirt completely off his back. He then tore it into shreds and wagged a finger in the helpless man's face. Adopting his best schoolteacher tones he delivered the final insult: 'And don't ever let me see you wearing a shirt like that again!'

The Strangler used to sit with another nutter, Ginner, or David, as his parents knew him. Ginner was equally crackers. We used to converge on The Precinct pub in Leeds before home games where Ginner would drink a pint of piss for a pound. Not just once, either. He would take a quid off of anyone as long as they were willing to fill the glass for him. And once it was full he would drink it. I have even seen him eat a bloke's underpants. But that was for a fiver. And he was drunk.

We were returning from the away match with Charlton Athletic on 19 March 1983. A lone John Sheridan goal meant Leeds had won 1–0 and we were in good spirits. Our bus pulled up in Garforth, just to the east of Leeds, and we walked into The Miners Arms for a beer. Immediately, we came face to face with a coach full of Manchester City supporters who had picked the same pub on their way home from a game in Sunderland. Initially the atmosphere was a little tense but gradually we began mingling, fuelled by a common hatred of manchester united and a love of the word 'Kippax' – as well as the name of our branch, it is the name of a grandstand at Maine Road. This mutual appreciation was very strange and unexpected. But even strangers were swapping phone numbers and arranging to play a football match against each other. To be honest, none of us really expected anything to come of it.

But on FA Cup final day 1983 the Leeds United Supporters Club, Kippax Branch lined up against Manchester City Supporters Club,

Denton & Gorton Branch. Leeds United kindly loaned us a Leeds kit and the use of one of the pitches at Fullerton Park at the back of the West Stand – formerly Leeds United's training ground, now dug up and replaced with cinders and rubble as a car park.

It was a good, hard-fought contest, and sadly City were the winners, by three goals to two. We decided to have a rematch the same time next year – Cup final day seemed an ideal date as it seemed unlikely that either of our respective teams would be in action at Wembley. But we lost that, too. In fact, City were the winners for the first four years. It was time for us to get serious.

We decided that, instead of playing lads off our coach – keen rather than fit, often drunk rather than sober – Kippax should put out a decent team. In 1987 our new policy worked and we ran out 4–1 winners – and went on to win the next two. It's a tradition that continues to this day, and as of 2003 has still not been interrupted by an FA Cup final featuring either Leeds or Man City.

After the first game in 1983, we all retired to The Beech pub in the Armley area of Leeds for food and beverages. Both sets of supporters sat cheering on Brighton against manchester united at Wembley. After Brighton had fought well and got a draw, we instigated a ceremony of speeches. First up was the organiser from City, Alan Potter, known affectionately as 'Disco Pants'. Alan is a big bloke weighing well over 25 stone so fortunately he wasn't too upset about not having a trophy to take home. We had bought a trophy – for obvious reasons it was called the Kippax Versus Kippax Trophy – but it hadn't made it to The Beech. Shortly after the game Dave Scobie kicked the ball straight at it, smashing it to bits.

In 1984, when we played the fixture at Man City, we made amends by presenting the winners with a highly polished toilet seat. Over the years, little metal shields bearing the names and dates of the winners have been added, so no one misses the one which Dave broke. The City fans were very happy with it and, I'm delighted to say, we didn't go home empty-handed either.

As we were leaving the club, having watched Everton stuff Watford in the final on the TV, we nabbed a stuffed duck, complete with feet painted in pink emulsion, from a shelf. The steward of the club came onto our coach to complain but after a bit of persuasion we were allowed to keep it and the duck has gone on to become the official runners-up trophy.

One year when Kippax were the holders of the duck, my dad saw it in the garage. He's a great singer but not an ornithologist and, assuming it was some wildfowl that had become lost and had sought shelter, approached it slowly with his arms spread wide. He got within a foot of the duck before he noticed that its feet were emulsioned and that it had been dead for about 50 years.

The fixtures continued to alternate between Fullerton Park and a Man City venue. City's venue varied but it was good of Leeds United to let us use the pitch and we even gained the benefit of their security in the form of Jack 'The Rottweiler' Williams. A bear of a man, he had been known to refuse entry to first-team players who couldn't produce any identification. As the years went by, the toilet seat collected more little shields and the duck got more and more dead.

In 1993, once more at Fullerton Park, Leeds and Man City were lined up before the kick-off. The referee, Steve Jones, called both teams to the centre and each player, wearing a black armband, stood side-by-side round the centre-circle. Steve blew the whistle for a minute's silence. During the silence I looked towards the touch-line and noticed that Jack had removed his hat and stood with head bowed respectfully. After the silence both teams went to their own halves in readiness for the kick-off and I ran to the touchline to throw my tracksuit top to Big John. Jack was stood next to him.

'Who was the silence for?' asked Jack

'It was to commemorate manchester united winning the league,' I replied.

'Well, I go to hell,' said Jack, ruffled. 'I thought someone had died!'

As I ran back onto the pitch I heard Big John utter solemnly: 'No Jack, it's much more serious than that.'

The many appearances by manchester united in the FA Cup finals of the '90s eventually put a strain on the relationship between the Kippax Branch and the City fans. It came to a head in 1996 when we were playing City, away. The after-match activities were taking place at the Denton Cricket Club. Everything was going well, we had won 3–2 and had just received the toilet seat – this was despite team manager Vince Donnelly deciding which team Phil Roberts would play for. Phil is a great Leeds fan but, despite his vigorous protests to the contrary, his accent has a very distinctive Lancashire twang to it. The City lads were making room for their duck. Then manchester united went ahead against Chelsea at Wembley and it all began to go wrong. Our lads immediately lost interest, and began playing cards. When it got to 2–0 at Wembley the atmosphere began to change. A couple of manchester united fans kept coming into our private room at the Denton to order drinks from our bar and have a little gloat. Suddenly the score was 3–0 and the gatecrashers were distinctly unwelcome. At the bar Alan Potter said to me, 'It's getting a bit ugly, Gary,' and nodding I suggested we abandon the tradition and turn the television off. 'It's not helping,' I said, 'and besides, no one's watching it.'

Before anyone could hit the off switch it became 4–0. Tico had had enough. He came running up to the bar and pushed a steak and kidney pie into the face of one of the manchester united fans. As the manchester united fan wiped pastry from his eyes, Wayne Procter came running past with a stuffed red devil he had taken from one of the other rooms. He was biting its head off. The manchester united fans looked at each other and motioned to leave. If they'd have gone sooner one of them would not have received a tray of pie and peas on the back of his head. Too depressed to join in and thinking this could only get worse, I got another pint and headed out onto the balcony.

It was a beautiful day and a cricket match was being played. I sat down to watch for half an hour while things calmed down inside. I had only been there a couple of minutes when I looked down at the players' bench. I did a double take but sure enough there was one of our lads, Steve Ella, getting padded up. He was arseholed.

With the pads buckled, he grabbed himself a bat and began walking out onto the pitch. He stumbled to the crease, held his bat to the floor and shouted at the umpire: 'Middle!' The umpire shook his head, the other batsman looked nervous, all the fielders sat down. 'Come on,' pleaded Steve. 'Just one bowl . . . come on!'

Steve refused to move and no one looked like persuading him. Presumably hoping that he'd be true to his word the bowler gave in

Arriving in Barcelona for the European Cup semi-final in 1975. Leeds won 3–2 on aggregate.

A chip fells Coke in China, 2002.

Eddie Stevens is accosted by a fan as he leaves the stage in Bradford, 1996.

Champions! The Kippax Branch celebrate the Championship win of 1992.

Jim Morrison's grave in Paris. 'No one here gets out alive.'

Athletics Champions! Me (second from right, middle row) and my sister Julie (second from right, back row) in Kippax Infants Athletics team, 1965.

Dogfight at the OK Moorgate.

Me, Sniffer and the 1972 FA Cup final shirt.

Me with Billy Bremner, two weeks before his untimely death.

I share a beer with Hotshot in Lisbon, 2001.

Fine wine and a fine woman. I can tell a joke – just ask Lesley.

Assorted members on the nudist beach in Varberg, Sweden, in 2001.

Me and Dad (far left) knock 'em dead in the Butlins father-and-son competition of 1964.

Me and some of the lads enjoy a cool beer on the holiday island of
Madeira after the game with Maritimo in 2001.

Melbourne, 2002. Me, The Kangaroo (Macca) and Robin (Procky).
Batman (Moose) had collapsed in the toilet.

'We're ready.' Jack and Jill in Leeds kit.

Men behaving badly. Me with Martin
Clunes in Dublin, 1996.

Stuart Hayward and other members of the Leeds United
Disabled Organisation (LUDO) in 1996.

Billy and I slip into Scotland unnoticed for the
Rangers–Leeds game in 1992.

and threw him 'just one bowl' – but under-arm. Eyes lit up, Steve took an almighty swing at the ball, and, as the ball rolled harmlessly past the stumps, Steve's bat ended up at mid-wicket. Satisfied, he staggered back to the pavilion. It was time to round everyone up and get the hell out of there.

A couple of weeks later, Alan Potter sent me a copy of a letter he had received from Denton Cricket Club. It wasn't very favourable. In fact, its writer was very cross and the incident looked like it could bring our annual event to an end.

But after a few telephone calls, Alan and I decided to risk another go, next cup final day. 'It's been going on too long to pack it all in now,' was our reasoning. However, when Leeds United arranged two games in Washington DC at the end of the season, I had to ring Alan and tell him we would be in America. We agreed we would abandon the fixture for a year although I think in the back of our minds we both believed the scenes at Denton Cricket Club had brought the curtain down on the Kippax Versus Kippax Trophy.

Then at Christmas 1998, I received another phone call from Alan. City were playing at York, and two coaches of their supporters would be stopping at The Miners Arms in Garforth again. Would we like to join them for a pint? Collar, Lunge and I got there ahead of them. We saw the buses draw up but only Alan came in. This was his usual party piece. Telling everyone to wait while he checked it was OK to bring in coach parties, he simply went to the bar and got himself two quick pints. He chatted with us then went out and gave the 'all clear'. In the couple of hours that followed, quips about City playing York ('In a League match?') the day before we played Arsenal, and the embarrassments of Denton were forgotten and Kippax Versus Kippax was fully back on track. And, until the unlikely event of one of our teams reaching the FA Cup final, it looks set to continue for many years to come.

- 11 -

Europe, We Come in Peace (Usually)

I'm not lucky, I've never been lucky. I just seem to get by. But
I do pick the wrong bar sometimes. When you go into as
many as I do, you're bound to.

The Leeds United Supporters Club of Scandinavia (LUSCOS) has
hundreds of members from all the Scandinavian countries. In the
summer of 1981, Leeds United's participation in a tournament in
Ikast, Denmark, gave some of them a chance to see their heroes in
the flesh. Our plan was to join them using a railcard that would
enable us to travel across on the North Sea ferry, and then afterwards
allow us to continue by train through Europe to where United were
playing Cologne FC in Germany. We would then fly back to England
and then onto La Linea in southern Spain, to watch Leeds play in a
tournament involving Real Madrid.

We arrived in Ikast – a small town with five bars, one nightclub
and a tiny police station – a week before the tournament began and
pitched our tent on a large campsite. On our way we passed the
police station and noticed a flag pole lying on the ground in front of
it. A few us went back later and 'borrowed' the pole. It took a
concerted team effort to fix it upright, after which our Leeds United

flag was attached and flew proudly throughout our stay. The police did come to investigate, but after an assurance by us that we would return the pole intact, we were allowed to keep it.

Ours was a modest four-berth tent, but there were at least ten of us in it – all blokes! One of them, Kenny Young from Middlesbrough, suggested we look for some more comfortable alternative. We noticed a number of caravans on the edge of the site that appeared to be vacant. After a discussion with the site manager all ten of us moved into relative luxury.

The other teams taking part in the tournament, apart from the hosts Ikast, were Utrecht from Holland, Start from Norway, Eintracht Braunschweig from West Germany and the Polish side Widzew Lodz. About 400 Leeds supporters had travelled to Denmark, but there were very few fans of the other teams.

Leeds fans began converging on the few bars. It was only a small town and the girls all seemed to have their own apartments; most of them were only 14, the legal age in Denmark for 'fooling around'. The local lads, however, seemed to resent the presence of the Leeds fans. It was understandable, as the girls seemed more than interested in the English lads. An uneasy atmosphere developed. Especially as our old blue tent had been left where we had pitched it and, as the days passed, it had become known as the 'shagging tent', used by dozens of other Leeds fans and the 'girl of their dreams'. The atmosphere on our campsite was great.

One night, four Utrecht fans came into Jacob's Well, the bar that we had nominated as our local. As the night wore on, some of the Leeds fans began chatting with them, so Pete Dillon and I wandered across to join in. They turned out to be bona fide Dutch football hooligans. They asked us to follow them out to their car. Me, Collar and Pete did as they asked. The boot of their car was full of weapons ranging from knives and knuckledusters to large axes. In their broken English they explained, 'We come to fight Leeds, but too many Leeds, we fight with Leeds against others.'

Pete took a second look at the hardware, sighed and said, 'Fucking hell, you're with us, all right!' We returned to the bar and had one or two beers with our new found 'allies'.

The following night, I was with Kenny and Pete, sat having a quiet drink in a different bar, not far from our campsite, when about a dozen local lads walked in. They told us we were not welcome and to leave or face the consequences. We explained that we were only here for the football and offered to buy them a drink. They shouted loudly in Danish and left, banging the table tops with their fists as they did so. After that, the trouble started.

We were walking to another bar when Greg Gater warned of a speeding motorbike coming towards us. At the last minute it swerved and narrowly missed Pete. We were just checking that everyone was all right when another bike came at us from the other direction. Pete had had enough. He was holding a Leeds flag and pole in his hands. As the bike drew nearer, Pete took a swing at it and the flag slipped out of Pete's hands and entangled with the rider. He sped off but came to halt at a level crossing about 40 yards away. He then unfurled the flag and waved it at us, gesturing for us to come and get it, then threw the flag on the ground and began to ride over it, doing 'wheelies' before picking it up and disappearing into the distance. This was to be round one of a ten-day feud.

The next day everyone on the site had heard of this episode. Ian Hewertson – a good Leeds fan from Blackpool, whose nickname is either Blackpool, or Pool for short – suggested that from now on we keep in small groups, just in case. Later that day, the last before the tournament began, even more Leeds fans arrived, among them Big Mick Hewitt with the South Kirby Branch bus, who were also staying on our site. Confusingly, there were two Leeds-supporting Mick Hewitts in Ikast. This one was Big Mick Hewitt, who runs South Kirby Branch, but already there was Little Mick Hewitt, who runs the Vine Branch. Things are never simple for me and Leeds United.

The first game of the tournament, Leeds versus Ikast, wasn't anything spectacular, but everything at the ground was relaxed, with only two policemen on duty. I've long since forgotten the score but remember that after the game a large group of us went back to Jacob's Well. The landlord by now knew us and greeted us warmly. Little Mick Hewitt was stood at the bar. After a few hours the atmosphere was good and numerous Leeds flags hung from the beams. At about ten o'clock at night a couple of local lads, dressed in leathers, walked in. They looked around and went back outside. They returned seconds later with another couple of lads. One of them then tried to pull one of the Leeds flags down from the ceiling. Alan 'Scouse' Upright ran over and suggested otherwise. The lads left again but trouble was definitely brewing. Then Kenny saw that outside the window gangs of bikers were gathering. We later learned that the locals had taken offence at our taking over their town and distracting their girls, and so almost 100 bikers had ridden 200 miles away from Copenhagen to explain the situation to us.

Minutes later there was an almighty crash. A smoke bomb had been thrown through the window. In seconds the whole pub was filled with dense smoke. More missiles followed. This was getting serious, but an uneasy stand-off ensued before the police, called by the landlord, arrived.

We liked the police in Ikast – and not just because they lent us their flag pole. They were very laid-back indeed. They finished work each day at four in the afternoon and didn't work weekends except for emergencies. This was an emergency. Even then, all that arrived were two cars, four officers and two dogs. By then we had all gathered outside the front of the pub to escape the smoke, the Danish bikers had moved back and the police were in the middle. I noticed that among the many motorbikes, there was a hearse with white curtains. Not a patch on my own back in Kippax, I remember being assured by Kenny.

An ambulance arrived to take the landlord, who had collapsed behind the bar, to hospital, where he spent the night in an oxygen tent. Eventually our tormentors dispersed and we were all escorted back to the campsite. But not before one of them produced a gun and shouted, 'We will get you, Leeds!' There was no doubt about it, we were now definitely going to keep in groups at all times.

The next morning we were in the shop when Blackpool came in and told us that the landlord had recovered and had stopped by to see us. We all went down to the gates to greet him and found him waiting with a crate of beer, saying we were welcome back in his bar any time. At lunch time we took up his invitation. The day passed off peacefully, although we did hear that over 100 more bikers were on their way up from Copenhagen. The battle was clearly not over.

As I was walking back into the campsite I noticed Kelvin Sutcliffe driving towards me in his green Citröen Diane car. I could see as he got nearer that he was heading straight for me. Unexpectedly, we were playing a game of 'chicken'. It was too late to do anything about it now. The next thing I heard was the sound of Kelvin skidding and loose chippings flying about. Then the car hit me head on as I bounced off the bonnet and went flying over the roof. He jumped out of the car and found me behind it, lying on my back with my hands still in my pockets.

'Are you all right?' he gasped. 'Why didn't you move?!'

I told him that I thought he'd stop.

'We'd better go get a beer,' I said. Amazingly there wasn't a mark on my body.

The next day brought our second match, against Widzew Lodz. Again the match wasn't spectacular. Again I forget the score. It was so boring, in fact, that Cockney Phil Ward, from Halifax, spent most of game asleep near the goalpost. He was fast asleep when all of a sudden the ball hit him and woke him up. He immediately ran on the pitch and began chasing the Polish keeper, who in turn, ran away. So too did most of the Polish defence. He quickly calmed down and decided to lay behind the net for the rest of the match. After the game, Alan Aries ran onto the pitch and made straight for his hero, Kevin Hird. He had his photo taken with Hird while holding up his beloved flag, a Union Jack with 'Kevin Hird' emblazoned across it.

After the game all supporters had been invited to a huge beer tent that had been erected in the town, where a 'small' amount of free beer was available. Word had spread that the bikers from Copenhagen had also arrived in town. Almost every Leeds fan there arrived at the beer tent together – on our way we had spotted the hearse cruising down the parallel street – and went inside. There was a bigger police presence than we had been used to – twelve officers and four dogs. The four Utrecht supporters were also with us. About a dozen bikers then appeared. They were looking around and it appeared as though we were being counted. We can only assume that there was more of us than them, because, luckily, the rest of the evening, and the rest of our stay, passed without further incident.

On our way to our final drink in Jacob's Well, we noticed the local newspapers carrying the match report and pictures. Every single one showed a photograph of Cockney Phil chasing the Polish keeper. Also in one newspaper was a full-page article on Scouse, who had sold his house to finance his trip to this tournament. We had a couple of beers with the Utrecht lads and then said our goodbyes. Before we left, we returned the flag pole to the police station and shook hands with the officers. Then we boarded the train and headed for Germany.

On our way to Cologne, we stopped at Hamburg to visit the famous Reeperbahn. This is an amazing place, like the Golden Mile at Blackpool, but instead of amusement arcades, it has wall-to-wall sex shops and bars. Coachloads of pensioners roam the streets taking in the sights and apart from the odd, 'Ooh!', never seem to bat an eyelid. At one point we found ourselves in what resembled a giant underground car park, except rather than cars it was full of girls waiting to be picked out. Each one of them would whisk you upstairs and give you whatever you wanted. Passing on this we opted for another establishment that proudly announced, 'Live sex on stage!' We paid our money, got our 'free' beer (it had cost us £15 to get in) and awaited the entertainment. The curtain opened and an absolutely gorgeous girl appeared. After a couple of minutes of introducing the audience to her body, she posed over a chair, with her arse poised high in the air. At that moment her partner was led on stage. It was an Alsatian dog. It was all his handler could do to keep him under control as he bounded over to his 'treat'. The hound wasted no time in getting acquainted with his lover and clasped his front legs round her body and gave her a real good seeing to. It was short but sweet, and then we had to leave. Before we did, the star of the next 'act' was introduced to the audience. It was a four-foot-long snake. Dave Fry and I looked at each other and, although tempted, decided to move on.

We hadn't booked a hotel in Hamburg, opting instead for somewhere quiet with our sleeping bags. After a brief recce, we settled for a large grassy area with a few trees as shelter. We were wakened at dawn by noisy rush-hour traffic, only in that light realising that we were camped in the middle of a large roundabout. It then began to rain. We wriggled under the trees like a dozen huge caterpillars, pulled our hats down over our ears and had an hour's lie-in.

The following night Celtic were playing Hamburg and we went along for an hour. Kevin Keegan was the Hamburg hero at the time. We were stood in the open end with some Celtic supporters. It quickly became apparent that there were more Leeds fans in the ground than Celtic. This, we were told by one of the Bhoys, was because the majority of them had gone straight to Rotterdam for the next match. We comforted him by saying that it was OK, and if there was any trouble, we would protect them. He seemed a bit miffed.

We arrived there around lunchtime. Every television set in every shop, bar or club was showing the wedding of Lady Diana and Prince Charles. We headed for the department store known as Kaufoff, similar to a Marks & Spencer, except for the added attraction of spit-roast chickens. We had discovered this on previous visits to West Germany in the '70s. Although they tasted delicious, it was to be many years before anywhere in Britain caught on to this idea.

Another German tradition, which still hasn't caught on in Britain, is of blood banks, where you can sell your blood for around £13 a pint. We had discovered these in the '70s, too, introduced to them by a group of Liverpool fans. We were in Leverkusen during the Leeds pre-season tour of 1978, and we came across these Scousers who recommended it as a way of gaining some extra finance. That very day we joined the queue. We all had our fingers pricked before receiving a ticket and were then ushered upstairs to the donor room. There would be a little yelp and a Hattie Jacques lookalike would come out of each cubicle with a bag of blood. The first one on his feet could look back on a long line of cubicles, each with a pair of Dr. Marten boots sticking out through the curtains.

The blood can't have been much use to anyone. We had consumed that much beer between us that most of the bags had a head on them. Nevertheless, we were given another ticket and shown to a little office where we received our 54 Deutschmarks. We did attempt to go back, half an hour later, with the other arm, but they sussed us and sent us 'mad English' on our way.

Despite our frequent trips to Germany it still took us a while to get used to it. In the 1979 pre-season trip to West Germany, five of us –

Brod, Mally King, Dave Fry, Dave Burrows and myself – hired a car. We were driving down the autobahn from Dusseldorf to Marburg, where Leeds were to play Schalke 04. Brod was taking his driving shift and after about four hours of watching the road and the signs he said, 'Fucking hell, this Ausfhart is a big place.' It was only afterwards that any of us found out that 'Ausfhart' meant exit.

From Cologne we flew back to England and into Heathrow Airport. A few hours later we were flying to the Costa del Sol, for the tournament in La Linea. Predictably the weather was brilliant and we emerged from our hotel in shorts and sunglasses. Time for a San Miguel. In the very first bar, we came across the local character, Chico. He was a portly gentleman, wearing a large Hawaiian shirt and using a walking stick. His most prominent feature, though, was his facial hair. He had shaved off the left-hand side of his beard and the right-hand side of his moustache. He immediately struck up a friendship with every Leeds fan in town – although there were only about 50 of us as most had returned to England after the game in Germany.

There were four teams taking part in this tournament. Along with Leeds were Real Madrid and Real Sporting Gijón from Spain and Partizan Belgrade from Yugoslavia. We had seen the trophy in the newspapers and it was huge. A fully grown man could easily sit in it. We were chatting away with our half-bearded friend when I was surprised to be interrupted by Phil Ella from Kippax. We continued talking to Chico, telling him just how good Leeds were and that we would win this tournament and its giant trophy, not knowing then that after the coming season we would be relegated. Chico told us that he hated Real Madrid, but he added that Madrid would win this tournament, without any doubt whatsoever.

'Real Madrid have not won a trophy all last season,' he explained. 'They will win these games and the Cup. It will already have been decided.'

Unlike Chico, the majority of the Spanish local people were supporting Real, even though Madrid was hundreds of miles away. At the time, the border between Spain and the British colony of Gibraltar had been closed by the King of Spain, prompting discontent between the two countries. However, La Linea was so close to the border that you could clearly see Union Jacks, some bearing the name of Leeds United, draped over the edges of the famous Rock.

Leeds won their first game, against Sporting Gijón, 3–2. They played really well, but during the game Real Madrid were allowed to walk around the pitch dressed in their all-white kit. With the Madrid team was Laurie Cunningham, who had recently signed for Real Madrid from West Bromwich Albion. Laurie tragically died in a car accident a couple of years later. The following night Real Madrid beat Partizan Belgrade, setting up a Leeds–Madrid final.

Hours before the kick-off we were socialising with Chico. Brod asked him if he still thought Madrid would beat Leeds.

'Without a doubt,' he replied. 'As I told you, it has already been decided.'

Such was the importance of this game to Real Madrid that it was shown live on Spanish television. To us it was just another friendly. Phil Ella, a friend of mine from Kippax, just happened to be on holiday in La Linea. I bumped into him in a little back street bar; he couldn't believe that Leeds were playing at this most southern part of Spain.

The game got under way in very humid conditions and the Union Jacks could still be clearly seen on Gibraltar – the British could see right down into the stadium from their vantage point on the Rock. It became obvious from the start that Chico may have been right about his prediction. To begin with, Leeds were playing in unfamiliar black-and-white stripes, their own kit having mysteriously disappeared shortly before kick-off, leaving Real free to wear their white colours. Leeds had to borrow the kit of Partizan Belgrade. Then, in the first minute, the referee awarded a free-kick to Real on the edge of the Leeds penalty area. It didn't look like a foul but Leeds set up a wall. The free-kick went flying, yards over the bar. The referee gave a corner. We were in for a great night here. Midway through the first half a harmless-looking challenge by Arthur Graham resulted in a lecture from the referee. No one could believe it when he then sent him off. Derek Parlane started laughing incredulously. The ref heard and ordered him off, too. By now the capacity crowd, full of the locals dressed in brand-new Real Madrid shirts, knew there was only one outcome to this game. It didn't get any better for Leeds in the second half and after a number of further dodgy decisions, our caretaker manager, Maurice Lindley, strode onto the pitch and signalled for his players to come off the field. Lindley was probably one of the mildest and quietest men in the game and was only acting manager for this trip. Eventually the team returned to the field of play but further stoppages meant that a game which had kicked off at nine o'clock at night finished, incredibly, at one o'clock in the morning. Real Madrid, not surprisingly, won 3–0, but near the end there was a bit of drama for the 20 of us Leeds fans standing in the corner.

A group of Spanish lads aged about 11 or 12 began taunting us. At first we ignored them but eventually Collar ran over and grabbed one of them. All the others scattered as Collar dragged his captive back up to where we stood. Then we all watched in disbelief as Collar put the young lad across his knee and smacked his arse.

The locals didn't like that. Not one bit. Angry Spanish supporters began coming towards us, all older than our previous tormentors. Their leader appeared to be the one in a wheelchair organising things from his vantage point on the stadium's running track. Everything began to get a bit freaky. Some Spanish lads were tugging at a huge Leeds flag that was draped over a wall to our left, but we couldn't see them. Collar did and vaulted over the wall to protect the flag. He disappeared. Unseen by him or us was a 25-foot drop the other side of the wall. A local broke his fall but Collar still broke his ankle.

Eventually the police intervened and calm was restored, momentarily. The police advised us not to go out the way we had come in and pointed across the pitch. Brod and I managed to reach Collar, and we laid him on an advertising board as a makeshift stretcher, which we began carrying across the pitch to seek medical attention. This just wasn't our night, however, and as we were halfway across the field, all the floodlights went out and left us in total darkness. We eventually spied a light and carried Collar towards it. This turned out to be down the players' tunnel. We got him into a deserted dressing-room and went to ask for some assistance. From outside, even then, we could still hear the sound of shouting. Bricks were being thrown, too, smashing windows.

Whether the locals were aiming for us or the Leeds team we'll never know. We found out later that the players had left as soon as the whistle had gone.

About an hour later someone arrived to tend to Collar. He got out his bag and proceeded to strap Collar's ankle, then his leg. He didn't stay long and left. The groundsman told us afterwards that this medical man was a horse doctor.

Apart from pushing Collar around, the following day was spent wallowing in the sunshine and having a farewell drink with Chico, who took no satisfaction whatsoever over his prediction of a Real Madrid victory. The next leg of our journey was to be Toronto in Canada where the team had another friendly to play, but we were in for further bad news. At the airport we discovered that Spanish Air Traffic Control was in the middle of a one-day strike. We could fly out eight hours later, but the time difference meant we would arrive four hours after the game in Toronto.

I still have my plane ticket to Toronto. It was the last and only Leeds game I have missed anywhere in the world to date. Just to put the icing on my bad-luck cake, a friend of mine, Kenny Bowers, was on holiday in Toronto at the time, and went to the match expecting to meet up with me. He never lets me forget that he saw the one match I missed.

It was no consolation that after the following season Leeds United were relegated and this proved to be the last pre-season tour for six years.

Leeds did, however, take part in a mid-season tournament in Djurgarden, Sweden, in 1984. Kippax took a full coach across on the ferry and despite other English teams such as Manchester City, Leicester City and West Brom being involved in the tournament, we were the only English on the ferry – with the exception of one West Brom fan who spent much of his time with us. It was an 18-hour crossing, but there was so much to do on board that the time flew by.

We experienced a bit of a culture shock when we arrived in Sweden. We had been informed that it was expensive, but we weren't expecting it to be quite this expensive. Or with bars so very few and far between. When we did eventually find one the beer was 26 krona

(£2.60, at a time when I'd pay about 70p at The Moorgate or The Royal Oak). Our coach driver, who was counting his pennies very carefully, said, 'Sod that, I'll just have a coffee.' When it arrived he nearly died – it was 36 krona. One of the South Kirby lads ordered a whisky and when that arrived it converted to almost a tenner. We soon discovered that the petrol stations sold beer much cheaper. It came in three different strengths, so we had to make sure we got the strong rather than regular – and avoid the non-alcohol variety at all costs. Our hotel was near a motorway and on the other side of it was a petrol station. One day a few of us were walking back to the hotel and, as the motorway was empty of traffic, decided to take a shortcut across it for some refuelling of our own. On the return trip we looked up at the hotel and saw some of our lads calling and waving to us out of their windows and, thinking they were being friendly, we waved back.

Kenny Young was the first to spot what they had been trying to indicate, calling over his shoulder as he broke into a run: 'These coppers don't look happy, come on!' The policemen were chasing us but we reached the other side of the motorway and scrambled down the banking towards our hotel. Just then, more police, who had driven through the motorway underpass to cut us off, confronted us. I don't speak Swedish but I could tell they were very upset about something. As they took their handcuffs from their belts, a woman officer said in English: 'Who are you, what are you doing?'

We spluttered something to the effect that we were visiting football fans and were simply going back to our hotel. She didn't seem impressed.

'Did you not notice that this motorway is closed?' she asked.

'Well,' I said, slightly confused, 'we noticed it wasn't very busy, so we decided to come across it instead of going all the way around. Silly, eh?'

She agreed with me.

'Yes, very silly. The King of Sweden is due to pass through here, at this very moment. But instead, his limousine is held up half a mile back. A police helicopter spotted you crossing the motorway, with weapons, so the procession was halted!'

Our 'weapons' were the two cans of beer that each of us had

bought. The police let us off with a caution and warned us that drinking in public was an offence. We thanked them and returned to the hotel, where we drank our beer in private watching *Blazing Saddles* on the telly.

The Leeds match against a local side – the first time I remember seeing them play indoors – was memorable only for one other thing, sadly, not the game. It was only a small arena and the small barriers had glass panes beneath them. One Leeds supporter slipped and fell head first through the glass. He later died in hospital.

This tragedy passed largely unnoticed and was soon overshadowed by the deaths of 39 Juventus fans during the 1985 European Cup final between the Italian side and Liverpool at the Heysel Stadium in Brussels. The result was major changes throughout European football. Not least that English clubs were banned from playing in any European matches. Or rather I should say that *Leeds United* were banned from playing in any European matches. Let me explain . . .

The ban, which had immediate effect, stated that English clubs would not be allowed to take part in any games in Europe, including friendlies. Yet that very summer, a ferry carrying West Ham and manchester united fans into Europe, was turned back when fighting broke out between the two. These fans were travelling to see their teams play friendlies in Holland and Belgium. Following this precedent Leeds applied several times to play on the continent but were repeatedly refused and reminded of the ban – even though several other English teams continued to travel into mainland Europe. The Welsh FA even cited the ban when refusing permission to allow Leeds into Wales, after they had been asked by Newport County to play in a testimonial to raise desperately needed funds.

A year later Leeds United played Genoa at Elland Road. The arrangement was that the teams would play each other home and away in exhibition matches. The game at Leeds took place, but the one in Italy was cancelled. If this wasn't bad enough, Liverpool *were* given permission to play in Italy, 60 miles down the coast from Genoa, at the same time. It was as if the decision-makers had forgotten which English club had been at the Heysel Stadium in 1985.

In July 1987, Leeds were invited to take part in a tournament in

Germany called Internationales Jubilaums – Fufballtournier. Three German teams, VFB Oldenburg, Borussia Mönchengladbach and FC Nuremburg, were the other sides involved. We made plans to travel over for the two-day festival. Then at the very last minute the FA ordered Leeds to withdraw, again repeating the ban on English clubs. Unbelievably, Luton Town took the place of Leeds United.

Batty is My Hero. And Shez. And Lorimer

In the '80s, all the players were great. They'd all come to the Kippax dos – whether they were invited or not!

I first saw David Batty play in 1985. He was 15 and part of a Leeds United XI assembled for a pre-season friendly against Thackley. It was obvious to everybody present that summer evening that this little blond-haired midfielder was going right to the top. He tackled everything and everybody that didn't have a Leeds shirt on, regardless of size. And Batty was easily the smallest player on the pitch.

Two and a half seasons later Bats made his debut for Leeds against Swindon Town at Elland Road. The same season he played for England Under-21s and in May 1991 he made it to the England senior team. None of us that had seen him in action against Thackley almost six years earlier were at all surprised.

During that period the LUSC Kippax Branch was thriving and our end-of-season dinner dance events were very popular. Most Leeds players we invited would attend our functions, which were usually held at a late-night pub-cum-nightclub called Upstairs Downstairs in Armley, near Leeds.

Among the favourites with our branch were Bats, Gary Speed, John Sheridan and Ian Baird. Tommy Wright and Neil Aspin were also regular, welcome visitors.

In 1988 we held our event in November on the same night as the draw for the FA Cup third round. At around eleven o'clock at night the place fell silent as everyone studied the televisions dotted around the club. The place erupted as Leeds were drawn away at Brighton. Big John Martin took the microphone from the disc jockey and promptly started a 'Wem-ber-ley! Wem-ber-ley! – We're the famous Leeds United and we're off to Wem-ber-ley!' Everyone had joined in as John Sheridan, ever so slightly drunk, took the microphone himself and shouted, 'No problem. Who's fuckin' Brighton?' Everyone cheered – and then Sheridan promptly tripped over one of the speakers and fell off the stage, dropping and breaking the microphone as he did so. (A few weeks later Leeds beat Brighton 2–0, thanks to a brace from Ian Baird.)

Meanwhile, back at Upstairs Downstairs, Shez was quickly back on his feet and drinking as though nothing had happened while a few of us stood chatting with Baird at the bar. Baird was born in Yorkshire, in Rotherham, but had grown up on the south coast and always considered himself to be a southerner. So he used to get really wound up when we would remind him that he was a Yorkshireman and there was nothing he could do about it. Pete Dillon put it better when he said to him, in the broadest accent he could muster, 'Tha's a Yorky mate, an' the's nowt tha can do abaht it.' Baird used to hate that.

The Snodin brothers, Ian and Glynn, also attended the Kippax functions, although never together because they played for the club at different times. But individually, they each left their mark. Ian was probably the best player at the club at the time, but left to join Everton in 1987. During the summer of that year Glynn joined us. It was Glynn who started the famous 'Leeds, Leeds, Leeds!' salute of the clenched fist and bending arm across the heart, which is still used today.

Bats regularly won Player of the Year awards – and not just from our branch. In 1989 the Wellingborough and Northampton branches made the same choice as us. Wellingborough were due to make their presentation on the same day that Leeds were away at Watford and as many of the lads – especially Tim Maguire, Ian 'Coke' Cockayne, Mark Belshaw and Trevor Smith (now sadly passed away) – are good friends of ours, we said that we would come along and personally bring Bats to their presentation.

After the game Bats boarded our coach in the fans' car park and, I have to admit, it was great looking at the faces of the Leeds fans on the other coaches as they watched him sit down and immediately open a can of lager that someone had handed him. Imagine that happening with our players these days! We basked in our glory as our coach squeezed away from the ground with the fans either side of us nudging each other and pointing.

When we reached Wellingborough, we began trawling round the pubs. There were quite a number of Leeds fans around and they couldn't believe it when Bats walked into their pub. Bats, I have to say, was totally unfazed by the whole thing.

An hour or so later, a group of Chelsea fans came into the pub. You could have cut the atmosphere with one of Carlton Palmer's legs. As another large group of Chelsea fans arrived, it looked like there was going to be a bit of trouble. Collar leant across to our guest and said, 'Look, Bats, you'd better fuck off, mate. This is gonna get naughty. The last thing we want is you splashed all over tomorrow's *News Of The World*.' Bats simply stuck out his chest, gave a little Glynn Snodin salute, and said, 'We are Leeds!' Fortunately for all concerned the Chelsea fans, perhaps realising they were outnumbered or simply not fancying their chances against Bats, supped up and left.

On our coach home after the presentation only the driver was sober. One of the most pissed was Stuart Smythe. Stuart is a proud Scotsman and a fan of Celtic. Or is it Rangers? I can never quite remember. But, anyway, he's Scottish and when he married Trisha in 1997, in Leeds, he proved it's true about what Scots are supposed to wear under their kilts by chasing people around with manhood gripped firmly in hand at the reception.

Just as drunk on the way back from Wellingborough was Stan Smith and he and Stuart soon fell fast asleep. Stan is another example of the kind of bizarre characters that the Kippax Branch seems to attract. He's very tiny, doesn't say much and has a habit of just turning up, as if by magic. It's hard to explain, but you could be having a conversation and you get the feeling that someone is watching you. Look around and there is Stan. Just watching. He's very weird.

Just like the big kids we are, we got out the marker pens. When we had finished they both looked like Spider-Man. Batty put the finishing touches to each face by signing his autograph on their foreheads.

Finally back in Leeds, we all piled into a late bar near the railway station. It was only then that Stuart looked at Stan and said: 'Look at the state of you – they've written all over your face!'

Stan looked back at Stuart and replied, 'They haven't, have they? The bastards!' But he never said a word about Stuart's face.

Half an hour later Stuart went into the toilet. Everyone around our tables fell silent. Then, as Stuart finally saw his reflection in the mirror, he began to yell: 'You bastards!' He came out of the toilet, his poor face red and raw from his ineffectual attempts to rub off the graffiti, still shouting: 'Bastards! Bastards! Bastards!'

Batty was helpless with laughter.

At the beginning of the 1991–92 season, I was stood waiting for the bus outside Elland Road. Leeds had just played Bradford City, I think, in a pre-season West Riding Senior Cup match, and I was stood chatting with John Martin and Pete Dillon. A white Escort XR3 pulled up and driving it was David Batty. The window opened. 'Going to town, lads?' We piled in and soon arrived at The Duck And Drake. Bats parked at the side of the pub and all four of us went in for a pint and sat down to drink it.

'Do you come in here a lot then, Bats?' I said.

He looked puzzled. 'Why, what's up?'

I pointed to an oil painting I'd just noticed on the wall. It was of The Duck And Drake, and in the side street was a white Ford Escort, exactly where Bats had parked his. Uncanny.

We began talking about an incident that had happened a few months before at about half past midnight on a Saturday when I was walking up The Headrow in Leeds city centre. I was with Dick Hazelgrave and we were going to The White Stag to a private party for Dick's lady, Trish. As we passed Mr Craig's nightclub we saw John Sheridan leant against the wall. He appeared a little worse for wear. He recognised us immediately. 'Hey, the Kippax boys are here!' he shouted. 'How's it goin', lads?' He had recently been transferred to Nottingham Forest so we were surprised to see him back in Leeds. I asked him where he'd been and, a bit unsteady on his feet, he replied, 'I've been to Tottenham with Forest.' I asked him the result and if he had scored. He put an arm around me. 'Scored? Scored?! I didn't even fuckin' play! That bastard Brian Clough doesn't like me. He doesn't even talk to me!' Shez was clearly upset. The word at the time was that Clough had been away on holiday when Forest signed Shez and the Forest manager seemed to resent this. Whether this was correct or not, Sheridan never kicked a ball for Forest. To make matters worse, the bouncers wouldn't let him in to the club. As we stood there, I heard a loud tapping on one of Mr Craig's large windows beside the stairs leading up to the main body of the club. I looked up and there were David Batty and Gary Speed, laughing and pointing at Shez. Sheridan responded with a two-fingered salute and a sneer: 'You bastards!'

So John Sheridan liked a drink, but don't we all? Besides, he was a brilliant bloke, always approachable, whether in the city centre or down at Elland Road.

I'm convinced that David Batty didn't want to leave Leeds United in October 1993. Just over a year earlier manager Howard Wilkinson had restored some much needed pride into the hearts of Leeds United fans everywhere when he led the side to the 1992 League Championship. Everything was looking healthy. Wilko had been in charge since September 1988 and in that time had dragged the team out of the old Second Division, as Champions, in 1990. I had been impressed since the first time I had met Wilkinson, when he was introduced to the fans at a special Leeds United supporters meeting in the old supporters club building on Elland Road, Fullerton Park. The place was absolutely packed as Wilkinson appeared on the small stage to huge applause.

'I don't know what you're all clapping at, you haven't seen anything yet,' were his very first words. Managing director Bill

Fotherby, who had claimed responsibility for capturing Wilko, and Eric Carlile, the popular secretary of the supporters club, flanked him. Wilko went on: 'I'm happy to be here. I first met with directors from Leeds United at a motorway service station, and can reveal here and now that they were all eating pork pies at the time.' This was an obvious reference to the many Jewish members of the board at that time. Fotherby looked a little uneasy and loosened his tie. The supporters lapped it up – here at last was a man who wasn't going to lick the arse of the directors. He then turned to the man on his other side. 'And Eric, dear old Eric, what can you say about Eric?' Eric gulped and loosened his tie, too, smiling uneasily. 'One thing is for sure. It has reinforced my belief that there is indeed life after death.'

Poor old Eric Carlile. It has to be said that he does the hardest job within the supporters club, and has done for 40 years or more. Not only that, he does it brilliantly, dealing with over 70 different branches. I have been to Eric's flat on many occasions to collect match tickets and it is an amazing sight. At any given time there are piles of tickets for different matches and different branches all over his lounge. But he knows where every one is. I've been sat there having a cup of tea with him when the telephone has rung, with someone asking about this or that ticket allocation. Over a period of ten minutes it would ring six or seven times. Each time he would go straight to the allocation in question and deal with it. All of this while watching the afternoon movie with the sound turned up very loud.

Alongside Eric in the LUSC building, Wilko answered questions for over two hours and left the throng with a very good feeling indeed.

So where did it all go wrong?

I believe Wilko's decline and subsequent loss of marbles started with the Batty transfer in October 1993. As I said, I am convinced Bats did not want to leave. But on the other hand, if you realise a club is prepared to sell you, then you must re-evaluate your situation. I lay the blame firmly at Wilko's door. It was obvious the directors were happy to sell Bats. Wilko claimed he was not. That should have been the end of the matter. Instead the manager told the player of the situation. For me that conversation should never have taken place. But the seeds were now sown in Batty's head and from then on, things could never be the same. The rest, as they say, is history. Bats went to Blackburn for just over £2.5m and was replaced by none other than Carlton fucking Palmer. The proverbial icing on the cake.

When I first saw David Batty in a Blackburn Rovers shirt, I swear I felt physically sick. Here was a true Yorkshire lad who had grown up shouting for his heroes from the Lowfields Road terracing, now wearing a red rose over his heart. It hurt. I knew deep down that he hadn't wanted to leave us, but I couldn't help feeling sad. It was almost like he was having an affair.

Bats had won the Kippax Player of the Year award for 1992, but had gone over the Pennines before we could present him with his trophy. Naturally, we couldn't give him it now and it is still in my house today. To show there were no hard feelings, Bats was invited to the 1993 Kippax Player of the Year event.

He sent the ticket back and wrote on the back, 'Gary, thanks for the invite but Blackburn play Chelsea on Sun, 5th Dec on TV. So I won't be able to come. Hope to see you at next year's presentation. All the best. Bats.'

So it was official. Bats now played for Blackburn and to prove it, he chose to play for them instead of attending a Kippax event and being with his friends.

The official Leeds United Supporters Club annual dinner dances are still popular but they have changed a lot over the years. Now held in Elland Road's impressive Banqueting Suite, built onto the back of the West Stand, they are far too official these days for my liking. Until recent years each branch would have a player of their choice sitting with them at their table. Afterwards the players would mix with everyone, drink (sensibly), dance and generally relax. Managers used to 'insist' that players attend these functions – not that it took much 'insisting' – and they were always a good time.

Nowadays the players all file in together and sit together at a long table. There they spend over an hour signing autographs before their meal. Once the meal is finished they leave, usually around nine o'clock. At the 2002 function, none of the players attended at all. They all chose a boxing match instead.

The good old days were definitely the best. One year, at a very posh restaurant in Leeds called The Allerton, we had both Noel Blake and Vince Hilaire on the Kippax table. Things were going well and Vinnie Jones came over and joined us. Vinnie went for a dance with one of our female guests and that is when I put my foot in it. I was getting on great with Blake and Hilaire when I blurted, 'Shouldn't you two be getting ready?' They both looked surprised. I went in deeper. 'Aren't you due on stage? Where are the other two?' They still looked surprised, then I just about signed my own death warrant. 'I'm sorry. You are the Four Tops, aren't you?' God only knows why I thought they would be amused. I received a stare from Blake that was usually reserved for opposing forwards. That was enough for me. 'Right then,' I said, standing up. 'Anyone for a drink?' Luckily, instead of punching me, Blake pointed to his and Hilaire's empty bottles. I've never been so happy to buy anyone a drink in my life.

That's another thing I admire about Wilko. It must have taken almighty courage to tell Noel Blake that the club no longer needed him.

Another popular annual supporters' function was the Menwith Hill Branch's. Situated near Harrogate, the American air base would put on a spread that was beyond belief. Huge beef and pork roasts would adorn the serving tables. And when I say huge, I mean American huge. English and American Leeds fans would mingle and generally be merry. It was at one of these events that I got the manager at the time, Eddie Gray, to sign my Kippax Flat Earth Society life-membership card.

On one occasion I was stood talking with members Tim Thorpe and Jack Frost, when John Sheridan joined us. Jack was talking with Shez when all of a sudden he slammed him up against the wall. Me and Tim looked at each other in surprise while Jack said, 'You are a fuckin' brilliant player, but you've got to get stuck in more.'

Sheridan was a bit taken aback but replied, 'Yeah, I know you're right. I know I have to get into tackles more.'

Jack dusted him down and said, 'Good boy!'

The very next game Sheridan went in for a crunching tackle and broke his leg.

Vinnie Jones was another player who always made time for Leeds fans. He attended many Kippax functions and when he was out on the pitch before a game would always go over and spend time with supporters in the disabled section. Mick Watson from Kippax was at Bournemouth for the crucial promotion game in 1990. Before the game he was with his son, Andy, who is disabled, behind one of the goals watching Leeds warm up. Vinnie went straight over to Andy and they had their photograph taken. Now enlarged and framed, that picture still has pride of place in Andy's room.

Before he signed for Leeds, in the days when he was still part of Wimbledon's Crazy Gang, a few of us were on the train on our way to an away match with Wimbledon when we noticed Vinnie in the next carriage. It was twenty to two and the kick-off was at three o'clock. 'Aren't you playing today, Vinnie?' I asked.

'Yeah, sure. There's plenty of time.'

As my mate Derek and his wife Tracie are massive Vinnie fans, I asked him if he would sign an autograph for Tracie. He looked around then tore off a piece of newspaper from a passenger opposite, took out a pen and said, 'Right, what's her name and address?' Sure enough a few days later, an autographed photo dropped through Tracie's letterbox.

We were planning to get off the train a few stops from the ground to go for a beer. As we were waiting to get off, Vinnie said, 'You don't want to get off here, lads, it's shite. Get off at the next stop and turn left out of the station. There's a few good pubs there.' As we got off where he had told us, he gave us the Leeds salute.

During the game, Vinnie had a good banter going with the Leeds fans, massed down one side. Every time he came to take a throw-in, he would give the Leeds fans the same salute.

I always thought it seemed a little cruel that Vinnie was sold before he got a chance to play with Leeds in the top flight. Especially as he had contributed so much to getting us there in the first place. Vinnie has a Leeds tattoo on his leg and it warms the cockles of my heart that these days he's strolling around Beverly Hills or Venice Beach in California, showing it to everyone. I can just picture him meeting Steven Spielberg to discuss a new film. Spielberg shakes Vinnie's hand and sits down. He starts to outline Vinnie's new role. But Vinnie immediately interrupts him and says, 'Hey, Steve, have you seen my Leeds United tattoo?'

I think Allan Clarke could have made it big in Hollywood, too. He would have made just as good a tough guy as Clint Eastwood or Sean Bean. 'Sniffer' is still a huge Leeds fan and makes no secret of the fact when he doesn't agree with things that happen at Elland Road. I met him not so long back and he still refers to Leeds as 'us' and 'we'. I like that. He goes to most Leeds games and only recently he was stood in the away end for the pre-season friendly at Halifax Town.

Peter Lorimer is another Leeds 'old boy' who still refers to Leeds as 'us'. I often pop into his pub, The Commercial, in Holbeck, Leeds. A few years back he was presenting trophies at our end of season bash for The Royal Oak football team. The evening didn't get off to the best of starts. The disc jockey arrived in a manchester united shirt. I immediately left the club and went up the road into another pub. About half an hour later, Steve Hartley came looking for me. 'Come on, mate, we've made the DJ take off his shirt. One of the lads has given him an old jumper – and Peter Lorimer has arrived.'

My dad had offered his services as a country and western singer for the evening, so we didn't use the disco much anyway. As the evening was drawing to a close, I was stood at the bar with Lorimer and thanked him for coming. 'No problem,' he said. 'Anyway, that singer was fucking brilliant.' Just then Dad walked past and I called him over. 'Hey, Dad, come here, this fella here says you were brilliant.'

He shook Peter's hand and said, 'You were pretty brilliant in your day, too, old lad!' A mutual admiration society holding its first meeting. I've seen Lorimer, even these days, turn out for the Leeds United Ex-Players Association and despite being somewhat larger and older, he still displays tremendous skill.

It is a pity that the present-day footballers do not show the same commitment to supporters as their predecessors did.

- 13 -

Rochdale Strippers and London Queens

We always looked at London as 'an eight-canner' – and Sheffield just one. Distances don't matter. It's who you're with and what you're doing.

Whenever Leeds played over the Pennines in the '80s and early '90s, we would always stop for a drink in Rochdale. Although long since closed and boarded up, The Derby was by far the favourite pub with the lads. The landlord would open up for us whatever time we arrived. When we used to play Oldham Athletic we would sometimes turn up at seven or eight in the morning.

One such instance was for a game at Boundary Park on Good Friday in 1986. It was my birthday and Dave Green's the following day. A stripper had been arranged for us both but, knowing we had been set up for a stage act, we did the brave thing and stayed well away. Instead we were drinking on our own in another pub, The Spread Eagle.

After an hour, when we thought it safe, we made our way to The Derby to meet the rest of the Kippax Branch. As we walked through the door it was absolute bedlam. One of the lads had just finished with the stripper but as they both got up off the tap-room floor, Para

Dave yelled, 'Me next!' Within seconds the stripper was back on her back on the floor. She was willing. She was good. And from where I stood, Para wasn't bad either. The DJ helped the proceedings with 'Sex Machine' and Dave Green and I felt safe. Even if we had wanted to have a go, there was a queue and there wouldn't have been time before leaving for the game.

Someone produced a camera but the DJ stepped in quickly: 'Not allowed!' It was only when we were all saying our farewells that we discovered that he was the stripper's husband. He obviously didn't mind playing music while his wife was being shafted, but he drew the line at taking a photo!

Later that night when I got home and told Lesley the story she quizzed me. 'Are you sure you didn't have a go?'

'Don't be stupid,' I retorted. 'Me?!'

She came back with a beauty. 'I wouldn't have minded, it was your birthday!'

Extremely cunning is my Mrs Edwards.

Many pubs in and around Leeds used to put strippers on, before and after games. At The Crown (now sadly closed) near Tetley's brewery, we'd watch one or two classy turns and then jump into taxis the mile and a half to Elland Road. It made for a perfect day, as long as Leeds won.

In The White Swan On The Calls, we were also regularly entertained, and just to make sure everything went off without a hitch, the local CID were nearly always in attendance. This pub has long since changed its name and style, but we still look back with fond memories. A similar venue was The Whip; the place would be absolutely packed and again the CID would drop in now and again to make sure everything was going smoothly. The Whip, too, has long since changed. Another such casualty was The Scotsman, now an amusement arcade. Before the machines moved in the place was something else. We were regularly invited in for 'breakfast' before boarding the coach for crucial '80s away games.

Panama Joe's (formerly the Hofbrauhaus) at the northern edge of Leeds city centre was another bar that latched onto the idea of mixing football and strippers. Every Saturday when there was a home game Leeds fans were invited to sample cut-price lager, free chips and three strippers on stage. For added entertainment, a huge screen showed the previous week's match. Hundreds of Leeds fans would turn up and the atmosphere was electric. It became so well known that after a few weeks customers other than Leeds fans began turning up. It wasn't long before the old-favourite sign went up on the door, 'No football colours', and the big screen began showing music videos. I got great satisfaction weeks later when leaflets began circulating, inviting Leeds United fans back to sample 'the brand new entertainment' at Panama Joe's – girls, half-price beer and a free burger and chips. Most Leeds fans by then had found new meeting places and very few went back. Shortly afterwards, Panama Joe's closed for 'refurbishment'. It opened three years later, with new owners and a new name.

Such harsh treatment towards Leeds fans in their own city sadly happened again in August 1988. We moved around a lot but by that year had been in The Horse And Trumpet on the Headrow, as guests of landlord Roy Peel, as often as we could for ten years. Leeds' first game of the season was at home to Oxford United. The Horse And Trumpet had undergone extensive refurbishment over the summer and seven or eight of us arrived looking forward to seeing the new decor. There was a new landlord, too, but the bar staff were much the same. We ordered pints all round only to hear one of them sheepishly explain, 'I can't serve those two with Leeds United shirts on, new Tetley policy. No football shirts allowed.' Ian Thornton, Pat Connor (both of whom have sadly now passed away) and Stevie Priestly were the 'guilty' men. 'Well, excuse us,' said Stevie. 'It's my fault, I thought I was in Leeds.' We were told the rest could have a drink but not the ones with the shirts on. There were six pints on the bar. They were still there as we all turned round and walked out. To this day none of us have ever been back.

Leeds city centre grew into a brilliant, vibrant area during the '90s, but it's a shame it didn't retain some of its more traditional watering holes.

I had a similar experience more recently, during the summer of 1999. Lesley and I took my nephew Scott to see his mam – my sister Julie – in Jimmy's Hospital, then on our way back we called at TGI's for lunch. Scott and I were wearing Leeds shirts and when I asked for a table for three our waiter, a dead-ringer for Basil Fawlty, replied: 'Certainly, sir! Just one thing, could you turn your football shirts inside out? Company policy, no football shirts.'

I told him not to bother with our table as we were leaving. I was prepared to leave the matter at that and never return, but I noticed a huge advert for TGI's in the Leeds United match-day programme. I was so annoyed I contacted the club chairman, Peter Ridsdale, who told me he would investigate. A few days later I received a letter from TGI's offering me an apology and a £30 meal voucher. Lesley used it while I was at an away match at Wimbledon. One pub we have drunk in consistently over the years, untroubled by police raids, refurbishments or 'No football shirts' policies is The Nag's Head on Vicar Lane in Leeds. John and Lorraine Mitchell have been the hosts there for many years.

The Market 'Madhouse' Tavern, now demolished to make way for a car park, was a pub of exceptional cuisine. Market traders such as butchers, greengrocers and fishmongers could always be seen plying their trade and drinking the odd glass before going to work at six o'clock in the morning. The Madhouse was a big favourite with the Kippax Branch. At the time we had a very good quiz team. When the team first started we used to hold the inter-branch competition upstairs in either The Three Legs or The Vine. Among the original team were Dillon, Big John, Greg Gater and myself. The team went on to have a number of successful years. Many of our successes were in the Madhouse where the intimidating atmosphere would invariably gain us extra points. During the '80s the official Leeds United Supporters Club quiz team was highly successful – often with our own Big John Martin among their number – winning the national quiz in 1982 against Barking and again in 1984 when Celtic were the beaten finalists. Big Mick Hewitt, our foreign travel arranger from the South Kirby branch, even won the individual national quiz that year and he collected his trophy from the former Blackpool and England legend Stan Mortenson.

Leeds United's Second Division years of the late '80s were short on glamour – strippers aside – but they did have their moments. I will always remember the 1986–87 season for Leeds FA Cup run.

The FA Cup third round draw in December saw Leeds drawn away to non-league Telford United. With Telford's full consent and co-operation, the tie, to be played on 12 January, was switched from their own ground, Bucks Head to West Brom's, The Hawthorns. This wasn't an ideal choice as there had been trouble there the last time Leeds played a league match. But, to prevent any repeat, Leeds United quickly introduced a self-imposed membership-card scheme and that ought to have been the end of it. But, the FA seemed to want more.

The game against Telford was a farce because the pitch was icy and rock hard. Any other game would have been postponed immediately. It was extremely dangerous and Leeds scraped through 2–1. In the following rounds, Leeds were forced to play at ridiculous times: midday, twelve thirty in the afternoon and so on, which is commonplace now but had never been done before. Even the opposing managers admitted things were being taken out of all proportion. For example when Leeds met Swindon Town in the fourth round the Swindon manager Lou Macari said before the game: 'I have no problem with the Leeds United fans, they are welcome here any time.' Leeds beat his side 2–1 and went on to beat Queens Park Rangers, also 2–1, at Elland Road, to reach the quarter-final.

For the semi-final – against Coventry City at Hillsborough – we hired a double-decker bus. We had breakfast at The Anchor, in Allerton Bywater near Kippax, before we set off for the quarter past twelve kick-off. Gord Findlay had made a 12-foot-high FA Cup out of hardboard and he brought it to me to be decorated. I sprayed it silver, put black shading on it and hung blue-and-gold ribbons through the handles. It looked fantastic even if I do say so myself. But it was so big that it wouldn't go in the bus and we had to take it in turns reaching out of upstairs and downstairs windows to hold it in place against the side of the bus. When we arrived we walked down the steep hill towards the ground, holding our cup aloft. As we reached the bottom of that hill, the authorities had one more anti-Leeds trick up their sleeve. All Leeds flags, even those without poles, were to be confiscated. (LUSC secretary, Eric Carlile, had hundreds and hundreds of returned Leeds flags in his spare bedroom for years.) We soon guessed our cup would not see the match.

Sure enough, two policemen approached us: 'Sorry gents, you can't go in with that.' Gord had had enough.

'No problem, mate,' he said. 'Here! It's yours.'

And so, as hundreds of Leeds fans walked past, laughing and pointing, his mate having left him to it, we left this red-faced copper holding a 12-foot hardboard FA Cup gently blowing in the wind.

He'd have had a lot more trouble holding on to it in October 1987 when I made the first of many trips to Ireland to watch Leeds United play friendlies.

It was six o'clock in the morning and still dark as we prepared to leave Leeds–Bradford Airport. Michael Fish had just famously announced to Great Britain and the lady who'd phoned the Met Office, that there was no need to panic – there were no hurricanes heading for our shores. Barely hours after his statement Britain was hit with winds of over 100 mph, causing deaths and millions of pounds worth of damage. It was certainly blowing a gale outside the terminal.

If I was worried our flight would be cancelled then I nearly died of shock when I saw the size of the plane we were getting on. I had seen bigger ones on the shelves in model shops. The stewardess at the top of the steps was holding on to her hat as she welcomed us aboard. Inside were only about 30 seats. There were enough to go round but not enough to fill me with confidence. As we fastened our seatbelts the Tannoy announced: 'Welcome to Capital Airlines. As you can see, it's a bit wild today – but we'll have a go and see how we get on!'

I gulped and looked around nervously as the voice continued: 'If you need to use the toilet, please move around the cabin carefully. And please do not all sit on the same side.'

Oh, great. As we taxied and took off it was like being on a ride at Blackpool Pleasure Beach. The plane was being buffeted all over the sky. We discovered afterwards that after we'd left, the airport had been closed.

As if things weren't frightening enough, David 'Ghandi' Sutcliffe fiddled with his watch and asked: 'Is Ireland an hour in front of us or an hour behind?' It was too windy to laugh. I just hoped the pilot had a better idea of which direction we were flying. It was one of the most frightening flights I've ever been on.

We arrived at Dublin, perhaps via Hong Kong and Australia, very windswept indeed. Having checked into our hotel we were soon making our acquaintance with a first pint of Guinness to calm our nerves. It was half past eight in the morning and all of Dublin must have been as scared as we were because the pubs were packed. On a return visit a year or so later we were even ejected (for being too noisy) at twenty to eight in the morning. Although I doubt we would have woken anyone up as they'd have all been on their way to a bar by then.

After that first flight, I've travelled to Ireland on the ferry from Holyhead a couple of times. Not everyone got the hang of it straight away. The first time we went, Lunge and I were sat out on the foredeck enjoying a beer when a message boomed out over the Tannoy: 'Could you two lads please leave the deck?'

We looked around. Did he mean us? Surely not. We carried on chatting and drinking. The voice was much louder next time.

'I really must insist that you two come inside immediately.'

We took the hint and went inside. We had just walked through the door when Lunge pointed through the window behind us. The deck where we had been sitting only seconds before was now raised and vertical, to allow the cars off.

On the way back we were waiting on the Dublin quayside when two of ours felt the need to cool off. As we stood nearby looking on in amazement, Trevor Hartford and Scotty suddenly threw off their shirts and jumped off the side of the harbour, plunging 20 yards down into the cold Irish Sea. They both disappeared below the icy waves and surfaced seconds later covered in green slime. When they climbed back up the ladder, laughing like school kids, they looked like two creatures from *Doctor Who*.

Television stars are everywhere in Dublin. Strolling up Grafton Street before a match with local side Shelbourne, Lesley and I came face to face with Martin Clunes, star of *Men Behaving Badly*. He was very friendly and we chatted for a few minutes and posed happily while Lesley took a photograph of us both. A Leeds fan in a bar up

160

the road took advantage of his good nature and quizzed him with a wink: 'Hey Martin, have you shagged Lesley Ash yet?' Clunes just smiled back and shook his head. The Leeds fan then added: 'Lee Chapman has!'

When I later got the photo developed I was horrified to see that Lesley, my wife, had also included in the background a little bastard, smiling into the camera, wearing a manchester united shirt. I could have cried. Instead I got a bottle of Tipp-Ex and a hand-drawn Thistle Hotels logo turned him into a Leeds fan. I still have a picture I can be proud of.

As well as in Dublin, Leeds have also played matches in Cork on a couple of occasions too. Cork is a brilliant place with hundreds of pubs and bars. We always stay at a really good hotel called Garnish House, run by the Lucey family.

Once in Cork, we got chatting to a group of very attractive Australian girls. Realising they were game for a laugh, Ian 'Skippy' Marsden bet them he was the only one in the bar who could scratch the middle of his back with his toes. Everyone put a couple of quid in the ashtray and began attempting to become the first to complete the challenge and pocket the cash. Soon the bar was full of would-be contortionists and after an unsuccessful attempt of my own, I settled down to watch the show. Our lads weren't too entertaining but the sight of the Aussie girls struggling to put their legs over their shoulders was a rare treat. After about 20 minutes everyone had given up. 'It's not possible!' said one of the girls. With that Skip dropped his jeans, unscrewed his false leg and proceeded to scratch his back with the toes. We all fell about laughing. Skip had lost his leg in a mining accident many years earlier and after fastening the falsie back on he took the full ashtray to the bar and bought drinks all round.

It was a novel way to get funds for the next round, but at Dublin Airport Derrick Holborn found an even easier way. Having fallen asleep on some terminal steps, his baseball cap had fallen off and landed upside down on the floor. As we got nearer, we could see that Del's hat contained about £10 in loose change.

There are several Irish branches of the Leeds United Supporters Club, both north and south of the border. As well as the Whites in

Dublin and Cork, there is always a large contingent from Northern Ireland led by Ian McKay and the aforementioned Belfast Bill – Mark Cosgrove. The popularity of Leeds means that the games at Tolka Park in Dublin and Musgrave Park in Cork are always sell-outs. In fact, the very first time we arrived at Tolka Park the ground was full and the gates were locked. An Irish Leeds fan had been drinking with Lunge and me all day and we'd ended in a couple of fantastic pubs near the ground, The Cat And Cage and The Ivy House. He told us to follow him as he knew another way in. He climbed up a drainpipe and over the wall. We waited for him to help us follow but instead he opened the two huge gates beside us. As the gates swung open hundreds of us swarmed into the ground to watch the match.

On the return ferry crossing after that game the beer was flowing as usual. The Guinness was beginning to take its toll and most of us hadn't had much sleep. If you want to get some shut-eye travelling with the Kippax Branch it is best to find somewhere quiet and private. I made the mistake of 'just having five' and woke up suddenly to the sight of the lads doing a very unconvincing job of smiling innocently. I quickly felt my face – the bastards had shaved off my eyebrows. But it was to get worse. On the way to the next Leeds match I heard much laughter and saw some of them handing photographs around the coach. I went to have a look. While I had slept on the ferry, they had not only shaved off my eyebrows but had written in red lipstick the words 'I love Scum' and 'manchester united for the Cup'. Just for good measure they'd coloured my nose red, too. And after taking the photos they'd wiped my face clean of any evidence.

Andy Brunton found a safer spot when he slipped away onto the top deck. He was spotted – or rather heard – by Chris Archer, who returned to the bar to announce that Andy was up top 'sawing wood'. Mick Colledge looked at me puzzled and whispered, 'What was Andy doing with a saw in the middle of the night?' We laughed so much we let Andy off the hook.

We were all wide awake on our way to Chelsea in April 1989 and looking for somewhere to stop for a light ale. Driver Dave Walker was our regular coach driver and announced he had spotted a likely candidate.

'This looks all right,' he said, steering us towards a raised barrier behind which was a club of some sort.

Outside it was parked a Rolls-Royce, an E-Type Jaguar and a couple of Range Rovers, so I suspected it might be a cut above our usual haunts.

'This looks a bit fuckin' posh,' said Stevie Priestley.

'Too right,' said Dave, suddenly realising where he'd brought us. 'Look, it's a bleedin' tennis club!'

To our left, tennis balls stopped in mid-air as the members gaped drop-jawed at a coach packed with 54 thirsty Leeds United fans. A commissionaire-type dressed in black uniform and cap appeared by the bus door. Craning his neck towards Dave – he was only about four feet tall – he shouted up at our driver. 'You can't come in here, this is private property!'

Big John checked the badge on his uniform.

'Shit! Look where we are – it's Queens Lawn Tennis Club! Even John McEnroe is banned from here.'

Dave waved the commissionaire away and put the coach into reverse. But while we'd been waiting a brand-new Audi had parked unseen behind us and the bus scraped its side.

'Oops!' said Dave and tried to get out another way. But the Audi had boxed him in and its driver was nowhere to be seen.

'We might as well go for a drink then,' I suggested. There was no objection and so everyone piled off the bus.

The little bloke in the uniform went berserk. 'No, no, no! You can't go in here – it's members only!' he shouted.

We held back. By now another car was blocking the other side of our bus. Our little friend was getting more upset, but Dave remained calm.

'Look, we can't get out – why don't you go and get the drivers of these cars?' he said.

He looked undecided but went away, shaking his head then looking over his shoulder nervously. We had of course supped a few cans on the bus and by now everyone definitely needed to pee. With the club itself off-limits we looked around anxiously for an alternative.

'Over there!' yelled Aidy Sharp. 'That wall will do!'

Everybody lined up against this black-painted wall and took out their todgers. A cry went up: 'No! No! Oh no!' It was our little friend, back again. 'That's the restaurant – and that wall is glass. People inside can see out even if you can't see in!'

It was a little late to tell us now. There we were, dozens of us all in a line, relieving ourselves in front of a roomful of people tucking into prawn cocktails and cucumber sandwiches. It was all too much for the commissionaire, who did what he should have done before we arrived and lowered the barrier at the entrance to the Queens Club car park. Walking back by our coach, he looked even redder in the face. 'That's it, I'm calling the police.'

'OK,' said Big John with a shrug. 'We're just leaving anyway.' And with that he led us all towards the barrier on foot.

The commissionaire was stopped in his tracks. 'Hang on! Where are you going?'

Dave handed him the coach keys.

'Here you are, mate. It's all yours,' he said and started walking with us.

The commissionaire looked like he was about to explode. 'Hang on, I'll get the drivers. Come back, please!'

This little bloke just didn't seem to be able to make up his mind. First he didn't want us there at all. Now he was having a fit because we were leaving. But that did the trick. The cars' owners were summoned and we were on our way. We never heard a thing about our application for membership.

Don Revie

It was Leeds United against everybody else. Backs against the wall. If he'd have been the manager of any other club he'd have been mentioned in the same breath as the greats. He's still one of the greatest managers of all time.

The greatest manager in Leeds United's history, Don Revie, OBE, died on 26 May 1989. Some of us decided to attend the funeral, held in Edinburgh. We agreed to travel in style, so at seven o'clock in the morning we met at Albert Van Hire in Leeds. I had offered to share the driving with Big John Martin. Once in the office, I glanced over at the large stack of lager the lads had brought and reluctantly offered my licence. 'Sorry, mate,' said the bloke behind the counter, 'you can't drive with this.'

Without waiting for an explanation, I quickly retrieved my licence and called to Dave: 'Pass me a can, ta!'

'Hold on, hold on!' cried Big John. 'What's up, why can't he drive?'

'There's a speeding endorsement on the licence.'

'What?!' He angrily snatched my licence off me to check. 'But that was eight years ago!'

'Doesn't matter, it's still on the licence. It should have been taken off.'

Big John glared at me. He was turning green and his shirt was beginning to tear. I shrugged my shoulders.

'Sorry, John, I'd love to help,' I lied and while he did the paperwork, I began to help the others load the ale into the van. I refrained from asking him to help us. Don't get me wrong. I like a drink as well as, if not a bit more than, the next man, but I would have walked to Edinburgh in my bare feet to be at Revie's funeral. This was just a bonus.

Five hours later we arrived in Edinburgh. We listened to the service relayed on loudspeakers outside the church. As well as many of his former players, there were many big names in attendance, including Laurie McMenemy, Kevin Keegan and the TV commentator Brian Moore. After the service we were talking to Harry Gration from the BBC, when Don's wife Elsie came over and asked us if we were the ones who had travelled up from Leeds in the van. We were a tad embarrassed and feeling a little out of our depth, but when someone muttered we were, Elsie was pleased.

'Thanks very much for coming,' she said. 'Please come to the reception.'

We arrived at the hotel where the reception was being held and went into the bar. Unusually, I went to buy the first round. 'Four pints of lager, please.'

Don Revie's son, Duncan, was at the bar. 'Those are paid for,' he told me.

'Thanks very much,' I replied and returned to the table with the drinks and the good news. Dave Green came back with his round and told us he hadn't paid, either. More bad news for Big John. It was a free bar for the entire day. There was good news for John, however, as the food was amazing. It looked as though Henry VIII was about to show up.

As we sat chatting, Pete Dillon, nudged me. 'I bet that's a right conversation there,' he said and nodded in the direction of the bar. There was Allan Clarke with Mick Jones in deep discussions with Johnny Giles and Billy Bremner. A while later, Joe Jordan accompanied, inevitably, by Gordon McQueen came over and began talking to us. It was embedded in our hearts how they'd defected to the 'enemy' years earlier. But to our credit we were polite.

A few hours later we thanked Mrs Revie and Duncan and quietly left. Big John, bless him, agreed to stop at an off-licence so we could replenish our supplies. Jack Pratt was still laughing over the Asian owners' strong Scottish accents when he came out.

As I sat in the back of the van with my beer, I thought of how angry I'd been (and still was), when only 8,000 had turned up at Don Revie's Testimonial at Elland Road just over a year before, in April 1988. I had tears in my eyes that day as they wheeled Don out onto the pitch, flanked by his 'boys': Bremner and co. Motor neurone disease had taken its toll but Don managed a short, heart-rending speech in which he thanked everyone for turning out. Looking round I was really upset. Elland Road's gates should have been locked long before kick-off, with thousands more still trying to get in. I will never forget the disappointment I felt that night. The next day I had Don Revie's name tattooed on my arm.

I met Don many times. The first time was in the late '60s. My dad had just got together a young football team from our neighbourhood and was looking around for friendlies until the following season when we entered a league. One of those games was away against a team in Knaresborough. As we travelled to the game in Dad's van, he made an announcement.

'Oh, I forgot to mention before,' he said, 'the president of the Knaresborough team is Don Revie.'

We all sat there in stunned silence then erupted as the reality sank in. Then we found our voices.

'Will he be there?'

'Can we meet him?'

'Please, Dad, please!'

Dad stopped us in our tracks.

'Whoa! He's only the president, I doubt he's gonna be here on a wet and windy Sunday morning.'

We went back to a disappointed silence. As we arrived at the pitch and began getting changed, I noticed a crowd of youngsters gathered around two men. They were Terry Hibbitt and Mike O'Grady, two of Don's famous squad from the '60s. Then Dad tapped me on the shoulder and pointed to another crowd of people by the changing-rooms.

'Seen who's over there?'

It was Don Revie. He had come to our friendly match after all.

Shortly afterwards he came over and met our players. My ma had sewn onto my yellow goalkeeper's shirt the famous Leeds owl badge. Don noticed it and spoke to me with a smile.

'That's a very good badge that, son. Wear it with pride.'

Don and the two Leeds players remained to watch the whole game which, embarrassingly, we won 5–0.

Don always had time for the supporters and always gave the impression that nothing was too much trouble. At a special function at the Irish Centre in Leeds to celebrate the 1972 FA Cup win, I had my photograph taken with him and he was happy to take the time to do this. On another occasion, beneath the terracing at half-time during a match with Fulham in the '80s, I remember him being shocked when the man he was talking to asked if he minded us talking to him. Don looked surprised at the question and simply said, 'No problem whatsoever.' With that he signed a couple of programmes and we left.

Don did this constantly. Everyone connected with Leeds United were important to him, the players, staff, laundry workers, cleaners – and the fans.

Revie was famous for his meticulous detail both on and off the pitch. He never forgot a birthday and when a player's wife or girlfriend was ill she would always receive flowers.

One of his players from the '60s, Rod Belfitt, a squad player rather than one of the big stars, once confirmed this to me. He told me that although he wasn't a regular first team player, Don always made him feel like one. Another player in this category was Nigel Davey. Nigel now lives close to me, and often speaks about his good relationship with Don. When Nigel, a full-back, was unlucky enough to break his leg in a reserve fixture, the first man to visit him in hospital was Don Revie. There is no doubt that Nigel and Rod, as with many of the other 'squad' players, would have been able to play in almost any other team in the old First Division, but they chose to play a part in Don Revie's Leeds.

Rod Johnson, another of Don's '60s players – who made his debut in 1962 – now lives in Kippax. He also recalls the manager's relationship with his staff. Rod was the substitute in the 1965 FA Cup final at Wembley against Liverpool and later went on to captain Bradford City and play for Rotherham United before moving to the States to play for Chicago Sting. 'The boss was totally professional in everything he did. His eye for detail was uncanny. And from first-teamers to apprentices, he treated everyone the same. In all my 20 years in professional football, I never met the boss's equal – nor am I ever likely to.'

Eric Thornton, a journalist, once recalled a meeting he had with Don in his office beneath the West Stand. Don called out to the tea-lady as she passed his office: 'Bring us two cups, luv, please.' But the tea-lady never heard him. Thornton told me: 'Don just shrugged his shoulders and stood up. "Never mind, I'll go and get them, she's probably busier than me."'

I once took my mate Rich Seymour and his young son Tom to spend an evening at Peter Lorimer's pub, The Commercial. Tom had just finished a school project on Leeds United and to add the finishing touch, wanted a picture of himself with the great Lorimer. Peter duly obliged and without any prompting chatted to the lad about his own love for Leeds and Revie.

Lorimer said: 'Leeds had spotted me whilst I was playing for my school team and the boss wasted no time in signing me for Leeds. Leeds United at the time were languishing in the Second Division, but there was something about Revie that impressed me greatly.'

Don was actually stopped by the police for speeding when on his way to Scotland to secure Lorimer's signature and later left the Lorimer household at three o'clock in the morning. 'If a club can take all that trouble about an unknown youngster,' concludes Lorimer, 'that club must be something rather special. Leeds and Revie certainly were.'

It really annoys me when people talk about Don Revie these days. They simply dismiss his phenomenal record at Leeds and immediately mention the United Arab Emirates issue. The fact is that Don knew the FA secretary Alan Hardaker and the rest of the England board were about to sack him. He decided to take up the Emirates manager's job, which he had been offered on more than one occasion.

It wasn't his first tempting offer. At the end of the 1972–73 season, Don, feeling that he had taken the Leeds team as far as he could, was on the verge of taking over as Everton's manager. Following the diabolical refereeing decisions that robbed Leeds of the European Cup-Winners' Cup, he decided to stay. Leeds went on to win the League Championship after a 29-match unbeaten run from the start of the season. Don had found he could take Leeds United even further.

In the '80s, James Whale had a late-night phone-in show on Leeds commercial station, Radio Aire, which was often quite entertaining. But then one night, when Leeds United were being discussed, Whale called Don Revie 'a pillock'. Whale was famous for being controversial but this was too much. Fuming, I dialled the station in an attempt to speak to him. I tried for over an hour to get through but the lines were seemingly jammed. Funnily enough, I hadn't had a problem months earlier when he'd asked me to ring in to discuss the Kippax Flat Earth Society that I'd founded.

And so Whale's name was in my little black book, as Jack Charlton once famously said, and I would not forget what he'd said.

A couple of days later, Leeds were at home, and as usual we all met up and headed for The Nag's Head. One of the lads, Willie Docherty, mentioned that James Whale was to open an amusement arcade in Leeds that same morning. This would be an ideal opportunity to confront him. On our way to the arcade we stopped off at the market and purchased three-dozen eggs. We stood opposite the arcade, on the Corn Exchange steps, and waited for Whale to arrive. He duly did, alone and on foot. He was wearing a red woollen scarf – that was even better. As he got to the door, we shouted, 'Oi James, this is for Don Revie!', and with that our barrage began. It was such bliss watching him ducking and cringing, all the while trying frantically to open the door, which had stuck. Egg after egg rained down. Sadly the last egg, launched by Kev Metcalfe, landed hopelessly off course three doors down, but Whale had been sufficiently pelted. As we ran out of ammunition he finally managed to open the door and scramble – excuse the pun – inside.

The following Monday evening on his show he briefly mentioned the incident, claiming he had been attacked by animal rights protesters. But believe me, he knew who his assailants had been.

Another media man who dared to insult Don Revie was Yorkshire Television's Richard Whiteley, the *Calendar* presenter now better known for his work on *Countdown*. Shortly after Revie had quit his job as England manager and left to take charge of the United Arab Emirates, Whiteley was interviewing Revie on a special half-hour programme made by Yorkshire Television. Throughout the interview, Whiteley persisted in asking about the alleged money deals involved in the switch from the England job.

Revie had been savagely attacked by the media for leaving England, but as I said, England were about to dismiss him anyway and were simply angered by the fact that he had beaten them to it and resigned. I always maintained that Revie's only mistake was to slip out of England in disguise – he should have left with his head held high.

As Whiteley continued to pry into Revie's financial affairs, Revie, on more than one occasion, threatened to end the interview. 'Look,' he pleaded, 'I'm here to talk about football, not money. Any more on that subject and I'm leaving.' Whiteley ignored the threat and persisted, and so Don unhitched his microphone and walked out of the studio, leaving an embarrassed Whiteley to deal with the viewers.

A couple of weeks later, when Leeds were at home to Sunderland, a few of us were walking behind the West Stand towards The Kop. As we did so a Jaguar pulled up and out of it stepped Whiteley with a minder.

Sid Johnson spotted him first and walked over to him in a rage. 'You've got a fucking cheek showing up here after what you said about Don Revie,' said Sid, pointing his finger right in Whiteley's face.

The minder stepped forward to diffuse the situation but Sid was on a roll. Pushing his finger onto Whiteley's nose, he deftly flicked the glasses from his face and stepped back as they fell to the ground.

Satisfied, Sid calmly walked away. It was hilarious, with everyone walking past laughing at Whiteley as he and his minder dropped hurriedly to their knees, getting in each other's way in an attempt to restore the presenter's glasses and dignity. Between them they managed the first, but in my eyes the second was gone forever.

In January 1994 Leeds United played Blackburn Rovers at Ewood Park. It had been requested that at all grounds a minute's silence be observed for Matt Busby who had passed away the previous week. Many clubs, including Chelsea and Everton, had deemed it 'inappropriate'. Leeds fans were still angry that no recognition had been given to the passing of Don Revie in 1989. It was agreed with certain sections that Don Revie's name would be chanted during the silence. Hundreds joined in.

In hindsight, the best thing would have been to have adhered to the minute's silence and to have chanted Revie's name after. But Leeds fans were angry. Angry that their manager had been ignored not only by football but, more hurtfully, by their own club. The night Don died was a Friday, the same night incidentally that Arsenal clinched the Championship at Anfield with a late Michael Thomas goal. Shortly after, England played Scotland at Wembley. There was no mention from the FA about Don Revie's death. Even worse, as thousands upon thousands of tributes were left all around Elland Road by supporters from all around the country and Europe, there was very little reaction from Leeds United. This is what angered Leeds fans. I can remember the disgust in some of the Leeds players' faces that day at Blackburn when Leeds fans were chanting Revie's name. They simply didn't understand the depth of feeling among the fans. I spoke to a number of players who played for Revie and they knew exactly where we were coming from. Under pressure from the media, Leeds United stated that they would ban for life anyone found to have been involved in the chanting at Ewood Park. I didn't wait to be called, I telephoned Alan Roberts who was the general manager at the time to tell him our supporters branch were involved. He asked me if I could deal with the matter 'internally'.

I wrote to Mr Roberts, giving my reasons for the incident at

Blackburn, I also asked why Leeds were so reluctant to defend the name of Don Revie. He wrote back:

> I fully endorse your sentiments, but unfortunately at times, this club does seem to show a lack of sincerity with many long-term employees as well as Don Revie. I would confirm that I have passed your letter to our chairman in order to show the feelings of many of our supporters. Many thanks both for bringing the matter to my attention and also for your continued work in the branch.
>
> Yours sincerely,
>
> Alan Roberts

A couple of newspapers (the *Daily Mirror* being one of them) tried to keep the pot boiling, but generally that was the end of the story. However, there was one final twist. Shortly afterwards, five years since Don had died, the Gelderd Road End stand, commonly known as The Kop, was formally renamed the Revie Stand. Amusingly it was claimed by the then managing director Bill Fotherby that the plan to rename the stand was his 'brainchild'. OK, Bill.

I chatted with Don's widow, Elsie, recently at a supporters club function and she said how grateful she was for the continued support for her and also for Don's memory. I assured her that Leeds United fans will always, in turn, be grateful to Don Revie.

– 15 –

From the Far East to a Drafty Corner of Ibrox

> There's only about a dozen of us make these long-haul pre-season trips. Some of the places that I've seen I would never have gone to if not for Leeds United.

In August 1991, 11 of us flew to Japan to watch Leeds play Brazil's Botafogo in an exhibition game. The travel was organised by our usual travel organiser, Big Mick Hewitt from the South Kirby Branch, who told us that the cheapest flights would be £600.

These days Big Mick books travel packages as a full-time occupation (although he also buys and sells football memorabilia) and naturally he is the organiser of most of our overseas trips. He does an excellent job, making use of contacts all over the world. In 2002, when the UEFA Cup draw was made that paired Leeds with Malaga, we were on a train to Pisa returning from the match against Hapoel Tel-Aviv in Florence. He got out a laptop and by the time we arrived at our destination had booked us all onto flights to Spain and sorted accommodation for everyone. For these games Mick will usually book one or two coaches, for about 100 people. For the long haul pre-season trips the party is smaller, such as the 11 who went to Japan.

While Mick did his stuff for Japan, I also asked Richard at my local travel agent, Kippax Travel, but he struggled to beat £600.

'That's a brilliant price,' said Richard. 'Who's it with?'

I told him it was the Russian airline, Aeroflot.

'Oh Christ,' he replied. 'Good luck!'

I was still thinking about what he had said when we boarded. The service looked basic, to say the least. No televisions, no radio, no nothing at all, really. But it was too late to change now so we took our seats and prepared for the flight, which would last 18 hours, including a three-hour stop-over in Moscow. Our first meal, however, was delicious. It was curried chicken. At least I think it was chicken. The next meal, a couple of hours later, was also curry. Curried fish. We had curry for our third meal, too. This time it was curried prawns. Little Mick Hewitt from The Vine Branch, a vegetarian, was struggling, to say the least. Despite his explanations, there was no vegetarian – or non-curry – option. He was finding it very difficult getting something he could eat. He finally got something – rice. With curry sauce. We all decided to make the best of a bad job and began consuming alcohol.

After a few cans I was ready for my next curry, which came about half past eleven at night. Curried beef. After a few more beers and a toilet visit, we all went to sleep. An hour before we were due to land, we were woken for breakfast. You've guessed it – curry. Curried corn flakes, in fact. Scrumptious!

A short while later we arrived at our hotel in Tokyo, the Takanawa Prince Hotel. It was a massive place with 6,000 rooms in all. We checked in, dumped our bags and were on the streets within 15 minutes. We were just in time for a lunch-time session sampling the local brew. The Japanese beer was very expensive, but we forced one down and then another and then another before returning to our hotel. Following a quick shower and change, we were out again. I went with Whitby John, Ralph from Scarborough and Bruce Musgrove from York.

Ralph is a unique character, to say the least. I first met him at the 1973 European Cup-Winners' Cup final in Thessalonki, Greece. I got to know Ralph much better on a Leeds United tour of West Germany. Ralph is an odd bloke. And very keen on sex. In fact, ask him about it and he'll proudly claim to be a pervert. I'm not sure about that myself but I have seen him sniffing bicycle seats recently vacated by girls outside shops and launderettes. He once attended a party in his local village of Thornton-le-Dale, near Scarborough. It wasn't an ordinary party, it was an orgy. Ralph figured prominently in the video of that very same party. Now Ralph is only small, probably about 5 ft 4 in., but he was disappointed when he auditioned to take part in a film to be made in Germany. The film was to be about the adventures of a well-endowed dwarf. Unfortunately, Ralph was turned down on both counts. He was too small and too tall! In 1998 Ralph bought a bar with a lad called Pencil in, predictably enough, Bangkok. It was in Pattaya and they re-named it The Yorky Bar. Although Pencil and the bar are still there, Ralph has since returned. He is now in charge of a popular theme-park ride in the north of England. But parents should not be afraid. As I've said, Ralph is not the tallest person on this planet and unless your children are taller than him, they cannot ride.

The Leeds game was to be played the following night (Monday) at the impressive Tokyo Dome. We learned that the game was a complete sell-out. This would have been good news – except we didn't have tickets. Pre-season friendlies are not usually that popular so we had happily travelled to the other side of the world for a Monday-night game without ever considering the possibility that we wouldn't get in. This could turn out, as Big Mick observed, to be 'a bit of a bastard'. He then suggested finding the Leeds players' hotel and asking one of them, or someone else in the party, to help us out. By the time we got there, it was around ten o'clock at night. Sat in the hotel lounge/bar was defender John McClelland and we asked him where everyone was. He told us that the gaffer (Howard Wilkinson) had got them out jogging. He'd been excused because he had a slight strain.

We apologised for the lateness of our visit but he shrugged. 'Everyone has been told to stay on English time,' he explained in his warm Belfast accent, 'so for us it's only one o'clock in the afternoon.'

John is a great bloke and when we told him we were after tickets, he said he'd go find the club's managing director, Bill Fotherby, and ask him to come to the bar to see us. Mr Fotherby had been in another of the hotel's bars and he came through to ours holding a huge glass of brandy in one hand and an even bigger cigar in the other. John had already explained to him that we needed tickets and the MD pulled out an envelope full of them from inside his jacket. He puffed on his cigar and blew the smoke into the air. Eleven of us sat there looking at him, expectantly. He waited, to be sure he had our full attention, then spoke. 'Before I let you have these tickets, lads,' he began, 'I need to know: how hard have you tried to get tickets yourself?'

I nearly choked on my beer, I couldn't believe what I was hearing. Big Mick seemed more ready for this question and took out his Filofax. Flicking to the relevant page he answered: 'I'll tell you how hard we've tried, Mr Fotherby. We've flown 3,000 miles, taking us 18 hours. We had to stay three hours in Moscow Airport, none of us has slept for almost 30 hours, the arses are just about hanging out of our shorts, I've been in touch with the Japanese FA, the Brazilian FA and the English FA, but everywhere we've tried, there are no tickets for sale. That's how hard we've tried.'

Fotherby looked at Mick and then said: 'That's OK then. Just one other thing, though. You have got your Premier Cards with you, haven't you?'

The Premier Card is a membership card required by all Leeds United fans before they can enter an away ground. No loyal supporter can follow the team without one. The question was absurd and he had been pompous to ask it. I jumped up, about to tell him to stick his tickets up his arse, but just in time thought better of it and instead stormed out of the hotel. I was sat on the wall outside, still fuming, when the lads came out and Mick gave me my ticket.

No one could quite believe what we had witnessed. As is my wont, I later drew a cartoon depicting the incident which Phil Barrett, from Scarborough, somehow got a copy of. Phil liked the cartoon so much, he faxed a copy directly to Fotherby himself. Phil then told me he had received a reply in which Fotherby had requested the identity of the cartoonist. I rang him at Elland Road, spoke to his secretary and upon being informed he was busy, I left my number and address. Over 20 years later, I am still waiting for Mr Fotherby to contact me.

As the night wore on I became more and more fascinated by Tokyo. Although not my favourite city, there was no doubt it certainly was different from most others. We trawled many different pubs and clubs, but got a bit of a shock when we decided to stop at one of the countless restaurants for something to eat. We didn't have a clue what it said on the menu, so we opted for a dish of fried noodles and a large beer to wash them down.

It was our best way to mix our culture with our hosts'. Wherever I go I always try to do the same, but sometimes I see things I can't accept – even if they are a long-held local custom. After eating, we moved on to another bar where – to put it mildly – we were a bit upset to discover that the contraption on the next table was used to secure a live monkey. Customers would then gather round and watch while the monkey's skull was smashed in before its brains were removed and then eaten by the morons at the table – all this while the monkey was still alive. If this disgusting ritual had taken place while we were in the bar we would have been forced to intervene. It didn't, so all we could do was leave immediately.

We had a better time in the other bars. I had noticed that in most of them, the drinks optics were on the outside of the bar itself. I pictured the scene as if it were the same in Leeds city centre – in a word, chaos. But not in Tokyo.

As we went down the stairs into a place called Pips, I looked around at the clientele and said to Whitby John, 'We're either gonna have a great time in here or we're gonna get our heads kicked in.' Pips was full of Hell's Angels, skinheads, punk rockers . . . you name it, they were in here. But the mix was brilliant. We ended up having a great time. While Ralph and Bruce took on two punk rockers at table football, I got talking to the owner, Marlborough. Like myself, he was a big fan of Jim Morrison and The Doors and so we found much to talk about. Eventually Whitby John and I decided to move on but I took Marlborough's address and promised to stay in touch, and I still write to him from time to time even now.

As we were walking to the next bar we passed Gary Speed and David Batty, both dressed in Hawaiian shirts and shorts. They were trying to get into a night club but the bouncers were having none of it. It was hardly surprising, wearing those shirts. A little further on we came across David Wetherall stood alone on the pavement. We spoke briefly as we passed then he called us back and said with a conspiratorial wink, 'By the way, lads . . . You ain't seen me, right?' We grinned and promised not to grass on him, then flagged down a taxi in search of our next watering hole.

That appeared as soon as we got out of the taxi. Each of us assumed one of the other three had paid, and by the time we discovered that none of us had we were about 20 yards from the car.

It wasn't a big fare so we didn't think the driver would care as we legged it down the first alley and out of the way. It might have been cheaper to have gone back and paid. We came to a door and went in. It was a lift. Three floors up all four of us got out and were immediately greeted by a girl with a tray full of beers. 'This is all right!' said Bruce and in we went. It took us five minutes to discover that the beers were going to cost us £10 each and realised that Bruce's knowledge of back-street Tokyo bars is not to be trusted. Insisting that there had been some mistake, we paid the bar owners 'all the money we had on us' and made tracks back to the hotel. Time flies when you're having fun and we were surprised to notice it was now half past seven in the morning, so in the spirit of checking out local cuisine we stopped for breakfast in a 24-hour Kentucky Fried Chicken.

The match was to be played later that day, so after some sleep and another trawl round a few bars, we settled in a nice-looking pub, just across the way from the Tokyo Dome. The locals were friendly and an English lad who worked in Hong Kong but had flown over to watch the game with some colleagues bought us all our first drink. Soon we had been there a couple of hours, having a good time. Then, posing for a group photograph sat on one of the tables outside, Mick Garner accidentally knocked one of the old folding tables over.

A repair would be simple. It just needed screwing back together, but Mick had left his screwdriver back home in Scunthorpe. So he did the next best thing and took it into the bar and apologised. The owner didn't seem unduly concerned and we continued drinking. But a little while later the English lad who'd flown in from Hong Kong came over looking worried. He could speak fluent Japanese and told us the bar owner wanted £500 for the table. We all laughed and said that it only needed a couple of screws and it would be as good as new. Besides, the table wasn't worth a quarter of that. He spoke to the owner on our behalf but returned looking grim. 'It's no good, lads,' he said. 'He's adamant he wants £500 or he's going to call in the police.'

Ralph was determined: 'Tell him to go get 'em. We're not paying that much.'

We thought that would be the end of it, but 15 minutes later we were treated to the sight of 20 policemen hurrying down the stairs into the pub. They were lined up from the top to the bottom of the stairs, each armed to the teeth with pistols and rifles. They didn't look too happy either. We protested to them, but apparently they couldn't speak English. The lad from Hong Kong had a go, but unfortunately for us he couldn't make much impression. Through him, though, we repeated our opinion and watched the resulting discussion between the owner and the police. Our valued interpreter returned to tell us they had decided that if we didn't pay, they were taking Mick Garner away with them. It had all got a little out of hand. If we allowed him to go with the police, we feared we might not see him again for months so, begrudgingly, we offered £150 for the table. The owner accepted. We all chipped in and the police left. I swear they were disappointed that we had paid.

Luckily, police treatment of English football fans in Japan had improved markedly come the 2002 World Cup. I like to think we did our bit with that episode with the table.

We arrived at the Tokyo Dome 20 minutes before kick-off. It is definitely the best stadium I have ever been to. Before or since. Although strangely, it was deemed too old to use come the 2002 World Cup. But like many of the stadiums we all admired at that event, it had a roof.

For spectators, it was very plush. There were carpets everywhere. Even the toilets were carpeted. There were televisions everywhere, relaying match action – and yes, they had them in the toilets, too. This was just as well. Having flown 18 hours all the way to Japan on a diet of nothing but curry, the only goal of the game was scored while I was in the toilet. To make matters worse it was a Botafogo penalty which Mervyn Day could not save.

Alcohol was served to you in your seat and there was a holder on the back of the seat in front of you where you could rest your pint while you read through the programme. And you would want to read it, too, having spent £7 on it at a time when a similar thing at Elland Road would cost you just £1.50 . . .

After the match, we got on a fast train back into Tokyo centre. It was another new experience for us. At every stop, cleaners would board the train, do a quick sweep up and jump off again just before the doors closed.

As night time turned into day, we headed to the Hard Rock Cafe. Almost all the Leeds players had done the same thing and Gary McAllister very kindly came over and took my hat, which he got all the players to sign, before he returned it. We had originally planned to spend a whole week in Tokyo, but a re-arranged West Riding Cup match with Halifax Town meant that we had to return home in time for that game at Elland Road on 7 August, the Wednesday night. Lesley cancelled her plan to accompany us and branded us idiots for electing to spend just two nights in Tokyo.

On the flight home, via Moscow, I reflected on the trip and thought about a good friend of mine, Mally King. He had been one of the founder members of the Kippax Branch, along with Gordon Findlay and myself, in 1978 and had been planning to come to Tokyo with us. Just two weeks earlier Mally was part of a salvage team working at Allerton Bywater Colliery, making the pit safe to abandon before it was finally closed. Sadly a pit floor above him collapsed and Mally was killed. A friend of both myself and Mally, Dave Colgan, was working with him at the time; Dave was one of the first to get to Mally, but it was too late. He was 31. We were all very sad and his mother gave me the key to the Chapel of Rest, where his body was taken, so I could pay my last respects. I had never been to one of these places before and wasn't sure what to expect. Soft music played in the background as I made my way to the room where Mally lay. I had a few minutes with him and before I left, I pinned a Leeds United Kippax Supporters Badge on his chest. Over 500 people attended his funeral, and just as he did when he was alive, he had the last word as he was laid to rest in the churchyard. Mally was a big lad, about 6 ft 4 in. Correspondingly, his coffin was enormous, and when the time came for it to be lowered into the ground, the coffin wouldn't fit. It had to be left there until after the service, when gravediggers made the hole that much larger. Mally would have liked that.

After the funeral we went to the wake at The Royal Oak in Kippax. It was heaving and after a couple of hours and many reminiscences later, everyone in the pub was singing Neil Innes's immortal song from *The Life Of Brian* soundtrack: 'Always Look On The Bright Side of Life'. It had been one of his favourites when we followed Leeds.

Contrary to a mythical belief, this brilliant song was not first sung at Old Trafford. They only began to adopt it in the late '80s. Leeds fans regularly sang it during our dark days of the mid '80s in the depths of the old Second Division. And Mally sang it louder than most of us as we watched our team wrestle with the likes of Cambridge and Shrewsbury. It was a great, great pity, that he never lived to see Leeds lift the First Division Championship in 1992. He deserved the change of scenery.

He'd helped me out in October 1980, when I got a change of scenery I hadn't bargained for. Just back from Romania after the UEFA Cup tie against Universitatea Craiova, I had a beer too many and found myself locked up in Millgarth Police Station. It was early Friday afternoon but I was already thinking about the next day. Leeds were playing away at Southampton – what if they kept me in custody overnight? At the time, our coach used to make an early start from Kippax, then pick up various members en route to Leeds city centre before making a final stop at The Marquis of Granby, conveniently situated over the road from the police station where I found myself.

I was allowed one phone call. I called Mally. I told him that it didn't look like I would be getting on at Kippax as usual, but would join him and the lads at the final staging post outside the Marquis. That sorted, I could return to more pressing matters, such as my release. Sadly for me this occurred at four o'clock in the morning, so by the time the coach arrived, I was frozen to the core.

Mally took one look at me and said: 'You look like you could do with a whisky. Is this the right road to Southampton?'

On the plane home from Tokyo, I was a lot more warm and comfortable. I smiled at the memory and ordered two more beers for myself and Whitby John. We toasted Mally and I remarked how much he would have been impressed by our Tokyo hotel – a very classy place. The bath robes, with the name of the hotel embroidered on them, seemed like the height of luxury. So much so, I explained to John, that I had taken one as a souvenir. Not my own, of course, in case I got charged for it later. This seemed like a good time to confess. I had taken Whitby John's, while we were all having a beer in his room one night. John smiled. 'Yeah, I know,' he said, 'and I took yours, from your room, the following night.'

Mally would have enjoyed this trip.

A year later Leeds United were drawn against Glasgow Rangers in the 1992 European Cup and the authorities immediately banned away fans from both ties. This obviously meant it was going to be difficult to get tickets. Difficult but not impossible.

After phone calls to a couple of contacts, including one at the *Yorkshire Evening Post*, we were able to come up with a few tickets for the first leg, to be played at Ibrox. Many other Leeds fans knew similar tricks so it meant quite a few of us made the trip to the big game. The tickets I had organised would have to be picked up in Darlington and Edinburgh. I travelled up the day before the game with a good mate of mine, Billy Burton.

Bill is a thalidomide, but believe me he is not handicapped. He receives money from the Thalidomide Association every year and the association has taken its members on trips all over the world. One year, they were taken for a week to New York.

As Bill says, 'I was in a group of about ten thalidomide-related people. One particular member of our party was a real nasty piece of work. I can't remember his real name, but we called him "Ian Dury" because he sounded just like him. He was more reliant on other people than any of us. He was only about three and a half foot tall, he had no arms or legs, just hands and feet, and therefore had to be pushed or lifted everywhere.'

One night Bill and his mates were in the hotel bar enjoying a few drinks. Ian had been placed, at his own request, on a stool near the bar, on which he balanced somewhat precariously. As people drank and shared jokes Ian was sat there hurling insults at everybody who happened to go near him. After so long Bill and the lads said enough was enough and picked Ian up from his stool and then took him up to one of the rooms. The bath was really deep, it was filled up, and Ian was placed in it. He was bobbing about like a toffee apple.

'You fuckin' bastards!' he shouted, as the lads left and returned to the bar.

The drinks soon started to flow again and everyone was having a brilliant time. They left the hotel and began a little pub crawl.

One of the only things Bill has difficulty with is handling those pint-glass jars, the dimply ones with a handle on the side. There's been many a time when we've been out drinking with him and one of the lads will come back from the bar with a round of drinks in normal straight glasses and just one of those pint jars, which as a wind-up, is inevitably placed in front of Billy. After his traditional response of 'You twats!', someone swaps theirs for a pint he can lift.

After a tour of some of the bars in New York, Bill and his lads ended up in a late-opening Irish bar. Everyone was in good humour until suddenly someone shouted, 'Oh shit – we forgot Ian!'

The lads hurried back to the hotel and up to the room where Ian was having his bath. The poor bugger had turned blue and was completely out of breath. They took him out and dried him off. He'd been in the water for nearly six hours. Bill did say, however, that he was as quiet as a mouse for the rest of their stay.

On our way to Darlington to pick up the first of our Ibrox tickets, we had to telephone someone in Edinburgh to arrange to pick up the others. Billy pulled up at a Little Chef and I went to the phone while he got some coffees. I was told that these tickets were coming from a Rangers director so we had to be very careful and not get into trouble as his name would be on them. With that made clear, I was directed to meet a man in a pub on Rose Street. A few hours later I was in the pub, and noticed a chap who fitted the description I'd been given. As luck would have it, he was the man I was looking for and he did have the tickets. He had a pint with us, I paid him and he left. Mine and Billy's tickets were for the Copland Road stand, the Rangers 'home' end. We found a hotel and went out on the town.

The next morning we set off for Glasgow. We found Ibrox Stadium and decided to get a hotel nearby. We eventually plumped for the Copland Hotel, which turned out to be where a lot of the Rangers fans drank. We would be mingling with the enemy.

We threw our bags in the room and headed out to the city centre. But before that we thought it best to go to the stadium and find out exactly which turnstile we would be going through so that when the time came we wouldn't stand out as Leeds fans. We found it and as we were about to leave a television crew spotted us. It was the *Calendar* team from Yorkshire Television. They asked if we would mind being interviewed in front of the cameras. We had no objection. They asked how we got tickets.

'We've just been lucky,' Bill said.

'Are there many more Leeds fans coming?' they asked.

'Hundreds!' Bill said. 'They'll be arriving shortly.'

I said that it was wrong to ban fans from either club from travelling to watch their team and this way could lead to more trouble. With that we left for the centre. We hadn't been there long when a Celtic fan, stood in a doorway, asked us if we were from Leeds. We told him we were and he showed us where there were some cheap bars. We asked if he wanted to come with us.

'I've nae money, pal,' he replied

'C'mon,' said Bill. 'We'll get you a drink.'

During the afternoon we met up with some more of our lads from Leeds and gave them their tickets. Seven hours later our Celtic friend was still with us and we were slightly pissed. No, we were steaming. We had a final drink with him. He wished us all the best against Rangers and we were on our way up to Ibrox. On our arrival we went through the turnstile we had earmarked earlier. The turnstile operator took our stub and we went to the bar. 'I'm just gonna have a look upstairs,' I said to Bill.

When I got there, I got a bit of a shock – our tickets were for behind the goal. We were on the halfway line. I reported back to Billy.

'We can't be!' he said, going back upstairs with me. 'Oh fuck!' he exclaimed when he saw for himself. 'We're on the halfway line.'

'Yep, now what?' I said.

'Let's go find a copper,' said Bill, rolling his sleeves up. I knew what we had to do. There is still an awkward reaction when people are confronted by a thalidomide and that is precisely what we were hoping for. We approached a policeman downstairs. Bill was to say nothing.

'Hello there,' I said to the officer, 'can I have a word.' He detected my Yorkshire accent immediately. I knew as he did that the police were under instructions to eject anyone suspected of being from Leeds. Or England for that matter.

'Yes, what is it?' he said, eyeing us up suspiciously.

'The thing is,' I began, 'we've come through the wrong turnstile with these tickets. I'm from Leeds, but I'm working up here in Glasgow. I'm a carer, I'm looking after William here. He's retarded and can't speak, but he's Leeds mad. I managed to get some tickets from the local authority and it's his big day.' My nose grew that long, that it nearly poked the copper's eye out. It was going well until Bill began to improvise. He started crying. This threw me completely. I was having to bite the inside of my mouth to stop myself from laughing. When the copper looked away, Bill winked at me. By now I was bursting inside. I had to hurry things along or I would blow it. 'What can we do now?' I said to the officer.

'Somebody's fucked up,' he said. 'You shouldn't have got in here with those tickets. Follow me, I'll take you to your proper seats.' With that he took us through the stand and onto the perimeter, leading us round the pitch and into our seats, where I shook his hand and thanked him politely.

We nearly blew our cover in the very first minute. Gary McAllister put Leeds ahead with almost the first kick of the match. As the ball hit the back of the net, me and Billy instinctively jumped up. Luckily for us, so did everyone else as the Rangers fans hurled loud abuse and were waving fists at the Leeds team celebrating right under their noses. Throughout the rest of the game the 'carer and his patient' had some lucky escapes, none more so than when Gordon Strachan scored what appeared to be the second for Leeds. It was immediately disallowed for offside. TV pictures showed after that it was a perfectly good goal; had that stood it would have made a lot of difference to the tie.

We were finally sussed, however, in the second half when the Leeds keeper John Lukic managed to punch the ball into his own net. I went mad. I jumped up with everyone else, but instead of cheering, I was shouting, 'You stupid bastard!' This was heard by the Rangers fans around us, but apparently too delirious to care they simply carried on celebrating. One Rangers fan sat behind us did say later that he'd known we were Leeds fans right from the start.

After the game we went back to the hotel bar and after few more drinks everyone there knew we were Leeds fans but were OK about it. This was probably due to the fact that we had lost 2–1. It might have been different had we won.

The second leg on 4 November 1992 turned out to be Billy's last Leeds game to date. After the 2–1 defeat at Elland Road by Rangers, Billy told me of a decision he'd made after a lot of thought. He was to end his relationship with his long-term girlfriend, with whom he shared a large detached house in Tockwith, near York, and head for the Far East. A few months earlier Bill had been leaving his house on his way to work in Wetherby. As he got into his car he said good morning to one of his neighbours. It was a lovely street, quiet and quite select. But Bill wasn't happy. He longed for a bit of excitement. He had discussed with his girlfriend about just going to the Far East and coming back only when they felt like it, but she wasn't having any of it. Within a week Bill was in Hong Kong. Alone. From there he went touring, visiting Vietnam, Malaysia and China among many other places. When he finally returned home, things were never the same in his relationship. So he'd decided after the Rangers games he was going to return to the Far East. No one at the time knew the dire consequences this would have on his life.

In his letters to me over the following months he told me of a lad from England he'd come across. 'I've met with this lad from Derby,' he wrote. 'We're both skinheads, we're in the bars every night and all the local girls think we are Gulf War veterans. I've told them my hands are like this because I was blown up by a land mine. We're not letting on. They're all over us, literally. It's brilliant! I've got to be on my toes, though,' he added, 'someone asked me how big the engine was in my amphibious landing craft – so a lot of bullshit is essential here.'

I received many more letters and postcards from Billy, but they suddenly stopped arriving over Christmas. The fact that he was on the move all the time meant it was difficult, if not impossible, to get in touch with him. I just had to wait for him to contact me. Then a letter arrived from him in February 1993. It wasn't good news. On Boxing Day he had been arrested at Manila Airport as he was about to board a plane to Australia.

He had fallen in with the wrong type of people and had agreed to carry some drugs through customs. He was discovered by airport police with 5.2 kg of hashish in his bag. He hadn't even reached customs before he was approached and subsequently led away. He was taken into a small room at the back of the airport and was stripped naked, apart from his boots. A gun was put in his mouth and he was told that when the next plane flew overhead, he was to be shot. Billy heard the droning of an engine and closed his eyes. The policeman pulled the trigger. He later wrote colourfully: 'The gun was empty – and so was my arse.'

After some brutal interrogation he was given his clothes back and taken to jail. Even after such an ordeal, Billy still managed a smile to himself while in the back of the police van. He still had some hashish down his boots which they hadn't found. One bit of good news for Bill was that only the previous year the death penalty had been abolished for such an offence. Instead he was told he would receive between 12 and 20 years imprisonment. That didn't really make him feel any better.

I firmly believe Billy was stitched up. He was stopped even before reaching customs, which makes me think he was used as a decoy. Billy's prosecutor in Manila had a very strange line of reasoning that suggested because his passport was issued in Liverpool, Billy must be familiar with Liverpool. And because The Beatles came from Liverpool and were big dope smokers in the '60s, Billy must also have been into dope before he came to the Philippines.

Billy's parents, Eddie and Teresa, have supported him through the last nine years as, too, have his friends. We regularly send him money and parcels. He is also sent the Leeds match reports every week. We just live in hope that each year will be his last in custody. The Foreign Office and the Thalidomide Association are trying desperately to obtain his release but so far without success. Ironically, in 1999, the king of the Philippines ordered the release of many murderers, rapists and arsonists, but stated all offenders convicted of drug-related crimes were to remain in custody.

When Bill first arrived at Manila jail he was the only European and was treated as a bit of a celebrity. He also had a bit of money so he was looked up to by the other inmates. Within a month of his internment he, a 5 ft 5 in. thalidomide, was given the job of coaching the prison basketball team.

Billy was always able to look after himself, but as he readily admits himself he has often used his disability to his own advantage. I remember a time at Wolves in the early '80s. We had arrived for the game and a group of us were walking towards the South Bank under the subway when we were ambushed by a large group of Wolves fans; we were heavily outnumbered. After what seemed like an age of fighting with our backs to the wall, someone shouted: 'The police are coming.'

Everyone who attends football matches know that the police tend to wade in first and ask questions later. So even though it wasn't our fault we thought it best to make our exit. I looked round for Billy and saw he had hold of this Wolves fan and was knocking seven bells out of him. 'Come on, Bill,' I shouted. 'Let's go!' Too late, the police arrived. Our lads and the Wolves fans had gone, leaving me, Billy and this hapless Wolves fan.

One officer grabbed Billy but, after seeing his arms, immediately let him go. He was confused. He grabbed the Wolves fan who was by now sliding down the subway wall, leaving a trail of blood as he slumped to the floor. Bill started crying.

The copper looked appalled. 'You low-life bastard!' he said to the Wolves fan, picking him up and handcuffing him in one swift movement. 'I've seen some things in my time, but attacking an invalid? Come on, you're nicked!'

I looked again at the mess the Wolves fan was in and quickly made our excuses. Promising the copper I'd look after Billy, we were allowed to go and make our way into the ground.

16

I Hate Carlton Palmer

He was so arrogant. And useless. But he thought he was Pelé.

Mark Aizlewood and Jimmy Floyd Hasselbaink are two of a very small number of players I have resented ever wearing the white of Leeds.

Whitby John – or, to use his preferred title, John of Whitby – and I spent a happy afternoon at Ripon races in 1988 and won handsomely on a horse called Markaizlewood. I realised afterwards, however, that our winning jockey rode in red, white and black colours. It was common knowledge that Aizlewood knew what the fans thought and it was clear that he wasn't happy playing for Leeds, but he overstepped the mark big style towards the end of the 1988–89 season. After scoring the winner against Walsall at Elland Road, he leapt onto the fence at the Gelderd End and raised two fingers to the Leeds fans. He was immediately substituted by manager Howard Wilkinson, stripped of the captaincy and banned for 14 days. Better yet, he never played for Leeds again and was sold to Bradford City.

Hasselbaink was a far better player but his greedy salary demands immediately before the start of the 1999–2000 campaign (leaving

Leeds no time to find a replacement) and his eventual move to Atletico Madrid irrevocably damaged his relationship with the vast majority of Leeds fans. Few were surprised when, after Madrid were relegated in that very season, he scampered back to England and to the biggest wage packet he could find – at Chelsea.

But as much as I dislike Aizlewood and Hasslebaink, there is only one Leeds player I can positively say I have hated: the one and only Carlton Palmer.

I've often tried to think of something constructive to say about Carlton bloody Palmer, but I can't. In my opinion he was far and away the worst footballer I have ever seen in my life.

I've started now, so I'll finish. He has the head the size of a tennis ball and I am convinced that if he lay on his back in the middle of the Isle of Wight and stretched out his arms and legs, he could touch the coastline in all directions.

The thing with old Carlton is, he thinks he is the business. No one else does, except Graham Taylor. Taylor, unbelievably, gave Palmer 18 England caps – the turnip. When one of his many passes would go astray, Palmer would point to someone else to get him out of trouble.

When Ron Atkinson was his manager at Hillsborough he christened him 'Miss Palmer' because of his ability to hit the corner flag from six yards in front of goal.

His manager at Southampton, David Jones, once said after another calamitous performance by Palmer, 'It was great that the fans were singing "There's only one Carlton Palmer" but I have to say thank God for that because I couldn't put up with two of them. He covers every blade of grass for us, but only because his first touch is so crap!'

One thing he is good at is hopscotch. He was once the world champion at it. And I'm not making this up.

Palmer was an egomaniac with his head so far up his own arse that he actually believed he could play. One TV pundit once summed up his abilities perfectly when he said, 'Palmer can trap a ball further than I could kick it.'

When Palmer first arrived at the club I didn't like him, although I must admit to being as stunned as most people that he was the man chosen by Howard Wilkinson to take over David Batty's number 4 shirt. Nevertheless, I have to admit I ignored my doubts and gave Palmer my full backing. It didn't last long.

In the summer of 1994 Leeds United (with Palmer in tow) were invited to take part in a tournament to commemorate the opening of a new stadium, the Shah Alam, in Kuala Lumpur, Malaysia. Our last away trip to watch Leeds had been to Swindon. Reluctantly, we made plans to try somewhere a little more exotic.

Kuala Lumpur is a big city. It is also extremely smelly in parts. When we were there the humidity and open sewers combined to create an aroma that was far from pleasant. Luckily, we were staying at the Swiss Garden Hotel – a very comfortable and sleek affair with welcome air conditioning. It came as a great relief after trooping round the hot streets to find that most of the bars had air conditioning, too.

One bar we liked was called Brannigan's. It was a huge music bar and very lively. The locals there were extremely friendly and insisted upon buying me drinks which, as I didn't want to come across as unfriendly, I gladly accepted. One night I was drinking with about half a dozen of them, who had been overly generous. I was just about to get carried away, literally, when Simon Featherstone and Nigel 'Nibbs' Bray came across and intervened. I was seconds away from being whisked off by six members of the local gay community. I still shudder now, every time I think about what might have happened.

Everywhere we went, the Malaysians were promoting their railway system as being the best in the world. One day we thought we'd put it to the test and go to Singapore, about four hours away to the south. But Whitby John pointed out that Penang, about the same distance in the other direction, was known as a popular holiday island, with girls, nightclubs and bars galore. We opted for there instead.

One hour into our journey, the train broke down. The buffet bar was closed. Just our luck. We were stranded for two hours, discussing the merits of the Malaysian railway system that the company continued to promote with constantly repeated advertising videos on the carriage's television screens. Finally the train began moving again, but our relief didn't last long. The train ground to a halt once more and we were held up again for another three hours. The videos continued. The Tannoy apologised for a mechanical fault but gave us no clue as to when, or even if, we might reach our destination. It was getting very frustrating. Perhaps trains to Singapore were having greater success.

We did eventually reach Penang, and though our journey took nine hours at least we could finally begin to enjoy ourselves. Then we discovered that the next, and only, train back to Kuala Lumpur left in just two hours time at half past six in the morning. We jumped straight in a taxi and asked to be taken to the nearest bar where there would be 'ladies'. He took us over a large bridge and onto the island of Penang. We hadn't been far when the taxi stopped beside a dark alley. 'Down there,' he said, pointing enthusiastically. We paid the fare and walked down the alley. At the end of it was the seediest bar I'd seen for a very long time. Inside was a corridor with bedrooms on either side. At the end of the corridor was a really dark bar area. One or two of the girls were playing on Space Invaders and pinball machines. Webby, knowing that time, tide and Malaysian railways wait for no man, went straight over and picked himself a girl. He paid the landlord and took her into one of the bedrooms. The rest of us had a beer or two and Webby came out half an hour later, sweating like a pig.

'Bye 'eck, that was all right!' he announced, romantically.

Reassured, one or two others followed while we moved on to a karaoke bar. We gave them a few songs, then, inspired by his earlier adventures, Webby gave a rendition of 'Hello' by Lionel Richie. It brought the house down. We just had time to move to another bar before catching the train back to Kuala Lumpur. Not before time too as Jeff was falling madly in love with one of the local ladies, who had more chest and arm hair than Richard Keys.

Back in the hotel bar later that night the resident pianist and guitarist were playing quietly in the background. Webby couldn't resist giving them the opportunity to repeat his performance of 'Hello'. He simply walked over, opened the song book at the chosen page, grabbed a microphone and began. The band were slick and picked it up immediately – even though he was doing it in an extraordinarily different key and accent to the original.

Everyone in the place was in stitches as he tried for all the high notes. His musicians simply looked on in disbelief, doing their best to follow. We still threaten to enter Webby for *Stars In Their Eyes* as Lionel Richie. Despite the fact that he is a 6 ft 4 in. white skinhead with tattoos.

In Brannigan's the next night we came across the local 'mafia'. We had been talking happily to one of them, who described himself as the main man, when suddenly he announced his love for manchester united. It killed the conversation instantly. He took exception to the fact that we simply stopped talking with him and insisted, menacingly, 'I only have to make one phone call, and my men will be here with guns.'

Ralph, possibly the smallest person in the world, stood on his tiptoes and replied, 'You'll have to get to the phone first, mate.'

The mobster left and we never saw him again.

In the Hard Rock Cafe I entered a beer-drinking competition and found myself on stage with about a dozen other drinkers. We were each given a yard of ale and told that upon the given signal, the quickest person to drink his ale was the winner. Now I like my ale too much to rush it so while the others rushed and spilled their beer, I simply began drinking mine and enjoying it. In fact, I took about 20 minutes to finish because it tasted so good. The judges weren't best pleased, though, but I reminded them that the rules stated, quite clearly, that if you drank all your beer, you did not have to pay for it.

Leeds' first game was against Flamengo of Brazil. It wouldn't prove to be a classic game but it did have its moments. Just before the kick-off, with the players out and doing their final stretches, five parachutists floated down out of the sky and landed on the pitch of the shiny new stadium. They gathered up their 'chutes, bowed and left the field to let the game get under way.

Seconds into the game, Leeds were awarded a penalty. As Gary Speed stepped forward to take it, a sixth parachutist appeared and landed right on top of him. Most teams settle for their goalie waving his arms about if they're trying to distract the taker.

Leeds' second game was even less memorable as they lost 2–1 to Australia's national side. The day after that game we found ourselves in a small outdoor bar relaxing in the sun with beers that were getting warmer by the second. For reasons that escape me now, we'd picked a bar by a large open sewer and from it a rat the size of a dog ran merrily by us as we chatted about last night's game. We were distracted when the bar's owner appeared, carrying a large basket full of live frogs. He placed the basket on the ground and went back inside. In the heat of the sun the poor frogs were about to be literally baked to death. Mick Garner and I challenged the owner about the cruelty, but he just shrugged his shoulders and called us '*loco*'. Later we found out that frogs' legs are a delicacy in some Malaysian restaurants and at this particular one they simply dismember each critter and dump the rest of its body, still alive, into a bin round the back of the kitchen. As we were repeating this sad tale to Russ back at the hotel, Nick 'Marshy' Marsh and Mark Palmer walked in and said, 'Hey, we've just had some frogs' legs. They were lovely.'

I wouldn't buy them a drink all evening.

As you may have heard, there is no shortage of prostitutes in Kuala Lumpur. In one bar we were shown to a table, about four feet high, surrounded by half-a-dozen tall chairs. Unusual furniture maybe, but what was really different was that hidden under the large tablecloth upon which we stood our beers were half-a-dozen girls giving customers oral sex as they drank and chatted away. As the customers were approached, their voices would go up a couple of octaves higher for a bit. When they returned to normal, the girls would crawl round on their knees and start at the next chair's occupant. The only snag I could discern was that it was important to check that your bar snacker was actually a woman.

For the equivalent of £20 a girl would come back to your hotel room and stay for as long as you wished. One or two of the single lads regularly took advantage of this offer. Robby picked one of the girls out, paid her pimp the money and off he went with her. Russ and I were sat downstairs in the hotel bar at six o'clock in the morning when Robby stepped out of the elevator with his girl.

'I'm just taking her back,' he explained. 'I'll be with you in a minute. Could you get me a beer?'

It was a small investment, knowing it would buy us all the details.

He returned five minutes later, took a big gulp out of his beer, and began.

'She was brilliant!' he began. 'At one stage, I had her feet in the lampshade on the wall . . .' We were still laughing when he said, 'The pimp asked me if she was all right and when I told him, "Not half!", he replied, "Good, she is my wife!"'

Malaysia really is a different planet.

One night we spent nearly half an hour convincing Ralph that the girl he fancied was not a girl at all. Although sometimes it is quite difficult to tell, this one wasn't very convincing. On almost every occasion that a 'girl' is wearing a choker, it is being worn to cover up their Adam's apple. In hindsight, it might have been funnier if we hadn't intervened.

We spent our final night in Kuala Lumpur in The Ship Inn. It was a massive pub, with a stage and a really good rock band. As the evening drew to a close, we were all singing the old Leeds favourites and our flags were flying proudly. The landlord called time, but no one took much notice. He grew more impatient as we continued to drink and sing. Finally he snapped and vaulted over the bar armed with a very large machete. To this day I don't know what the hell I was thinking about, but I tried to reason with him. As I approached him, he swung at me, and swiped my right hand. I didn't dare look at my hand but I knew it was bleeding. Someone rushed over and wrapped it in a beer towel. Amazingly, I soon learned it was only a minor cut and all my fingers were still attached. That certainly beats ringing the bell for last orders.

Our journey home was an absolute nightmare. From the hotel foyer to Leeds took us just over 30 hours. We landed at five different airports en route but by far the worst one was Dhaka in Bangladesh. There was no air conditioning and the whole place stank. There was even a cat running round, inside the airport, with a lizard in its mouth. At about one o'clock in the morning I noticed a crowd gathering outside. Some were doing building work perched very precariously on a high, flimsy scaffold made out of bamboo. Others stood around looking up at them. I asked an airport official what was going on. He explained casually that the ones on the ground were waiting for the ones on the scaffold to fall off so they could take over their jobs. Our stopover in Dubai was more pleasant, with a massive range of duty-free items at extremely cheap prices.

We arrived back in Leeds thirsty and shattered. We had just one day to recharge our batteries before flying out to Italy for two games there.

When we arrived at Pisa Airport the following night at midnight, there wasn't a soul in sight. No taxis, nothing. We managed to find a couple of airport staff in another terminal and they arranged for a fleet of taxis for us. They hadn't heard of our hotel, Piccollo Palace, but they said the taxi drivers would know where it was. They did – it was 'a very long way, at a place called Massa'. They were right, it was a long way. Each taxi had cost us nearly £70. That said, it was worth the trip. Massa is a seaside town and quite lively.

However, we soon discovered that the match might be cancelled because the team Leeds had flown out to play had just gone bankrupt. Great! Manager Howard Wilkinson had apparently been less than amused but we had chatted with Gary McAllister in Kuala Lumpur and he gave me a number to ring once we arrived in Italy to find out about the game. If they were going to play at all. The number wasn't much help given the changed circumstances but some brilliant detective work by our organizer, Big Mick Hewitt, and the hotel owner, came up with the answer we were after. Leeds were to play a hastily arranged match against a team of amateurs, US Lampo. But it took us hours to find out where the game was.

We eventually found the ground. It was in the middle of a forest. It was about an hour before kick-off and some of the Leeds players were out on the pitch. McAllister noticed us and came over.

'How the hell did you find us here?' he laughed. 'We didn't know where we were playing ourselves until two hours ago!'

The truth was, we didn't know either until we had found them.

Once the game kicked off, it was obvious Leeds were in for an easy ride. Even Carlton Palmer was in with a chance. The linesman on the far side was no thinner than Demis Roussos. Leeds ran out 10–0 winners and could easily have had more.

Our troubles weren't over, though, as Leeds' next game was to be on the opposite, east coast, against Ascoli. The drive would take around six hours. At least we had a couple of days to enjoy Massa.

In Italy, a lot of the beaches are sectioned off and are privately owned. Our hotel owned a section and we enjoyed a couple of days drinking and swimming in the glorious sunshine. Because she likes Italy, Lesley had come with me on this trip. Webby liked it too, a little too much, and soon got sunstroke. His head turned a horrible red colour and you could see him coming down the seafront from five miles away. He was sharing a room with Keith Gaunt, who offered Webby no sympathy at all by being the last one to return to the room each night. Webby didn't like that one bit.

The day before the game with Ascoli we were in the hotel bar at half past three in the morning. There was a police convention going on in the hotel that night and the landlord was tired and ready for bed. We insisted on one more drink. One of the officers took his side. 'You go to bed, now!' he suggested. We explained we were just having one more. He took his revolver out and began spinning the chambers as though he was in a western. We all yawned heavily and hit the sack.

The next day we boarded the transport Big Mick had arranged and headed for the east coast and Ascoli. With the kick-off approaching we were in a sports bar outside the ground when the Leeds team coach arrived. We still hadn't got tickets for the game, but didn't expect any problem getting in. Nonetheless, Webby decided to speak to Bill Fotherby as he got off the bus and asked if he had any tickets for us. Webby returned looking cross. Fotherby had no tickets but, generous as ever, had given him a tenner to get us all some drinks. There were 12 of us.

We shrugged and added enough to buy one more round. Little Mick Hewitt celebrated by flinging his Leeds hat, James Bond-style, onto one of the optics at the first attempt and we left the bar. Leeds lost 2–0 and we didn't get back to our hotel until four in the morning. We were leaving for the airport at six. But Italy, after Malaysia, had still been one of the best trips of recent years. Then 1994–95 got under way and I was brought down to earth by our man in the number four shirt.

Palmer had signed for Leeds in the summer of 1994. A few weeks after the season had started, in November, they travelled to Cork to play a friendly on a wet Monday night and I went to watch with Webby, Jeff and Pencil. After the game we ended up outside the same nightclub that most of the team had gone to. The bouncers knew we had come all the way from Leeds but insisted it was a private party and they weren't going to let us in. The arrival of reinforcements in the shape of Whitby John and a few other lads didn't persuade them, either, so I tried a new approach.

'Would you let us in if one of the players vouched for us?' I asked.

The bouncer merely smiled and said, 'Sure, who?'

'Gary McAllister,' I said. 'Just tell him some of the Kippax Branch are outside.'

The bouncer disappeared and a few minutes later McAllister came to the door. 'Hi, big man, how's it going? You coming in?'

Behind him the bouncer, looking a bit perturbed, waved us in. Once inside, we bought ourselves beers and relaxed. We didn't pester them but many of the players spoke to us and bought us drinks. The atmosphere was relaxed and we were having a good time. It was then I noticed Carlton Palmer stood on his own at one of the other bars, I walked over to him. The previous Saturday we'd played Wimbledon and Palmer had looked to have got away with handling the ball on his own goal-line. We'd smiled about that so from where I stood, behind him, I put my hand on his shoulder and said: 'Hey up, Carlton, was it handball or what?'

Without looking over his shoulder he replied: 'Whoever's got their hand on me, let go now.' And without looking round he walked off towards the toilet.

When he returned I was still gobsmacked and said, 'What's up with you, mate?'

But he was so arrogant he wouldn't even look at me. At that moment Gary Speed, a good friend to the Kippax Branch over the years, came over and asked me to join his table for a drink. He could see I was annoyed and was there to calm things down. I went with Speed and sat with him and some of the other lads and players.

McAllister said, 'Take no notice.'

Speedo nodded. Palmer had only been at Leeds two weeks and it hadn't taken his fellow professionals long to weigh him up.

That should have been the end of it. But at around three o'clock in the morning a few of us were outside a chicken-and-chips cafe when sauntering down the road, with a girl on each arm, came Carlton Palmer. He saw me and came over to speak to me.

'C'mon, mate, we're all Leeds!' he said and playfully pushed the peak of my Leeds baseball cap down over my eyes.

'Leeds?' I replied, pushing my peak back up with one finger. 'You don't know the meaning of the word. The sooner you fuck off from our club, the better.'

His two 'dates' looked away. Whitby John was stood behind him, grinning at me and mouthing the words 'Smack him!' It was tempting. Palmer was thick-skinned, however, and reached over and tried to grab one of Pencil's chips. Pencil wasn't feeling generous, swore at Palmer and pulled his supper out of the player's reach, adding, 'Get yer own!' with such calm insistence that Palmer took the hint and hurried away down the road with his entourage. I'm not a hateful person, but Carlton Palmer really got to me that night. And he did it again in 1996.

It was during a pre-season tour of Germany. Mick Hewitt had arranged our trip, as usual, and travelled with us. We had a good base, nestled at the bottom of the Rhine Valley in a little place called Freiberg. One of the games was against Pforzheim, from one of Germany's lower divisions in a small but attractive ground. Well, it's main attraction was the large bar overlooking the pitch, in which you could sit at a table and watch the match. Whitby John and around 30 Leeds fans had gathered behind one of the goals. Dave and I had taken our ladies along and were enjoying a drink in the bar. Also on the trip was the Doctor, so nicknamed due to his resemblance to Tom Baker of *Doctor Who* fame. Anyone who has met our Doctor, and many have, will testify he's no ordinary character. If he had two hearts and travelled in a Tardis he couldn't be any more unusual. About half an hour into the game I noticed him in the main stand and excused myself from Lesley to spend ten minutes with him. As the Doctor and I were sharing a beer, I noticed Leeds United's managing director Bill Fotherby sitting a few rows behind us. The Doctor didn't like Fotherby. Not many fans did. I couldn't resist pointing him out. Within seconds Fotherby was getting a visit.

'You bastards have taken my card off me!' yelled the Doctor. He was talking about his LUFC Premier Card – needed for away games.

Fotherby looked worried. 'Come and see me when we get back and I'll see what I can do,' he replied.

The Doctor was not convinced. 'Oh yeah, sure . . . You'll extend it!' he replied, sarcastically.

'No, I promise,' said the MD, trying not to look flustered. 'You're obviously a loyal fan – coming all the way out here to watch a friendly. Come and see me.'

I almost believed him myself. The Doctor wasn't so sure but returned to his seat, and I returned to the bar to rejoin Lesley. At half-time one of the lads wandered over to our table. 'Isn't that the Doctor?' he said.

I turned to confirm but noticed he wasn't looking in the direction of the Doctor's seat. Following his gaze I looked, instead, out of the bar window. On the pitch, running about with nothing on except his socks, was the Doctor. The German substitutes were kicking a ball about in the goalmouth so he made a beeline for them. Racing over he stuck out a foot and whipped the ball off them with no resistance at all. He then feinted left and right, skipped around a stunned German defender, before smacking a blistering shot past the bewildered keeper. Yelling, 'Goooaaaalll!!' he raced over to the Leeds fans behind the goal to celebrate.

I was laughing so much I had tears in my eyes and could see there was no one on hand to arrest him. After a while, he simply grew bored and returned to his clothes. His streak put everyone in a carnival mood, but Carlton Palmer was about to put a stop to that.

During the second half, the Leeds fans behind the goal were barracking him and feelings were running high. As the half wore on Palmer lost patience and was gesticulating to the fans with increasing regularity. As the referee blew for full-time, I flipped and began shouting at him.

'Sit down, you idiot,' suggested Lesley but I wasn't listening and shot down the stairs, heading straight for the pitch and Palmer. After signing an autograph for a young fan (who didn't know better) he looked up and saw me coming. He didn't seem keen to talk and immediately ran off – with the kid's pen. This incensed me more. I chased after him but he stepped up a gear and disappeared down the players' tunnel.

But there was no stopping me now. Having run this far I decided I might as well continue. I followed Palmer down the tunnel. He skipped into the dressing-room and I saw Howard Wilkinson shut the door behind him. I ran up to the door and started banging on it. I was still banging when two out-of-breath security guards and a policeman arrived. Suddenly it dawned on me what I was doing. In my mind's eye I saw handcuffs and protracted Foreign Office negotiations to get me out of a German jail. I needed to think fast. As the copper drew nearer I heard myself say five of the daftest words I had ever uttered: 'I just want his autograph.'

I wasn't sure they believed me – perhaps Carlton Palmer's reputation had reached Germany, too. Whatever, my insane plea got me off the hook. One of them shook his head and directed me back out of the tunnel. What else could I do but return to the bar? Lesley would not speak to me. She maintained her stony silence for the final three days of the trip. So it wasn't all bad news.

But it could have been worse, Palmer might have opened the dressing-room door . . .

17

Into Africa . . . And a Police Cell in London

I don't know what my life would be like without Leeds. It would be different, that's for sure. I haven't missed a match since Nelson Mandela was put in jail. Look how his life has changed since then!

Leeds United's pre-season tour for 1995 included two games in South Africa. A dozen of us opted to travel with Big Mick Hewitt's party and we arrived at our hotel just outside Johannesburg three days before the first game.

Once the bags were in the room, we were in the nearest bar. It was lunchtime but Late Night Al's, part of the hotel complex, seemed like the perfect place to taste our first Tiger beer. In Late Night Al's we got talking to an English bloke about good places to visit. We had only been there about half an hour and ten of us were in two cars driven by this English bloke and his mate heading for a district called Hillbrow. Before the trip we had all been given an itinerary stating the places we were advised to avoid and the places definitely to avoid. At the top of this second list was Hillbrow. The itinerary made it perfectly clear: on no account should we visit Hillbrow. It was about two in the afternoon, and the only advice the bloke we met in the hotel gave us was to leave before dark. To fortify ourselves for the experience we went into a pub called The Jungle.

We had to ring a bell on the door to gain entrance. Once inside, we quickly noticed we were the only white people in the place, with the exception of the landlord, who came from Middlesbrough. After a few beers we were relaxed and having a good time. Our lads were circulating, some taking on the locals at pool, while the rest of us were sat at the bar. Some of the local girls arrived with only one thing on their minds. What they were selling was really cheap, but we didn't fancy any exercise. We declined, and told them they were more than welcome to join us for a drink. From the barstool behind me, the girl called Wendy asked me again if I was sure I didn't want to take her up on her generous offer; as I turned to answer her she had a condom, still in the packet, stuck to her forehead. You had to admire her persistence.

One of the lads, Russ Townend, came over and pointed to one of the locals in the corner and told me that the man had just pulled a gun out.

'On you?!' I said.

'No,' Russ replied, 'but he asked me who had brought us in here, then produced the gun and said, "Show me and I'll blow his fucking head off!"'

Luckily, the bloke who did bring us had already gone. It turned out that the lad with the gun was originally from Castleford – only three miles from where we live. When we finally left, we realised that we had stuck to the advice that our friend had given us about leaving before it was dark. It was half past six the next morning and the sun was up.

South Africa was really cheap and it was possible to get a large steak, with all the trimmings, and a couple of beers for around a fiver. Travel was cheap too; we were there for 11 days and we paid about £70 for a coach to take us wherever we wanted, with the same driver. One of our first outings was to a safari park. Rather foolishly we arrived about midday when just about all the animals were asleep. We saw a warthog running about, which was good until we saw another and then another. After a while, one warthog looked exactly the same as the other and the novelty wore off. It was the same with the gazelles. We did see a load of hippopotamuses around a small pond, but they just resembled a bunch of motionless rocks. One or two took photographs – this was about as exiting as it got. Deciding that the marvels of African wildlife weren't for us, we stopped off at a bar in the middle of the park and then left.

Leeds' first game was at the Loftus Stadium, in Pretoria, against Kaiser Chiefs – the side that Leeds had signed Lucas Radebe from the year before. We arrived early and sampled the local brew. The first bar belonged to the local rugby club. The owner didn't care for black people at all. He told us that four years ago they weren't allowed out on the street. 'Look at them,' he said, pointing out of the window, 'they're all over the place now.' We quickly learned that rugby was for the whites and football was for the blacks. This was apparent once we entered the stadium. There were only a handful of whites in the sell-out crowd of almost 65,000. Inside, the fanatical Chiefs supporters, all dressed in their colours of black and yellow, chanted and danced. As we entered our turnstile, we noticed a sign which read: 'All firearms must be left here'. Many, behind the goal to our left, still had spears and shields. I could just imagine them getting off the train at Leeds City Station for a game at Elland Road. The day was quite an experience, and would have been all the more enjoyable if Leeds hadn't lost 1–0.

The next day, our coach took us to Sun City – the holiday, sports and entertainment location controversially visited by westerners during apartheid sanctions. The driver had arranged to take us through Soweto on the way. As we passed through, some of the sights were unbelievable. There were millions of people living there. It looked no better equipped than a giant garden allotment. Most houses had no electricity, some didn't even have four walls. Groups gathered round burning tyres hurriedly eating scraps of food. Somewhere in this sprawling mass Lucas Radebe had been shot. He was a professional footballer at the time. We passed the football ground of Orlando Pirates, situated deep into Soweto. 'There is much fighting there,' said the driver, pointing to the stadium, 'many deaths.' Our stunned and respectful silence was ended by Whitby John: 'Just our bleedin' luck to draw them in Europe, then.'

As Sun City was a long distance from our hotel, the driver had brought along his mate to share the driving. He quickly set the pace and after an hour, he took a break, spark-out in the aisle, having smoked two massive joints. Summer being the closed season in South Africa, much of Sun City was not open but there was still plenty of activity. We went into Alligator Park, where men wrestled with alligators, and fed them whole, dead chickens. Alligator was on the menu and the waiters would come to your table with live baby 'gators for you to choose from. These would then be killed and cooked to your liking. None of us are what you'd call the sensitive kind, but we all declined. When the time came to leave, Ralph from Scarborough was missing. 'The pervert will be in one of the cinemas showing blueys,' said Jeff, and promptly volunteered to go get him. Half an hour later Jeff returned with Ralph in tow. He'd found him straight away in the cinema but had sat down with him, watched the film for half an hour and then remembered: 'Oh, by the way, everybody is waiting for you on the coach.' The return journey was hairy to say the least. By now both our drivers had been smoking marijuana all day and were completely out of their heads. We were driving through small towns at up to 100 mph. Everyone on the coach, including whichever driver wasn't at the wheel, kept his head down, afraid to look. When we arrived back at the hotel we headed straight into Late Night Al's for a calming nightcap.

On the Saturday we had a day at the races. In between races we watched a football match on the television in the bar. It was at the Orlando Pirates' ground, which we had passed the day before. As the camera scanned round the crowd, it focused on the only two white faces in the entire stadium. They belonged to Keith Gaunt and Mick Garner. Now I like my footie, but these two are football mad. Whenever we travel to see Leeds, they try and get to another game as well. But the Orlando Pirates? Where people are killed for supporting the wrong team? These are two silly white men, without any doubt. We couldn't help laughing, as time and again the cameraman kept going back to Keith and Mick, as if he too, couldn't believe what he was seeing.

Our second match was in Johannesburg, at Ellis Park. Because Leeds lost their first game, they were here to meet Benfica in a play-off, while the 'final' was to be between Kaiser Chiefs and Mamelodi

Sundowns (who ex-Leeds striker Philomen Masinga had once played for). After our game, a 1–1 draw, we left, leaving another sell-out crowd whipping itself up to a frenzy.

The only drawback of our visit to South Africa was that all the bars closed at half past eight on Sundays. And this was a Sunday. We headed back to Late Night Al's to see how late it would stay open. The man behind the bar was the spitting image of Rod Wallace, so we had been calling him Rod. We asked if it was possible to stay open a little later than usual. He said he would have to ring Al. Up to now no one had seen Al, in fact we didn't even know if he existed at all. He came back and said we were OK until half past ten. It was a start. When half past ten arrived we asked Rod for another hour or so. We had been giving him generous tips and he was putting them all in a cardboard cup on his bar. He rang Al again, who said it was OK to stay open till midnight. Rod also had to ring his wife for permission for him to stay. Once he told her how much in tips he was getting, he too received the OK. He must have been very poorly paid as he said his tips already amounted to four times his weekly wage.

As midnight approached we asked Al, through Rod, for a further extension and at half past one in the morning he decided to come to his own bar to see what all the fuss was about. When he saw a dozen Leeds fans drinking plenty and with no trouble, he had no hesitation in allowing us to stay for as long as we wanted. For good measure, he bought everyone a drink. Rod was like a dog with two knobs with the tips he was getting. Al was white and had come originally from Halifax. He told us that a lot of blacks had recently begun showing resentment towards white-owned bars and he went home a different way each evening. He told us that a few weeks earlier a white landlord had been found, stabbed to death, in his own freezer. The man responsible had been a black barman. We looked across at Rod without saying anything. 'Oh, he's all right,' said Al, 'he's been with me during all my ten years here.' At about five o'clock in the morning we all shook hands with Al and Rod and made our way back to our beds. It was our last night and had been a good evening all round, a fine send-off before the morning's long flight back to England. And an eight-hour wait for a connecting flight to Germany for the Leeds game in Dusseldorf.

Arriving at Heathrow, we decided to kill time in a King's Cross snooker hall. I left the lads there and nipped out for a newspaper. Bill Fotherby had promised major signings during the summer of 1995. He had, of course, promised us major signings every summer for the last ten years, but we lived in hope. In 1987 he'd told us Maradona was all set to sign. Brazil's Rivaldo was another of the many players Fotherby said he was bringing to Leeds. Ever the optimist, I was eager to see if there had been any developments since we'd been in South Africa. There had.

I returned to the snooker hall waving my newspaper and announced: 'We've signed a new player!'

Webby and Jeff stood down their cues and asked who.

'Paul Beesley – £600,000!' I replied.

They both stared at me in silence before both saying, again, 'Who?!'

Exciting times lay ahead. But not necessarily involving an ex-Sheffield United defender.

I came close to missing a game back in the 1990–91 season. It was at Chelsea on 30 March. We had got off our coach and were gathered by the turnstile talking among ourselves and with other supporters branches. Suddenly the police charged at us, demanding we get inside the ground. In the melee that followed a few Leeds fans were arrested. Foolishly, perhaps, I intervened and I became part of their number. My mate Lunge questioned my treatment and he too was arrested. As a result, eight of our members were nicked in one minute! As I was being led away I wrestled my arm from the officer who was applying extremely hard pressure for no reason. This was interpreted as an escape attempt and all hell broke loose. Coppers jumped on me from everywhere, booting me and punching me from all sides. Bystanders were complaining and I heard the supporters club treasurer, Roy Schofield, say that he'd seen everything and to ring him if required. I was bundled into the back of the van, my hands handcuffed behind my back. The van then drove to the other side of the stadium and I was taken into the detention area. I obviously hadn't seen my face, but I could tell from the reaction of others that I was in a pretty bad way. I was having difficulty breathing or seeing. Ironically this was to work in my favour.

A woman police officer asked me to come with her. 'I haven't done anything wrong,' I protested. 'I just want to go to the game.' She said nothing, only repeated her instruction to follow her away from the detention area. I was led to a room and she opened the door and instructed me to go in.

Pointing to the wash basin she said: 'Get yourself cleaned up. I'll be with you shortly.' I was about to protest again when she pointed at the window, said nothing and closed the door behind her. I peered through the blind to find I could see the whole pitch! The players had just come out but I still had time for a wash and brush up before the kick-off. I looked in the mirror. What a sight! Both my eyes were bruised and blackening by the second and my nose was all over the place. There were cuts all over my face. I washed myself the best I could; it was hurting like hell. I settled down to watch the match.

After about half an hour the woman officer returned. 'Everything OK?' she asked. I pretended not to be too interested in the game and told her again that I hadn't done anything wrong. 'I have something to attend to,' she said. 'I'll be back in about an hour.' I went back to watching the match.

Just before the end of the game – which Leeds won 2–1 – two officers came, said I was being charged and I was led off and driven to Fulham Police Station. After I was formally charged I was led to a cell. Five minutes later I was visited by the police doctor. He took photographs of my injuries and asked how I got them. I told him I had tripped and fallen, but he didn't believe me. I was only in custody for about an hour and then I was released. I asked the desk sergeant if there were any more of our branch in this prison. I was told that another four were in custody and he asked where I would be when they were released. 'Out of the door, first pub on the left,' I said. 'Can you tell them I'll be in there, please?' He said he would.

I got some concerned looks when I ordered a pint at the bar. It must have been obvious I had just come out of the nick. I had a couple of pints and then Big John arrived. He'd been arrested trying to help Lunge. Barry Hope came in next. He'd been nicked helping me. Lunge came in about ten o'clock with another lad, Phil from Ossett. We moved to another pub until closing time and then we discussed how we would get home. The next train to Leeds was half past five in the morning – six hours away.

At Victoria Station I spotted a private-hire taxi and asked the driver if he would take us to Leeds for £200. 'Yeah, no problem!' he said, eagerly. Then he noticed there were five of us and he could only take four. He seemed more disappointed than we were. A London cabbie had been listening in. 'I'll take you to Leeds for £50 each,' he offered. We agreed and piled in. But as we were heading up the M1 he had a change of heart and said he would take us to Luton and get someone to take us on from there. We had given him £250 up front. 'Nothing doing!' we argued. So he carried on chugging up the motorway. He dropped Phil off at the Ossett turn-off, Barry at Swillington and then myself in Kippax at about six o'clock in the morning. As I got out I noticed that the meter read £373.00. I'll never forget the sight of the London black cab disappearing into the early morning fog, with two more passengers still to drop off at Garforth and Seacroft.

The court appearance that followed came about a month later at West London Magistrates Court. The precise charge was the old favourite: 'Drunk while attempting to enter a designated sporting arena'. This is the charge that police can use when all else fails. It has always amazed me how people escape such a punishment at sporting arenas such as racecourses and cricket grounds. Both, incidentally, which I attend regularly.

When I arrived at court, without a solicitor, I told an officer that I wanted to speak to the duty solicitor. He asked me my name and charge, and said that for such a 'minimal' charge, I really didn't need to see one, that I would be 'in and out in no time, small fine and on my way'. Foolishly I took his advice. I received a £200 fine and more importantly an 18-month ban from football grounds in England and Wales. To say I was devastated would be an understatement. I left the court and went straight over the road to see a solicitor (something I should have done in the first place) and immediately filed an appeal. I was told that an appeal may not be accepted, so a couple of tense weeks lay ahead.

In the meantime, I had been ordered to appear at my local police station the following Saturday at three o'clock in the afternoon. Leeds' match that day was at home against Liverpool. I worked all week on a cunning plan and come Saturday morning, prepared to put it into action.

I asked my wife Lesley to drive me to the police station at two o'clock. I was to tell them I was early because I had finished with football and was taking the wife away on holiday. It turned out I didn't need to say anything. The station was all but deserted with only a handful of officers about (the others were probably all at the match). A woman officer dealt with me. I told her of my conviction and consequent ban and that I had been ordered to surrender myself and have my photograph taken. This was then to be circulated to every football ground in the country. She didn't have a clue what I was talking about. 'Right then,' she said, 'you'd better come with me.' She led me into the back and asked me to sit on a stool, while she set a camera up on a tripod. Now, as anyone who has met me will verify, I haven't got the smartest appearance on the planet at the best of times, but as the officer was occupied preparing the camera, I carried out the next stage of my plan. I tugged vigorously at my straggly locks and beard. When I had finished, my hair was sticking out at all angles and I looked like Captain Caveman. I sat there and waited.

'Right then,' said the officer, still checking the settings. 'I think that's it . . .' She looked up and saw me. She was visibly shaken at what she saw. I may have overdone it a bit. She looked down into the viewfinder and then looked back at me, not quite believing what she was looking at. She quickly took the photo, said that was it and told me I could go. I guessed she could not wait to get rid of me. Which was fine. I could not wait to get out.

I rushed out of the station and jumped into the car. 'Go! Go! Go!' I yelled to Lesley, sounding like someone out of *The Sweeney*. I then arrived at Kevin's barber shop. A quick haircut and a very close shave later, I headed on to Elland Road. Lesley pulled up at the ground about five minutes before kick-off. I jumped out and headed for the Gelderd End. At the time, I had a seat in the north-east corner stand. But being ever suspicious, I thought the police might be

211

watching my seat so I had swapped my own ticket with that of my mate, Barry Hope, and used his to go in The Kop. I made my way, right up into the far corner. I was wearing a flat cap and was sure I'd done everything possible to make my arrival and presence as incognito as possible.

I was a bit disappointed, then, when as I walked all the way up the steps to my new place at the back, people everywhere were nodding to me and saying, 'All right, Gary? Nice cap!' My heart sank further when I got to the back of the stand and saw a mate of mine, Steve Pratt. Steve is a great lad but, like myself, does tend to get a bit carried away sometimes. The last thing I wanted today was attention. I just hoped he was due a quiet game. No such luck. In the first five minutes Liverpool scored. Steve started shouting and bawling. Minutes later, Liverpool scored a second. Steve became even more animated. To make things worse, a lad near us stood there clapping the goal. I grimaced in anticipation of Steve's next move. 'What the fuck are you clapping at?' he demanded.

Our sportsmanlike neighbour looked sideways at Steve and explained: 'It was a good goal!'

'Good goal? Good goal?!' Steve was furious. 'There's no such fucking thing as a good goal against Leeds United!'

I happened to agree with him, but this was not the right time or place. Then disaster struck, Liverpool scored another. I closed my eyes and then cringed as our man started clapping again. I still had them closed when I heard an almighty smack. Steve had punched this lad right in the face, knocking him completely off of his feet. This caught the attention of the police nearby. I pulled my cap right down over my face as they made their way over. Luckily people around us closed ranks and the coppers were unable to get any nearer. The injured lad slipped away, holding his bloodied nose, never to return. In the second half Leeds mounted an impressive assault on the Liverpool goal and were narrowly beaten 5–4. Had it not been for a very dubious decision that ruled out a Lee Chapman effort, Leeds would have finished with a well-earned point.

The incident reminded me of the home game with Queens Park Rangers, earlier that same season, in October 1990. Leeds were leading 2–0 when Roy Wegerle pulled one back for Rangers, and my mate Neil 'Spender' Moseley started clapping. I leant over and asked him what he was doing. 'It was a good goal, Snake,' he said. 'Don't be daft,' I replied. QPR went on to equalise and finally win the game 3–2. Spender didn't clap anymore. The following week, at the match away to Aston Villa, I gave Spender a present. He took the bag I offered him and removed a baseball cap. On top of it were two massive hands with a piece of string attached. When pulled, the string made the two hands clap together. Sportingly he wore it for the whole of the match, but he never needed it. The game ended in a 0–0 draw and we never saw that hat again.

I learned from my solicitor that my appeal had been granted and would be heard on Friday, 31 May 1991 at Knightsbridge Crown Court. Lesley and I travelled down the night before and we stayed in a hotel near Harrods. On our arrival, Wub went to reception to check in, while I looked for a parking space. It took some time to find one, so by the time I arrived at reception, she had gone to the room. There was nobody about at all.

I looked around and shouted for someone. Then I thought I saw something out of the corner of my eye. I looked round but saw nothing. Confused, I looked around once more and saw it again – but then it vanished. I stayed focused on this spot until the head I presume I had glimpsed before appeared from round the corner, about half-way up the wall – only to disappear again. It then came back and said, 'Can I help you?' I was just about to speak and the head went out of sight again. Things were getting rather surreal.

When the head reappeared, I spoke to it quickly: 'Mr Edwards. I have a room booked.'

The head disappeared yet again. Unable to guess what on earth was going on I just stood there bemused, wondering what I should do next. Presently the head appeared again and said, politely, 'Room number seven, your wife has gone up, sir,' before it vanished again.

As I made my way to the stairs, the mystery was solved when the head came round the corner attached to the body of a Muslim. The penny dropped. He had been praying at the time of my arrival and had therefore, been unable to deal with me until he had finished.

When I eventually arrived at our room, Wub asked where I'd been. When I explained the delay she simply shrugged and said, 'Oh, right.' I'm not sure, to this day, what she thought.

Next morning I was up in front of three judges at the Crown Court. They heard my case and took my references away into the back room, to read in private. I had brought 20 with me, ranging from other supporters clubs, including Sunderland, courtesy of secretary of the supporters club Harry Brass, and Manchester City, as well as from branches of our own supporters club. I also had one from my local councillor, Keith Parker, who later went on to become Lord Mayor of Leeds. I had one from Rod Johnson, a friend and former player in Don Revie's great sides of the 1960s. We had to rise as the judges returned. My appeal had been upheld, they saw no reason why I should be banned from watching Leeds United and also added that they were surprised that I had gone to such lengths 'just to follow a football team'. I was elated and didn't see the need to explain.

There were a couple of police officers at court and I recognised one of my arresting officers; they had not objected in any way to my appeal. There was also a ginger-haired woman officer. I recognised her as being the one who had taken me into that small room at Stamford Bridge. She came over to me and Wub. She asked how I was and said that she hadn't thought I would be charged in the first place and was glad things had worked out in the end. I thanked her for giving me the opportunity to watch the match that day.

Over the following weeks, after the appeal hearing, I received numerous letters and phone calls from the Police Complaints Authority, urging me to press charges against the officers responsible. Much to the annoyance of Wub, I refused. I told one of the investigating officers that I was glad it was all over and that was the end of it as far as I was concerned. I was a Leeds fan who attended every game and if I were to press charges I believed I would suffer from retribution by London police in future visits to the capital. Despite assurances to the contrary, I stuck to my decision.

Before the beginning of the following season I was at Leeds Road in Huddersfield watching Leeds United play a friendly against Huddersfield Town. Only days earlier I had been in Tokyo watching

Leeds. So it goes. The beer was cheaper here, anyway.

Just before half-time I was approached by half-a-dozen policemen. I was asked my name. 'Gary Edwards,' I replied.

This so excited one of them, he had to be steadied by his senior officer. 'Could you come with me a moment, please sir?' Fearing the worst, I followed them downstairs. 'Do you realise you are the subject of an exclusion order?' continued the senior officer. I explained about my successful appeal back in May. 'Have you any proof?' snapped one of the other officers. I said I hadn't. I was really glad that this senior officer was there and I am convinced, that had he not been, I would have been carted away and locked up until my story was verified, which doubtless would have been after the game. 'I will give you the benefit of doubt on this occasion, sir. Go on back to your friends and watch the match. I will check your details and take the appropriate action. In the meantime I would advise you to carry your documentation with you until this matter is cleared up.' I thanked him and rejoined the lads.

'Have they gone?' said Lunge, looking worried.

'Yes,' I said, 'why? What's up?'

Lunge reminded me: 'I'm still banned, aren't I?!'

It just goes to prove: you can never trust the police to do their job right.

- 18 -

Billy Bremner

Loyalty.

When Billy Bremner died, I was devastated. It was Sunday, 7 December 1997. I had been with my local team, The Royal Oak, to a cup match in Huddersfield. We were in the home team's local having after-match drinks and sandwiches. The day before, it had been reported that Billy had suffered a minor heart attack, but was now doing fine. At about four o'clock, on the television in the bar, Sky News reported that Billy had suffered another attack and died.

It is perhaps hard for someone not as involved as I was to understand, but I just could not stop myself from crying. I tried to look away hoping that no one had noticed, but one of the lads, Derek Parker, came over with a large whisky and said, ''Ere, mate, get that down you. He was the best.'

I felt such an idiot. Here I was crying over a man I'd met just four times in my entire life. But I simply couldn't help it. He was Leeds United through and through. I remembered him saying, when he returned to Elland Road as manager, 'Every time we concede a goal, I feel like I have been stabbed in my heart.'

My mind wandered back to one of the first matches at Elland

Road after Billy took over as manager. It was actually his third in charge, against Portsmouth, on 2 November 1985. Leeds won 2–1. We were stood in our usual spot on The Kop, about 30 of us. Another hero of Don Revie's side, Eddie Gray, had been sacked as manager a little over a week earlier, after three years in the job. Many of the younger supporters who now congregated at the back of The Kop, where we had stood many years before, understandably, weren't happy at a new manager coming in. Perhaps many had only heard of Bremner through their parents' memories. There were a couple of flags bearing the name of Eddie Gray, another proclaiming, 'I love Eddie Gray'. I, too, thought he was very unfairly treated by the directors but was unprepared for what happened next. Minutes before the teams were due out on the pitch, the chanting began at the back of The Kop: 'Fuck off, Bremner! Fuck off, Bremner! Fuck off, Bremner!' I could not believe my ears.

Almost to a man, our group of 30 charged up to the back and began dishing out 'punishment' to the young upstarts who dared to call themselves Leeds fans. One of our lads, Lunge, had a bad leg and was having to use a walking stick, but that didn't slow him down any. They scattered in all directions, genuinely unaware of what they had done wrong. Soon it seemed that the entire Gelderd End had them surrounded. Then a very strange thing happened. Instead of kicking the shit out of them, the young ones were being taken to one side in small groups and were being lectured by the knowledgeable that what they had just done was very naughty and they shouldn't do it again. After a few more tales about the great Billy Bremner, someone remarked that the teams were out.

It wasn't too long into the match that the name of Bremner was being chanted without the expletives.

Twelve years later my thoughts were interrupted with another drink. It was the captain of The Royal Oak, Barry Hope. 'He'll be up there with Don now. What a team that'll be.'

The funeral was held a few days later at the small St Mary's church in Edlington, near Doncaster. It was attended by many supporters and players alike.

I remember feeling that there weren't many representatives from the current Leeds United, but almost all the old boys were there.

Allan Clarke looked particularly upset – he and Billy had been very close – and he solemnly said a few words during the service. Asa Hartford, a man who never played for Leeds but had almost signed until a medical detected a heart condition, came and stood with us. Then he was asked to go in the church, and did so, reluctantly. Denis Law looked very upset and was crying . . . He was a long-time opponent and friend of Billy's. Another of Billy's former opponents, Nobby Stiles, arrived late – much like in his playing days – and dashed into the church minutes before the hearse arrived.

Stood opposite us on the other side of the road was a man in his 30s wearing a red Scum shirt. I had seen him arrive and was very angry. 'Cheeky bastard,' I thought but decided to ignore him. Just then someone behind me noticed him and wasn't so tolerant. 'Oi, you, yer twat!' he screamed, quickly adding: 'Zip yer fuckin' coat up!'

The man defiantly pulled his zip up only a few inches. Not enough.

'If you don't zip that coat right up, I'll come over there and kick your fuckin' 'ead in.' Not very subtle but that did the trick. The coat was duly zipped up.

I was just picturing the thought of the two of them brawling over the hearse's bonnet, when Webby nudged me in the back. 'I don't believe it, look who's here . . .'

I leant forward and looked back up the road. Walking down, as large as life, was Alex Ferguson. I had another vision, this time of me being hauled away after jumping on him as he walked past. Scum had been playing in Italy the previous night and, although I shall say this only once, I admired him for coming. George Graham, our own manager at the time, had seen fit not to attend.

Once Billy had been taken inside the church, the speakers that had been erected outside to convey the service to those unable to fit in echoed with the voice of Billy's closest friend, Alex Smith. Alex had been a life-long friend of Billy's. Alex had also had a distinguished football career and was Billy's best man at his wedding to Vicky in 1961. It was a very moving speech; they were obviously great friends. He talked at length about them growing up together.

A great memory I have of Billy Bremner is of when he was

manager at Leeds. He and his assistant at the time, Norman Hunter, gave a question-and-answer session in the old supporters club building on Elland Road one evening.

The event was a brilliant success and among the many memories is of the two reciting a tale by Billy about our old favourite, Liverpool's Emlyn Hughes. It dated from when Leeds were playing Liverpool at Anfield in the very early '70s.

'It was midway through the second half,' recalled Bremner, 'the scores were level, and we were defending a corner. I was at the near post and as the ball flew over my head I heard this almighty crash. I looked round and saw Emlyn Hughes sprawled out in the back of our net.

'I noticed Clarkey (Allan Clarke) heading back to the halfway line, dusting himself down. It was then I saw Tommy Smith, the Liverpool hard man, making his way towards Clarke. I ran after him to intervene. Smith ran past Clarke and took up his position in the defence. I looked at Smith rather puzzled, and when I got nearer to him he simply said, "Not a bad bloke after all, that Clarke, is he?" Apparently, not many of the Liverpool players liked Hughes, either.'

Throughout the evening, Bremner kept making adverse comments about the former Leeds keeper, the notoriously punchy Gary Sprake. Like the time at Blackpool when Gary had just flattened a Blackpool forward.

'The referee had seen it and was on his way to Sprake to no doubt send him off,' recalled Bremner. 'The forward was lying face-down, motionless, in the six-yard box. I went past him and stood on the backs of his hands. Within a flash he sprang to his feet and chased me 50 yards. This diverted the attention from Sprake and both players were booked. We were always getting Gary out of trouble, like the time he punched Bobby Gould. That was in a 2–1 win at Highbury in April 1969, the season we went on to win the title. The game was only five minutes old when Sprake, seen by everyone in the Clock End, threw a left hook at Gould and knocked him out cold. Terry Cooper actually caught him before he hit the ground. Luckily for Leeds, Sprake's teammates protested so much to referee Ken Burns – whose dislike of Leeds wasn't exactly a top secret – that the keeper escaped with only a booking.'

There were many more stories involving Sprake, and Bremner made it clear throughout that he had no friends anymore at Elland Road. This was a clear reference to Gary Sprake selling a story to a national newspaper that named certain people at Elland Road in bribery allegations (all of which were later challenged and successfully dismissed, resulting in large libel payments). The parting shot of the evening came, of course, from Billy, who said, 'Thank you all, ladies and gentlemen, and if you've got the impression that I don't like Gary Sprake, you're 100 per cent right!'

In the summer of 2000, on our way home from a holiday in Oban, Scotland, I had my football anorak head on. I asked Lesley if she'd mind if we stopped off at Stirling and visited the street where Bremner lived and was brought up. She tutted but agreed. We headed for the city's tough Raploch district. Turning into Weir Street felt weird; this was where the king of Leeds United grew up. I honestly didn't know why I was there, it was just something I wanted to do. I was disappointed to find that the only house in the street that was no longer there was the very one I'd come to see – Billy's number 35a. Instead I had my photograph taken standing on the grass patch that had been the Bremner household for four decades from the 1930s. An ice cream van was parked nearby and its owner was watching my every move. He must have thought I'd cracked up (he may have been right). I went over to him.

'This is where Billy Bremner lived, isn't it?' I said, fearing I'd made a big mistake.

'Aye, that was it, right there,' he replied. 'Some wee fella that, right enough. I grew up wi' Billy.'

I told him I was a Leeds fan having a look at a piece of our history.

'Y'know,' he continued, 'he was the most loyal man you could wish to meet. Do him a good turn and he never forgot it. Back in the late '50s and early '60s, Leeds gave him his chance. Once it was obvious he was going to make it, all the big boys wanted him – Celtic, Arsenal, Chelsea, Sheffield Wednesday–' Wednesday were, believe it or not, a good side in the '50s, or so my mate Jurgen says anyway '–and Aston Villa. Loads of 'em!'

'We were struggling at the bottom of Division Two, then,' I said.

'Aye,' replied the ice cream man, 'but he would never leave Leeds

United. They were his team. When he used to come home, we'd tek the mickey oot of him. We knew he was missing home and Celtic was inviting, but he'd pledged his allegiance and that was it.'

'There's a big statue of him at Elland Road,' I told him.

'Aye, I've heard. He'll like that.'

And with that, he shook my hand, and went on his way to find some more customers.

As I watched him go I looked around once again at the very street in which Don Revie had arrived in the dead of night in 1961 to persuade Billy to return to Leeds after Billy had suffered from severe homesickness.

I'm glad I called at 35a Weir Street.

- 19 -

From Stardom to Outrage

I do do other things. I was watching The Bootleg Beatles a
few years ago and someone came up to me and said: 'I know
you, you're the bastard that won't paint red!'

Early in the 1997–98 season I was contacted by the BBC who asked
if I would be filmed for a documentary – a one-off half-hour film
called *Shoot* by Adam Wishart that went out on BBC2 – on my love
for Leeds United and my hatred of manchester united. It wasn't hard
to say yes. Their plan was to interview me at home on Saturday, 27
September and then film me on my way to Elland Road (where
Leeds just happened to be playing manchester united). I was to go
about my business as usual, visiting the same pubs I would normally.
The crew would continue to film me during and after the game. The
week before I told everyone about this and to expect some cameras.
John at The Nag's Head simply shrugged and said, 'No problem,
they can take us as they find us.' It was the same response from the
rest of the bar staff. Everyone assured me they'd play it very casual
and unaffected.

The big day arrived and the BBC turned up at my house. They
set up cameras both inside and outside – to get shots of the Leeds

222

United flag that flies from a pole on the roof. Stewart Webb had turned up at the house for action and was lapping up the coverage. A couple of hours later we set off for Leeds. As we walked into The Nag's Head, it was packed, even more so than usual, and everyone cheered as I walked in. I then looked behind the bar and nearly died laughing. John was dressed up like John Travolta. The younger barmaids were done up like Barbie dolls with false nails and high heels. The older barmaids had hairstyles that a family of four could have lived in. Between them the girls had enough war paint on to frighten away a whole army. If this was supposed to be casual, it wasn't fooling me. Or anyone else. Every one of them made constant glances in the mirrors behind and the sight of them leaning sideways to get into camera shot as they tried to pull pints was hilarious.

But it wasn't only the staff who were acting up. The Nag's regulars are not exactly the best-dressed crab in the tray, but today all this had changed. Almost every one of them had worn a clean suit and shoes to match. No harm in that. However, among the men, the huge amount of war medals on display did seem slightly over the top. Likewise they suddenly acquired a taste for the finer things in life. The firm that supplied John with his cherries, oranges, lemons and cocktail umbrellas must have thought it was Christmas. With all the overloaded drinks on the bar, every time the door opened people expected 'Del Boy' Trotter to walk in.

The camera team, though, were loving it and after some initial shyness – that in some cases lasted for a full ten seconds – people were giving interviews at the drop of a hat. In fact, the customers became so keen that when it reached the time to leave for the match each member of the crew had a local clinging to his or her legs. But these people were professionals and as they dragged them across the floor to the door, they were easily able to ignore the cries of, 'Don't go yet, I haven't told you about the time I was on *Follyfoot*!'

Once the camera crew had recorded Stewart's and my brief visit to The Peacock on Elland Road, after having persuaded them not to film a bunch of Leeds fans roughing up a minibus of visiting supporters, they tracked us across Elland Road and into the ground's supporters' club bar for one last pint before kick-off. The day had gone well but was about to get better. A headed winner by the now-legendary David Wetherall made it complete. Almost. On leaving the ground, the BBC were just in time to catch a group of Leeds fans 'mooning' to Mark Hughes and Paul Ince on their team bus.

The television appearance was a laugh, but it didn't change my life. I simply got back to the serious routine of following Leeds whenever and wherever they played. In early August 1999 I was in Thirsk for a race meeting with some of the lads. Leeds fan Ian McKay from Belfast always likes to come over for this particular meeting and he sat with us in a pub in the main square as we watched, live, the draw for the coming season's UEFA Cup.

As usual, it was a long-drawn out affair and we were just losing interest when Simon Lackey shouted, 'This is us!'

We were pitched against Partizan Belgrade and the first leg was to be in Belgrade. 'There's a fuckin' war going on there!' said Matty, our landlord back at The Royal Oak.

War or not, it looked like Belgrade was where Leeds were going. As we all walked out of the small market town and up to the racecourse, we passed a toyshop.

'Here, this is what we want for Belgrade,' said Wayne Procter, pointing to a couple of children's toy soldier hats.

'They'll have to be bit harder than that,' said Haggis.

I got the feeling he could be right. Over the next couple of weeks, as a debate raged over whether Leeds United should be expected to travel into a war-torn country to play a football match, Mick Hewitt provisionally booked some flights. Leeds said they didn't particularly want to travel to Belgrade, but would abide by UEFA's decision. Partizan immediately suggested that Leeds 'were scared'. But as the mud-slinging began, UEFA broke the habit of a lifetime and sided with Leeds. It was decided to play the first-leg game in a neutral country, Holland, with the match to be played at the home of Heerenveen. Their ground was near to Amsterdam, which would be OK with us.

Mick rebooked the flights and booked a hotel right in the middle of Amsterdam. The city proved a popular location with Leeds fans. A quick glance out of our window revealed numerous Leeds flags hanging out of various hotel windows. I was sharing a room with three others – my regular roommate from the Kippax, Jeff Verrill, plus Colin and Duggie from the Ripon Branch.

After an evening sampling the local brew we got up the next morning to board a coach for the trip to Heerenveen. The locals had really made an effort to make us welcome, setting up beer tents and live music, and dedicating the whole town square to the visiting fans of both teams. Unsurprisingly, given what was going on at home, there weren't many Partizan fans to be seen but the couple I spotted mingled good-naturedly with the thousand or so Leeds supporters who dominated the square. Countless Leeds flags were draped over anything that didn't move. Much singing and drinking took place and there wasn't a hint of any trouble. Local and British television companies were interviewing fans and locals were saying they were 'impressed' by the behaviour of the Leeds fans. The local mayor stated, 'Leeds fans are welcome back any time.'

Lunge and I were in fine spirits as we made our way to the ground and stopped off at one last bar en route to order two beers and Jagermeister chasers. Jagermeister, a very strong German liqueur that tastes a bit like cough medicine, is my favourite tipple whenever I'm abroad. However, the bar tender said he didn't have any Jager (or 'buttercup syrup' as Lunge and I called it) and offered us an alternative. It was more than adequate and when he saw we liked it he left us almost a full bottle, compliments of the bar; it would have been an insult not to drink it all.

There were Leeds fans everywhere. We strolled up to the ground with John Gibson and met up with Neil Hudson and Steve Bailey just outside it. Once inside, most Leeds fans took their shirts off and sang. The shirts were still off at the end of a 3–1 victory and the singing continued, inspired both by the result and a 'spectacular' goal scored by Lucas Radebe, who fell over on his arse in the box but still somehow managed to score with an overhead kick.

At about three o'clock the following morning, after trawling round numerous bars in Amsterdam, I found myself with Nigel from the South West Branch squeezing into a bar to investigate the blues band whose music had been leaking out into the street. A couple of hours later, with Nigel asleep at the bar and myself not much better, I thought it best to make our way back to the hotel, and at the second attempt, fell into bed. Three hours later it was time to leave for the airport and the bathroom mirror showed that I had a lovely graze down the side of my face from my first attempt.

At the airport, among the thousands of happy Leeds fans, was Ray Stubbs, who had been covering the game for the BBC. We chatted with him and he said that he had been impressed with the Leeds performance and even more so by the size and passion of their supporting contingent. Leeds' next destination, in the second round, would present that contingent with some unique challenges – Lokomotiv Moscow were Leeds' next opponents.

I have been all over the world and can say, without a shadow of a doubt, that Russia is the most corrupt country I have ever been to. And its capital, Moscow, is the most corrupt part of it. We stayed in the large Intourist Hotel and it was immediately apparent that the secret police were responsible for organising everything – from the general running of the hotel, money exchange, the police and even the 'ladies'. The secret police, it seemed, oversaw the lot. Many Leeds fans were confronted on the streets and asked if they had their passports with them. Whether they had, or whether they'd left them in the hotel, it didn't seem to matter. Whichever answer was given was the wrong one and an instant fine (of whatever cash the person had on them – Tony Green was relieved of almost £200) was imposed. The general rule became: whenever you saw more than one policeman – stay clear. Many Russian bars, however, were cheap compared to prices in Britain. We discovered these after initially falling into the trap of visiting the 'tourist' bars and nightclubs. One famous one was called Nightflight and in it you could get absolutely anything that took your fancy – but at a price! Leaving overpriced drinks, food and hookers behind we eventually got ourselves on the right track and were drinking vodka for less than 20p for a large shot. Fortified and encouraged by the local spirit many Leeds fans were enticed by the steady supply of pretty Russian girls looking to sell themselves to improve Russia's balance of trade. The reception in the hotel, at times, resembled a Miss World contest with the contestants regularly disappearing with the British judges for half-hour 'interview' sessions.

In the match, played on 4 November in freezing conditions, Leeds ran out convincing winners, beating Lokomotiv 3–0 to add to the 4–1 victory two weeks earlier. Leeds cruised through to the next round. On the flight home I wore a Russian police hat which I had acquired. The draw for the next stage of the competition was made while we waited to take off and as the news filtered through Mick Hewitt told me: 'Keep your hat on, we've just got Spartak Moscow in the third round.'

If it was cold in Moscow for the Lokomotiv match, the temperature was positively tropical compared to when we skidded into Moscow Airport for the Spartak game two weeks later. Thermometers recorded –23 °C as we entered the same hotel we had stayed in during our last visit. Although Spartak kept telling the media that everything was all right and there was no danger that the game would be postponed, it was obvious to every one of us that there was no way the game could take place the following evening. We had given up hope of seeing a football match. On our travels we had come across Stan, the man in charge of the Leeds police contingent, who told us that the players had trained on the pitch but it was frozen solid and there seemed no chance that the match could be played tomorrow.

We had arranged to meet some of the other lads in another hotel, so once we had checked in, Jeff and I took a stroll across the horribly named Red Square to a hotel at the opposite end. A police car full of officers pulled up alongside of us. Remembering their tactics on our previous visit, we didn't stop and just carried on walking. Although one of them shouted something out of the window at us, we continued on to the hotel and nipped inside. Some of the other Kippax lads were already there. John Gibson looked very handsome in his newly bought fur hat but then again, didn't everyone? Almost every Leeds fan in Moscow was wearing one of these furry hats as they could be bought off any street vendor for a fiver. You needed them, though. It was that cold.

As we all walked back across Red Square to our hotel I discovered my face had no feeling in it at all. I feared at first I was having a stroke but through my super-chilled fingertips I discovered that my beard was freezing over. By the time we reached the first bar, my beard had literally frozen solid. It was time for antifreeze. We strolled in and ordered vodkas all round. We ordered more a short while later in a lap-dancing bar but there the price had gone up to 30p a shot – we could live with that level of extortion given that we'd been taught by some of the locals how to save money on cab fares. They told us that instead of hailing a taxi, we should simply get an ordinary car to pull over and then make the owner an offer. The first time we tried it, it worked a treat. An old Lada pulled over at the first time of asking and the driver took us to a bar just outside of the centre. We gave him something like a fiver and he was chuffed to bits.

The next morning Stan came into the hotel lounge and confirmed that the game had been cancelled. We were already expecting this news, but it was still a disappointment. We consoled ourselves by making plans for another 'vodka frenzy' over a pizza in the hotel restaurant. Joining Jason Hirst and I was Trevor Horsley, now chairman of Nationwide Conference League side, Forest Green, but formerly one of Leeds United's original Harehills Boys who used to terrorise opposition fans in the '60s. Those hooligans wrote the book long before the notorious Service Crew was formed. These days Trevor is a successful businessman and well-informed pillar of the community. He had heard that Leeds' and Spartak's game would be re-arranged in Bulgaria. He turned out to be right.

Sofia turned out to be even cheaper than Moscow. At our first port of call on a cold and sunny day, Lunge and I argued over who should get the first round in. We eventually compromised: he got the beers and I got the whiskys. The whole round was less than a pound.

This was my first time in Sofia but the number of prostitutes eager for Western cash was, after Moscow, familiar. The arrangement here, though, was unique. All a customer needed to do was simply hail a taxi and state his preference. The drivers would then whisk him off to their headquarters, where girls were waiting in the back rooms, all included in the price of the fare.

The game itself, played in an almost derelict stadium that looked far short of the standards of most European countries, ended in a disappointing 2–1 defeat, but most Leeds fans were optimistic for the return at Elland Road.

After the game we were all in a nightclub-cum-strip bar where the price of beers was a little higher than we had been paying elsewhere, but still only £1.50 a pint. The entertainment was good though and the girls mingled freely among the lads. I was sat at one of the bars, about three yards from a beautiful blonde girl in a large cage. She was performing extremely naughty acts on herself. Then without warning she 'escaped' from her cage and began crawling on all fours, on the bar, towards me. She snuggled up to me, began rubbing her hands up and down my groin and then started kissing and licking my earlobes. The lads were shouting, 'Go on, Snake. Sort her out!' I leant across and pushed her hair away from her ears, and said, 'I'll tell you what, love, we didn't half miss David Batty in midfield tonight.' Everyone just fell about laughing. A little offended, my 'girlfriend' returned to her cage.

In the return match at Elland Road a last-minute winner by Lucas Radebe ensured Leeds' passage through to the next round, where they would face Roma.

Italy is a great place to visit, but not when it involves football. The police presence is overwhelming and intimidating. Almost all bars are closed down, much against the wishes of the owners and freedom of movement is very restricted. As Lesley is a big fan of Italy, she came along on the trip. I had warned her beforehand of the police tactics, but I don't think she realised the scale of their operations until our party arrived at Rome Airport, the night before the game. We were met by well over 1,000 riot police all dressed as though they were going into battle against Cromwell's army, armed to the teeth with guns, tear gas and large batons. Lesley couldn't believe it.

'Welcome to Italy, dear,' I sighed as we were ushered onto our awaiting coach and escorted at high speed by police cars – lights flashing and sirens wailing – through the city centre to our hotel. Once we had checked in we called into a small bar nearby, with Dave and Debbie Green. Knowing that the police would close the bars down on match day, we had a quiet word with the owner and he agreed to allow us in through the rear entrance after the match.

Dave and I went with our party to the match the following night, leaving the girls in this bar. All Leeds fans had been ordered to arrive at the Olympic Stadium early and, duly, the 50 of us were inside the ground three hours before kick-off. We were mugs. Our party was the only one who adhered to these rules, much to the amusement of everyone else who strolled in ten minutes before the start. To make thing worse, after a 0–0 draw, Leeds fans had to remain in the ground for another two hours. I knew the stadium pretty well by then. Fortunately, an impromptu sing-along between the thousands of Leeds fans and the Leeds team, led by Gary Kelly and Peter Ridsdale, helped pass the time. At the same time, Ridsdale also let us know that David O'Leary was the new manager.

Richard Watson turned to me and said, 'C'mon, Snake. Get the keys. We opened the ground, we might as well lock the bastard.'

We arrived back at our hotel and, as arranged, Dave and I slipped in through the back door to meet up with the girls, who had been drinking all night and by then were quite merry! One of the locals treated us all to his repertoire of Beatles and Rolling Stones songs on his guitar. There were a number of other Leeds fans in the bar and the atmosphere was brilliant. The bar owner, apart from an unfortunate resemblance to Mick Hucknall, was a great chap.

For the return leg at Elland Road, I managed to get a ticket in another part of the ground for my friend Alan Osborne. We arrived at the LUSC entrance and made arrangements with big Dave Jennings on the door to allow Al in then and again after the game.

Another brilliant display by Leeds at Elland Road saw them win 1–0 with a fantastic Harry Kewell goal and progress to the quarter-final. After the match I met up with Al and we both enjoyed a celebratory drink. Although a Hammers fan through and through, he was genuinely pleased at Leeds' success.

It is LUSC policy that at the end of every session, any food at the bar that remains unsold – pies, pasties and such like – is placed on the bar and is free to anyone who wants them. Al loves meat pies and his eyes lit up when this happened. I suggested he grab one and put it in his pocket for later. The next morning, as he prepared to drive to Hull on business, he put on his coat and instantly developed a serious list to the right. He was puzzled by this and put his hand in the pocket to see what had added so much extra weight to the garment. His search revealed that rather than just a single pie, he had shovelled in so many that they burst the pocket's stitching and spilled on into the lining. He unloaded them and cancelled all shopping expeditions for a couple of weeks.

The quarter-final draw paired us with Slavia Prague. I had been to the city in 1971 for a tie in the old Inter-Cities Fairs Cup against Sparta Prague, but I was too young then to enjoy the delights of the night life. This time I was determined to make the most it.

The nightclubs were great but there was a trick or two to learn. Entrance was reasonably priced and, usually, showing your ticket at the bar gave you not one but two free drinks. After the second most Leeds fans made plans to move on – just spending a couple more minutes enjoying a few more free eyefuls of the delightful females strutting their stuff on stage. But upon leaving the club they would be asked to produce the tickets once more. If they couldn't – and none of us were told we would need them again – the doormen would demand some extortionate fee to cover the cost of drinks we may or may not have drunk. This led to some heated exchanges and although in our case Collar played peacemaker and negotiated a nominal exit fee, others weren't quite so lucky. Once the lesson was learned, we stuck to our tickets like glue.

Gary Patrick and Kenny Pearce were among those who had had to pay an exit fee – around £100 each – and when they spoke to me later at another club they were in no mood for a repeat performance. Attempts to reason with the bouncers had drawn a blank so they organised all Leeds fans present who had lost their tickets to join together and storm the doors to get out. Extra doormen were assigned and – thanks to the bouncers' use of batons – a few heads were cracked but with a medical team mopping up and the police arriving, they backed off and allowed the Leeds fans to pass them and disappear into the night. The following night, large notices were prominently displayed at all the clubs explaining their rules carefully and in English. There was no further trouble.

Leeds lost the game 2–1 but thanks to a 3–0 win in the first leg at Elland Road went through to the semi-finals on aggregate. This was the team's best performance in Europe since reaching the European Cup final in 1975 and we were in the mood to celebrate. Another nightclub, another sex show. It's a dirty job and we were the men to do it. The place we chose was packed with Leeds fans, who were treated to a full-on one-on-one performance enjoyed by both the man and the girl beneath him. Tico must have enjoyed it, too, as we noticed he was stood right at the front, only a yard from the action on stage, totally mesmerised. Later, as we teased and asked why he hadn't got any closer, all he could say was: 'I'll tell you what – that bloke's feet really stank!'

In the semi-finals, Leeds were paired with Galatasaray of Istanbul – a club whose supporters were famous for producing a hostile atmosphere. We were about to witness it first hand.

As we touched down at Istanbul Airport and passed through customs, we were met by hundreds of Turkish people hissing and spitting at us, all with the apparent consent of the police who stood by and watched. Many of our welcoming party were jumping up and down or threatening us by gesturing with a finger dragged across the throat. I couldn't believe the large number that had turned out to 'welcome' us. It was midnight. As we turned the corner and headed into the airport foyer, we were met by more demonstrators and a flag draped over a barrier which read, 'Welcome to Hell!' Webby and I had expected this and responded by unfurling our own banner, which read, 'Hello Hell – We are Leeds!' They didn't like that one bit.

As the coach headed to our hotel, dozens of mobile phones started ringing. It quickly became apparent that there had been major disturbances in the city centre and reports of fatalities filtered through.

Details of exactly what had happened still weren't clear as we pulled up at our hotel, under a heavily armed escort. The tense atmosphere continued as we checked in and then all met up in the lobby. We thought it best to stay in groups of no less than 12 and cautiously began visiting a few of the local bars, not too far from our hotel.

A small police escort, consisting of a car and a small van monitored our every move. Conversations with other Leeds fans along the way established that there had been trouble in Taksim Square in the centre of the city and there had definitely been two Leeds fans killed. As yet, no one we spoke to knew their names.

At breakfast the next morning we discovered that we were all under 'hotel arrest'. No one would be allowed to leave until our coach arrived that evening to take us to the match. The situation was ridiculous, and became farcical as scores of media and television crews were allowed into the hotel to attempt to interview us. Apart from the fact that none of us knew exactly what had happened, no one was prepared to give interviews anyway. The media people, from all over the world, became very tiresome indeed. Webby summed up our mood when he told a lovely Australian girl, 'I'll give you an interview, sweetheart,' and a swarm of cameras scrambled to surround him. This 6 ft 4 in. skinhead with tattoos dropped his tracksuit bottoms and showed his arse to the bewildered camera teams. They left us alone for a while after that.

Mick Hewitt came over from reception with very sad news. The two Leeds fans who had been murdered were Kevin Speight (Spag) and Chris Loftus. I knew them both. Kev was the landlord of The New Inn at Farsley in Leeds and Chris was from the Burmantofts area of Leeds. Everyone was stunned. Most of our lads knew them both and a feeling of anger was building.

All the time, phones were ringing as friends and families back home called to make sure we were all right. Lesley rang me and said she had received many calls asking if I was OK.

Although hundreds of police surrounded our hotel, someone came into the bar with the news that it was possible to escape through the door of the hotel restaurant, but most decided to stay put for the time being. To try and diffuse the situation, the hotel had reduced the price of the beer, but our resilience was tested further when the bar ran out. Worried staff met with their superiors, and within half an hour, a lorry from the local brewery arrived with fresh supplies. By now the media were realising that they weren't going to get much from us and were keeping a low profile. However, they did remain in the hotel.

The next rumour was that the game may now be postponed in light of what had happened, but an hour later it was confirmed that it would definitely go ahead. None of us were in the mood for it. Our coach duly arrived and we had to pass through scores of police to board it. There was a simmering feeling of real anger that two of our lads had been murdered but we were being treated as though we were the murderers. It was scandalous.

All the way to the Ali Sami Yen Stadium we were being jeered, missiles were constantly being thrown at our bus and cars would pull alongside with people gesticulating at us. Our police 'escort' did nothing to discourage all this abuse.

I remember thinking, as I looked out of our window, that this was what it must be like for a child murderer, or something just as vile, while being driven from court after receiving a life sentence. But we were innocent.

In a traffic jam yards from the stadium, a brick was thrown through the coach window. By now most people's anger had reached boiling point and a few of the lads opened the emergency door. Upon seeing this the Turks nearest to the door, somewhat taken aback, retreated. Within seconds, however, the police, whom up to now had been taking a back seat to the Turkish hostilities, rushed to our coach and slammed the door shut and began hitting our coach with batons. It really was quite unbelievable.

Entering the stadium was an experience itself. We had to pass through hundreds of police lining our entrance, but all the time, as missiles rained over our heads, the police were simply laughing at us.

Once inside, the end holding the Leeds fans was the focus for more Turkish hostilities and the now familiar 'finger across the throat' gesture. But the greatest insult was the total lack of remorse from the home crowd or the police over the tragic events that had occurred only the night before. This lack of respect was reinforced when Galatasaray refused to hold a minute's silence before the game. The Leeds players wore black armbands but the home side chose not to. At the kick-off all the Leeds fans turned their backs on the game for two minutes in recognition of the two murdered Leeds lads, Kevin and Chris. We also discovered that hundreds of Leeds fans, who had been waiting to take off from all over England, had been denied permission to fly to Istanbul 'to prevent further escalation of any violence'.

As the game unfurled, it was clear that the Leeds team just wasn't up for it. The events had clearly had an effect and although they tried to raise their game, their usual passion just would not surface. Many Leeds players later said that they simply could not focus on a football match following the deaths the night before. Many had received abusive phonecalls in their hotel rooms, too.

After a 2–0 defeat, we faced more abuse as we stood waiting for our coach. Other Leeds fans boarded their buses and left but ours was nowhere in sight. An hour later, all the Leeds buses had left, but we were still stood there, surrounded by a hundred police. Dozens of police vans, buses and even a police tank were still lined up all along the road outside the stadium. As we gazed at these in disbelief we were informed by one of the policemen that our coach had refused to return to pick us up because of the emergency door incident. It was nothing to do with the damage caused by the brick – rather that some of our lads had been prepared to get off and retaliate against the people who had thrown it. Our driver had called us '*loco*' and insisted he would not return to pick us up in his coach. To call us '*loco*' whilst all the abuse was going on all around us, for me just summed up the Turkish attitude that night that seemed to suggest nothing was the fault of the Turkish people.

Eventually, a police coach came forward and drove us back to our hotel. There were about a dozen policemen on board. Mark Palmer began chatting with one of them. The policeman looked barely 18 years old yet was in possession of a high-velocity machine gun, a large baton and a hand pistol. He was clearly proud of his hardware. So proud in fact that he allowed Palmer to hold the machine gun. I was sat in the seat behind him and, along with the rest of the occupants, ducked as he pointed the gun all over the coach and out of the window saying, 'You won't mess with us now, you Turkish bastards!' All the time, the owner of the gun sat smiling proudly. When Palmer returned the machine gun, the policeman then gave him his pistol to play with. It was unreal. We returned to our hotel and spent the rest of the evening in the hotel bar and restaurant.

The next day we were still under hotel arrest and despite our protests were told that it would stay that way until we left for the airport later that evening. Everyone had just about had enough, so over breakfast we discussed an escape. The restaurant door was still an option and we were going to use it. The problem, as with any military operation, was that inevitably there would be some that didn't make it. We arranged a rendezvous: the harbour at 10:00 a.m. Apart from a couple who were caught acting as decoys going through the front revolving door everyone made it and soon we were on a pleasure cruise heading out of the bay. Sadly, with the exception of a very small minority, all the Turks we spoke to acted as though nothing untoward had happened. After about an hour the boat moored outside a restaurant and the captain said he would return in two hours. As a result of our hotel incarceration we had quite a lot of spending money left so didn't mind so much that the prices seemed so high. We also left with a bottle of Raki, the local firewater, compliments of the management. The bottle was empty as we returned to the harbour. Four hours later we were on the plane home.

The little trip on the boat had helped take everyone's mind off the Taksim Square atrocities for a while, but they soon returned as we were bid farewell by groups of Turks at the airport. They were much smaller than our welcoming party had been, but still vociferous nonetheless. I prayed that we would beat them back at Elland Road.

On the day of that match, despite an appeal for calm from Leeds United chairman Peter Ridsdale, Leeds city centre was brimming with hundreds of angry Leeds fans. As it turned out, Galatasaray fans were banned by UEFA from the game and therefore only a very small number of representatives from Turkey were allowed to attend. In hindsight it was better for Leeds United that this action had been taken by UEFA, but there was a general feeling, not just among Leeds supporters but fans around the country as a whole, that if the situation was reversed and the murders had been committed by Leeds fans in Leeds, then within hours, Leeds United would have been kicked out of the competition. Trouble by Galatasaray fans had happened many times prior to the Leeds game and has continued ever since. But yet, apart from a very weak ban imposed in 2001 on Galatasaray playing European games at home (imposed after they had been knocked out of Europe so it had little or no effect) the top brass at UEFA have failed to do anything to inspire the Turkish side to bring its fans into line. Before the game I was in the LUSC bar at Elland Road when the small delegation arrived from Istanbul. Out of the window it was possible to see into the car park as one coach pulled up surrounded by hundreds of police. Most of them were dressed in suits and apart from one individual defiantly shouting back at the Leeds fans yelling angrily at them and being held behind lines of police officers, they entered the ground in complete silence.

Sadly, there was to be no revenge on the pitch for Leeds that night. They started badly and although they rallied, the 2–2 draw meant that Galatasaray went through to the final in Copenhagen against Arsenal. That final attracted world-wide attention. Almost inevitably there was trouble with fans of Arsenal and Galatasaray fighting in the streets. Disappointingly, Arsenal lost the game and as the Turks paraded the UEFA Cup it was impossible to have any other feelings but anger.

Meanwhile, most of the Leeds players, along with Ridsdale and manager David O'Leary, were at Elland Road adding their own wreaths of condolences among the thousands of tributes from all over the world for Kevin Speight and Christopher Loftus.

Champions of Europe (?)

Peter Ridsdale said we lived the dream. It was a great adventure but it wasn't a dream. It would've been a dream if we'd won it – but we didn't. And that's the story of our lives.

Much has been written about Leeds United's excellent achievement in becoming the first British club to reach the semi-final stage of the Champions League at the first attempt. This is my version of that great adventure.

It all started with a tough qualifier against German side 1860 Munich. Some atrocious refereeing by Costas Kapitanis from Cyprus spoiled the first leg at Elland Road. He crowned his performance by conjuring up four minutes of injury time, which allowed Munich to pull a goal back, leaving the score 2–1 to Leeds. For the second leg I travelled, as usual, with Mick Hewitt's party. We were based just outside Munich and a short train ride took us into the centre of the city on match day. Germany is one of the best countries in the world for drinking beer and Munich is one of the best cities in Germany for it. We were soon throwing steins of the stuff down our throats as though it was our last day on earth. At one stage we met up with Brod and Bill Raddings. They weren't hard to find. They were in a bar that had all its windows open and 'Glory Glory, Leeds United' blasting out from a large cassette player that a Leeds fan had brought along with him.

On arrival at the Olympic Stadium we met up with Webby, who was with Ray and Dean from Barnsley. Despite being easily the shortest grown man I've ever met, Dean is a big Leeds fan. He likes a wet of the old alcohol now and again, too. On one occasion when we had beaten manchester united (again), he returned home – well almost. He was approaching his house from the back, down a large embankment when he slipped and was too pissed to get up. He lay there with his Leeds flag unable to move. He managed to get his mobile phone out of his pocket and after one or two wrong numbers finally got through to his lass in the house.

She was told to come to the back door and look towards the banking. It was dark but she could just make out his flag fluttering halfway up the slope. His ingenious signal enabled his rescue to take place.

Ray, an entrepreneur in every sense of the word, has been a Leeds (and Stones Bitter) fan all his life. He recently dyed his hair blond after his hero Alan Smith. Or it could have been Jimmy Saville. I would only do it in honour of Smithy. Years ago I was driving along the Leeds ring-road one Sunday afternoon listening to Jimmy Saville on Radio One. I pulled up at some traffic lights and who jogged past me? Jimmy Saville. I'd listened all those years and not known his radio show was recorded.

And so in August 2000 blond Ray, Dean, Webby and I were having a beer outside the ground, as our Belgian troops arrived. Seigfreid van Doren (Ziggy to his friends) is a supporter of Beerschot FC back in Belgium, but he's almost as fanatical about Leeds United. So too is fellow Belgian, Frank Janssens. A couple of seasons ago, Frank missed his own honeymoon in order to travel across the Channel to watch Leeds at Ipswich. Ziggy lives near Lierse and in the centre of town there is a bar called Elland Road. Owned by a Leeds fan, all the walls are decorated with Leeds United pictures and pride of place behind the bar is a life-size cardboard cut-out of David Batty. Beerschot fans are notorious and are by far the most feared of all supporters in Belgium, despite being only a Second Division side.

They recently merged with Germinal Ekeren and are now called Germinal Beerschot Antwerp, but the vast majority of the fans are Beerschot. We have made a number of trips across the Channel to watch Beerschot.

Once, after a game at Chelsea, we took our coach across to see them play the following day. We had special shirts made, white with the names of both Leeds and Beerschot across the front. This particular time, Beerschot were away, so after a night out in Antwerp, we travelled 40 miles south to the game. As we arrived at the ground, all the bars were full with the purple-shirted Beerschot fans. We got off the coach and all 50 of us headed up a street to a bar that was at the top. As we got nearer, I said to Collar, 'This lot don't look too friendly to me,' as about 20 Beerschot fans emerged from the bar and began walking slowly towards us. As we came face to face with them they noticed their club's name on our shirts; they looked a little puzzled, but one of the Belgians recognised us and told the rest of our welcoming committee. None of us bought a drink all day as we were supplied with endless trays of beers throughout the game.

In Munich, it was our turn to buy for Ziggy and Frank and we recalled how the last time we'd met, in Belgium, Kev 'Mouse' Broadbent had borrowed a push-bike but had fallen off after pedalling only two feet. It wasn't until we went into the ground that we realised that the home team played in white. The Beerschot fans at the bar had almost mistaken us for home fans and were about to engage us in battle. Later that night I was sat in a bar with Russ Townend. The locals were still buying us beer, even though we were no longer wearing our colours. We had been there about half an hour when I looked around and said to Russ, 'Have you seen any birds in here?' He looked around and replied, 'Oh shit, we're in a gay bar.' We quickly drank our last beers and left. On our way out we noticed Stuart Smythe in the far corner, surrounded by about a dozen lads plying him with free beers whilst all clapping and cheering him as each beer was thrown down his throat. I said to Russ, 'Shall we tell him?' We looked at each other and in unison both said, 'Nah!'

Back in Munich, we were joined by the Dutch contingent of Leeds fans. Frank van Grunsen and his mates have been fans for many years and regularly travel to England to watch their beloved English team. Their team in Holland is TOP Oss from the Second Division.

The Germans in the bars had been friendly but were supremely confident that their team would progress to the next round, the Champions League proper, but a brilliant goal by Alan Smith gave Leeds a deserved 3–1 aggregate victory. After the game Kev Snaith and I went back into Munich with the Dutch Lads and celebrated with good German ale.

In the first group stage Leeds were drawn with Barcelona, AC Milan and Besiktas from Istanbul. First up was Barcelona. I'd been to the Nou Camp on three previous occasions to watch Leeds – the play-off for the old Inter-Cities Fairs Cup in 1971, the European Cup semi-final in 1975 and the re-arranged European Cup tie with Stuttgart in 1992. That 1992 fixture, four years before the competition was expanded into the Champions League as we know it today, was an odd one . . . UEFA have never done Leeds United any favours over the years – quite the opposite in fact – but don't get me started on that. At Elland Road in the second leg a late substitution meant that Stuttgart had played one too many foreigners and broken UEFA rules. But instead of awarding the game to Leeds, which is what should have happened, we were made to play a one-off tie on a neutral ground, which happened to be the Nou Camp. So at very short notice the shorts and sunglasses were thrown into a bag and it was off to sunny Spain. On the plane our steward introduced himself as Steve Humphreys and said he was a Leeds fan. 'If there is anything I can get for you, don't hesitate to ask.' It was an invitation we couldn't refuse. John 'Bremner' Greenhill and I asked for some whisky. Our new friend promptly returned with a carrier-bag of miniature bottles. We opened it to discover about 20 of them. Once they were polished off the steward returned with fresh supplies. As we were nearing Barcelona he asked if there was anything else he could get for us.

'I've always wanted to sit in the cockpit when coming in to land,' I said.

'Oh, I wish you'd mentioned it earlier,' he replied. 'That lad over there has already asked.' It was little Mick Hewitt from the Vine branch.

'Never mind,' I said, 'We'll just have some more whiskies then.'

Another carrier-bag duly arrived. Bremner and I made our way down the steps of the plane very precariously. That night Bremner, Mick Hewitt, and Steve the steward went out on Las Ramblas. We soon met up with two of the finest and most famous of Leeds fans, Marion Fudge and Trisha McMullan, and hit the town. Sadly, Marion passed away in April 2003 after a short illness.

In the market on Las Ramblas we came across a poor live lobster, all trussed up and awaiting its fate, sat on a huge pile of ice. Mick is a vegetarian and we are both animal lovers, so we asked to buy the hapless crustacean. After agreeing a price we asked the fishmonger for a bucket. He looked puzzled. 'Bucket?' he asked, but when we explained we intended to put it back in the sea he got a bit angry and put the lobster back on the ice, muttering '*Loco!*' as he shooed us away. The following evening Leeds beat Stuttgart 2–1 and left the Nou Camp with two fingers in the air to UEFA.

Six years later, Leeds didn't do too well at the Nou Camp. Barcelona gave us an uncomfortable welcome to the Champions League when they beat us 4–0. After the game we went back to the small seaside town near Barcelona to drown our sorrows in the bars near our hotel. To cheer us up, we had been given a trumpet by some Barcelona fans that we christened Trevor. I can't remember why. At four o'clock in the morning, after a few more drinks, I took Trevor for a swim in the sea and began blowing him for all I was worth. We had a photograph taken of Trevor and made him a passport so we could bring him through customs and back to Leeds.

A month later I was arming myself with paintbrushes, ready for work when my phone rang. It was the daughter, Spoonhead.

'If I entered you for a competition and you won £1,000, would we share it?' she asked.

'That depends,' I replied. 'What competition would it be?'

'Leeds United's Fan of the Year.'

I laughed, 'Yeah, sure, whoever wins that will be a right anorak!'

'Well, Mr Anorak, we've just won £1,000!' said Spoon.

Without telling me a thing about it she had entered me for a competition to find the Fan of the Year in my part of Yorkshire. I'd won and we were getting some money. I asked her to tell me more about it.

'It's been organised by the market research people at Nisa Today's,' she began. 'You're one of ten finalists from all over the country.'

'So, we haven't won £1,000 then?' I asked.

'Yes, and if you win the overall final, we get another grand!' Spoon was very excited.

I found out later that there were fans from Aston Villa, Everton, Man City, Sunderland, Newcastle United, Liverpool, Sheffield United, Grimsby Town and Leicester City in the final.

I then received a confirmation letter asking if I would be available for a 'special event and presentation night' on 7 October at a hotel in London, 'details to follow'. I looked at my Leeds United fixture list and it didn't need a rocket scientist to work out that 7 October was the day England played their World Cup qualifier against Germany at Wembley, the last ever England game there before the famous Twin Towers would be demolished and the stadium rebuilt. Tickets for the match were very hard to come by so I rang the phone number on the letter and said yes.

A few days later I received another letter confirming my guess – I had been given a ticket for the England game. Although only one ticket was allocated, I could bring along another person to share the weekend's activities. Enclosed were two return tickets from Leeds to King's Cross and directions from there to the Thistle Hotel beside Tower Bridge. So at eight o'clock on the day of the game, Wub and I boarded our train.

At the hotel we were met by Jill Morris, a representative from Nisa Today's. We were the first to arrive. Jill handed me our itinerary and asked us to meet her in the restaurant bar at about half past 11 for introductions.

At 11.29 we entered the restaurant. Jill met us and said, 'Find yourselves a table and a waiter will be with you shortly. Everything, including drinks, is free.' We sat at our table and when the waiter arrived we ordered our meals.

'Anything to drink, sir?' asked the waiter.

'A pint of lager and a Diet Coke, please,' I replied.

'Would you like to see the wine list, sir? All complimentary, of course . . .'

Being quite partial to a nice Shiraz, I said yes and a bottle of fine Shiraz Cabernet Sauvignon duly arrived.

'Just pour, thank you,' I said to our waiter.

I held my glass up to Wub's: 'This is all quite civilised. And on match day, too!'

Some of the other fans arrived, but as yet no one was being introduced.

Jill came over to our table with a parcel. 'Here, Gary, we'd like you to have this with our compliments and wear it today at the match – and outside shortly for a photograph.'

I opened what I felt sure was an England shirt. It was – but a red one! Wub started laughing, and knowing my aversion to the colour red, cheekily got the camera out and said, 'Put it on then.' You don't need me to tell you what my response was.

As I shook my head at the abomination of a shirt, the Everton fan came over to our table clutching his England shirt. Like mine it was still in its package. He recognised my pain and said in a broad Scouse accent: 'They can have their fuckin' grand back. I'm not wearing a Liverpool shirt for no bastard!' I liked him instantly.

Jill then asked if we would all go outside and have a group photograph taken for the publicity. I and the Everton fan explained to Jill our reservations and she kindly agreed that we would all wear our own team's colours. But we could keep our shirts as a momento of the occasion.

A photograph was taken of the ten of us with Tower Bridge in the background.

After a few more drinks, we walked outside to be greeted by the two white stretch-limousines that would take us to Wembley. I noticed that some of the winners had put their England shirts on, but predictably only those whose club team played in red. Inside each limo was a television and bottles of champagne on ice. Watching the build-up to the match on TV whilst drinking champagne and being chauffeured to the game was an experience I could get used to. As we neared the stadium we were stopped in traffic and I noticed fans trying to look inside our limousine through the smoked glass of its windows. I flicked the switch and opened the window a little. The England fan beside the window looked in and seemed surprised to see a group of lads all wearing different football shirts and sipping champagne.

'Who the fuck are you?' he said.

'Go away, peasant,' I said and hit the switch again, watching the window glide up as his face fell. We had to pose for a few more photographs outside the stadium, and once inside, I sat next to the Everton fan, who by now I knew as Barry. I've remained in touch with him and have enjoyed the odd pint with him in The Stanley Arms pub just outside Goodison Park. Back at Wembley, the game itself was a major disappointment with England losing 1–0 to a goal by Dietmar Hamman. We left Wembley with the Tannoy system blasting out 'That's Life' by Frank Sinatra.

Back in our limo the champagne supply had been replenished so we began to drown our sorrows while stuck in heavy traffic. I telephoned Wub back at the hotel and the rest were laughing as I delivered a once-in-a-lifetime excuse: 'I'm sorry, darling, the limousine is stuck in traffic. I'll be there 15 minutes later than expected.'

The driver opened the glass panel that separated him from us and grinned over his shoulder.

'Funny that, Sir,' he said, 'that's just what Bruce Willis said last week from that very seat.'

I made a mental note to ask Wub how long she'd known Bruce Willis. Back at the hotel Wub recounted the stress of her evening: 'Oh, you know, socialising in the cocktail bar, nothing special.'

I showered while she lay on the bed watching a variety show on television. When I came out of the shower she urged me to hurry: 'There's going to be some aquabatics after the adverts.'

We settled down expecting a unique display by underwater gymnasts. But when the programme returned and Jonathon Ross introduced a bunch of ordinary gymnasts with not a drop of water to be seen, Wub was a bit miffed.

'Jonathon Ross has a speech impediment,' I reminded her.

After a three-course dinner in the restaurant, all the winners and their partners retired to a special lounge for the Fan of the Year final. Barry's friend made an impromptu speech to thank the sponsors, Nisa Today's, for their hospitality and the final got under way. I did my best, but couldn't compete with the Aston Villa fan – a girl – who won and received a further £1,000. Her dedication shamed every man in the room as she explained how she'd gone to watch Villa just three days after giving birth. The judges were very impressed.

Later, I got talking at the bar to the Sunderland fan, Gary, who had changed his name by deed poll to Gary Sunderland Lamb. Gary Sunderland is what I call a top supporter and totally devoted to his club. As were all of us present. I still keep in touch with Gary and have met with him a couple of times when our teams played each other.

'You should have won that, mate,' he told me.

But I honestly wasn't bothered. We had been wined and dined, driven to and from Wembley in a limousine with champagne, been given a match ticket, a luxurious double room on the executive floor, two return train tickets and been given £1,000 for our trouble. We had done all right. Even allowing for the red England shirt.

UEFA certainly remained consistent when the draw was made for Leeds' group. Less than 12 months after the tragic events in Istanbul before the Galatasaray game, we were being forced to return to the same city to play Besiktas. To be honest, I'd never even heard of the team. First indications were that no away fans would be allowed to travel to either game. (The teams met first at Elland Road when Leeds romped home as 6–0 winners.) It was while we were making plans to travel overland to the return fixture in Istanbul and enter the country via the 'back door' that we discovered that a small number of Leeds fans would, after all, be allowed to travel to Besiktas. The condition, however, was that they go as part of the official Leeds United travel party. It would be a one-day visit, straight in and straight out. And, it was stressed, it would be an alcohol-free trip. Yeah, right.

Among the 138 Leeds fans who boarded the plane from Leeds was our small group clutching heavily improved cartons of orange juice. Collar had stayed up almost all the previous night injecting vodka into dozens of these and re-sealing them. It all looked quite professional. So good, in fact, that we decided to keep Collar's stash intact and take it into the ground where we would be ready for a good little slurp. When we landed in Turkey we weren't allowed to get off the plane; we soon discovered that the Galatasaray team had just touched down after returning from their Champions League game with Glasgow Rangers. We had to wait until the Turkish players had gone through and left the airport. Peter Ridsdale met the Leeds fans at the airport, but with all the media presence and hype we were all getting a bit wound up. We had heard that once in Istanbul we were to be herded onto a boat that would sail up and down the Bosporus until just before the kick-off. I decided to honour the occasion with a new flag. On the last trip to Istanbul I had taken a flag saying 'Hello Hell – We are Leeds'. This time I went for the more light-hearted approach and as we boarded our vessel – surrounded by police boats and cameras as our every move was being broadcast live on Turkish television – I unfurled my flag and hung it over the side. It read: 'LUFSea'. The flag, incidentally, was mentioned by David O'Leary in his book *Leeds United on Trial.* Cameras were still clicking away when I opened my bag and produced a dozen pirate hats, which we all put on, much to the amusement of the media. By now, our secret stash was diminishing by the minute and it was relief all round when Whitby John spotted a dozen bottles of red wine behind the bar. Now the bar was closed but it wasn't locked, so we liberated it. We were on our fourth bottle before a security man came over and gave us a bollocking for nicking it. John gave him a bottle back and said, 'Here, that's all you're getting, now sod off!'

People often ask me how, given my aversion to the colour red, I can drink red wine. The simple answer to that is that it is my mission in life to rid the world of all its red wine. They keep re-stacking my local supermarket shelves, but rest assured, people, I will stick to my task.

The organisation as we got off the boat was a total farce. The stadium was only 100 yards away yet we were made to get on coaches to ride to the ground, whilst hundreds of police walked by the side of the buses. Once inside the small stadium we tucked into Collar's remaining 'refreshments' and were joined by about a dozen supporters of another Istanbul club, Fenerbahce, who were all wearing Leeds shirts. A couple of years ago I'd read an article in a football magazine that had a picture of Fenerbahce supporters lit up by a storm of rockets and flares. Right in the middle of them were a couple of fans wearing Leeds shirts. The bunch who were here tonight apologised for the behaviour of Galatasaray fans and said most Fenerbahce supporters aligned themselves with Leeds, even before the tragic events at Istanbul the year before. That news was much more heartening than the 0–0 draw we were about to watch – but at least the result left Leeds with a great chance of progressing to the second group stage, when Collar's skills with orange juice cartons would not be required.

It is always difficult for fans travelling to Italy for football matches and the game with AC Milan was no exception. We knew that the police would impose an alcohol ban on match day, so we decided to make camp in a side-street bar well before the 'ban' was enforced. None of the bar owners agree with the police action so it's just a matter of getting to know the landlord and behaving yourself long enough to persuade him that you will cause no trouble. We were tucking into a few cold ones in our adopted local when I noticed a woman, who I assumed was the landlord's wife, call our host over. They exchanged heated words, but as usual the woman won. The bar owner reluctantly told us that he could no longer serve us with alcohol. He seemed more upset than us.

'Just one more?' I asked.

'Yes, OK, no problem.' He beamed, as if in defiance of his wife. I bet he got a clout, though, when we'd gone.

We had arranged with the rest of the lads that if we couldn't get a drink, we would all meet at an Indian restaurant we had spotted earlier. The owner was delighted to welcome our party of 25. We explained to him about the alcohol ban and simply asked if we could just remain in his restaurant and drink till match time. He was more than happy as we scanned the menu ordering beer and wine all round. For good measure, he even let us have the first two bottles of wine on the house.

After a couple of hours we were still there, but the kick-off was approaching. Just before we left, he brought the visitor's book and asked us all to sign it. I simply couldn't resist drawing a cartoon of

Carlton Palmer, accompanied by the words: 'If you see this man, tell him he is a wanker!' I don't know if the owner fully understood it, but he was still laughing at it as we left and headed for the San Siro Stadium.

Leeds needed only a point against AC Milan to ensure passage into the second phase. A goal by Dominic Matteo gave us a deserved 1–1 draw and sparked off some of the best scenes I have ever witnessed at a football match. After the match, around 7,000 Leeds fans, kept behind at one end for 'security reasons', chanted for the team to come back out onto the pitch. Chairman Peter Ridsdale disappeared down the tunnel and returned with the players. The fans chanted for the team to 'Give us a song' and up stepped Gary Kelly who began jumping up and down singing 'Let's go fuckin' mental, let's go fuckin' mental, na, na, na, na!' Everyone joined in. The large police contingent could only stand and stare in disbelief as one by one the players all took it in turns to start the fans off with a song. Ridsdale had a go, too. Finally Kelly took centre stage again and shushed all the fans before shouting, 'Sit down if you hate man u, sit down if you hate man u. . . .' With that, all 7,000 fans sat down, followed by all the Leeds players down on the pitch. It was a truly incredible sight and one that we later heard prompted Alan Green, commentator at the game for Radio 5 Live, to say it was 'the best example of player–fan bonding he had ever seen'.

A home defeat by Real Madrid signalled an uphill fight for Leeds in the second phase. A return visit to Italy and a fantastic 1–0 victory over Lazio in Rome ensured that we were back on track. After the game there was another sing-song between the players and fans and all believed we could go somewhere in this competition.

Anderlecht were the next opponents and a scrappy, but a well-earned 2–1 victory to Leeds at Elland Road left the Belgian coach Aime Anthuenis claiming that 'Leeds are not a good team' and 'We have nothing to fear in Brussels next week.' We arrived the following week and made camp in Ostend. We travelled on to Antwerp where we again met up with Ziggy and his Belgian buddies. Antwerp is a lively old town with something for everyone and the following day we travelled to Brussels for the clash with Anderlecht. The atmosphere in the centre was fantastic, with hundreds of Leeds fans converging on the many bars. I had a few beers with the Garforth lads Dean Beecroft and Shane Thewliss before moving on just before the Belgian police decided to break up the party. Inside the ground we located our Dutch friends Frank Grunsen and co. I was looking out for Webby and Ray from Barnsley and soon discovered they hadn't made it. In the afternoon they had gone to bed for a couple of hours, separately I presumed, but overslept and awoke facing a mad dash to get to the game. They had been told by the hotel receptionist to get the number 6 tram and get off at stop number 12. In their haste they caught tram 12 and got off at stop 6. They ended up watching the game several miles away in an Irish bar.

The comments by the Belgian coach had an impressive effect on the Leeds team, who were absolutely magnificent as they hammered the home side 4–1. This meant that Leeds had already qualified for the quarter-finals and could travel to Real Madrid without pressure. I believe that Barcelona's Nou Camp Stadium is by far the best in Europe, but Real Madrid's Bernabeu is an impressive sight nonetheless. That said, I very nearly didn't see it. On the day of the match I had been drinking steadily with the rest of the lads and felt fine. As the afternoon wore on I was enjoying whisky with the locals and Kev Snaith and Lunge. Richard Roberts from Garforth had nipped off to do some shopping. Suffice to say when I arrived at the stadium I must have looked a bit worse for wear and the police refused to let me in. Collar came to my rescue and ushered me into a nearby bar. The game was just kicking off live on television; this was my cue to get my head right and get into the stadium. Whitby John's mate Graham was in the bar and just as I was about to leave, a Madrid fan came charging in, punched Graham in the face and darted out before anyone could grab him. The locals were upset by this and bought Graham his drinks all night.

Duly sobered I walked across the road to the stadium. It was then I felt my back pocket and discovered my wallet containing my money and, more importantly, my match ticket, had gone. Collar did the honourable thing and, said, 'Soz, mate, you're on your own, I'm off in.' My first attempt at getting past the security was dismal. I explained that I was English and had lost my ticket, so could I come in please? No chance. I walked up to the next entrance and received the same response. The third time I just walked straight past the two stewards who were chatting away while enjoying a cigarette. I slipped past them unnoticed and as they called me back I just said, '*Adios amigos*,' and ran like hell down the steps. I slipped into the crowd and spotted Marie, Steve Mortimer and Dean from Barnsley. Fortunately, someone had picked my wallet up outside the ground, recognised my photograph inside and handed it to my friend Chris 'Poison' Archer.

Despite a brave performance Leeds went down 3–2, due both to a freak bounce beating keeper Nigel Martyn and a goal scored with the aid of Raul's hand. After seeing the handball on TV replays soon after the final whistle, the referee even apologised to the Leeds team in the dressing-room. Too late.

More Spanish opposition awaited Leeds in the quarter-final. Deportivo La Coruna had emerged as one of the best teams in Spain and almost impossible to beat at home, but they did themselves no favours with the Leeds camp when they dismissed us as the weakest team left in the competition.

ITV got in touch with me before the home leg and asked if I would take part in a small documentary as part of their Champions League programme. We arranged for them to meet me in The Royal Oak. Ian McKay was over from Carrickfergus in Belfast so he joined me in a drink as the TV crew set up. Landlord Matty Sherlock and his wife Julie had kindly allowed the camera team to mingle freely in the pub.

On the day of my interview George the gardener, not the sharpest tool in the shed, had been told a crew were filming in the pub and not to come in through the back door where all the cameras were set up. Two minutes into the interview, in walked George, six feet tall, bald, large dark glasses held on by a pair of ears so large that he can receive satellite messages from Mars, with the watering can in his hand. He wandered straight through the bar, oblivious to all the equipment.

A couple of hours later we headed for Elland Road – but not before I had visited my regular watering holes in the city centre, still accompanied by the film crew. They proceeded to film me throughout the game and it was made all the more enjoyable when Leeds rammed the arrogant taunts back down the throats of

Deportivo with a 3–0 victory. Top Leeds fan Keith Boseley-Yemm was also being filmed for a television documentary that day. He had been commissioned by Channel 4 to take part in an experiment that forbade him from watching football, live or otherwise, for two whole weeks. His television set was removed and he wasn't allowed to read a newspaper or have any contact with anyone who may reveal any of the scores to him. He completed the experiment but he told me some time afterwards that it had been sheer hell and that he would never go through anything like that again.

I know I couldn't. I've always maintained that when I do eventually miss a game, it won't be of my own choosing. Unless the plc force me to think again.

We arrived at La Coruna a week later for the second leg. It was a small seaside town with plenty of bars and their Riazor Stadium was situated right on the seafront. Almost every Deportivo fan we met was supremely confident that their team would overturn the 3–0 deficit from the first leg. They came agonisingly close to their predictions as Leeds hung on and went through 3–2 on aggregate. After the game, relieved to say the least, we headed into town for a few celebratory San Miguels. On the way we stopped off at a Chinese restaurant where we shared a table with Barry Mortimer who has travelled with the Kippax Branch along with Eric Barnes since its formation back in 1978. Also with us was James Rowlands, a British Airways pilot whose profession allows him to attend many Leeds games across Europe. We proceeded to drink well into the night and why not? Leeds had reached the semi-final of the Champions League – the furthest any British team had gone at the first attempt. The next day at the airport, as we waited for the return flight home, I got chatting to old Leeds favourite Duncan McKenzie. He had been covering the game for Sky TV and agreed that despite the result Leeds had earned their right to go through.

We returned to Spain, yet again, for the semi-final. A 0–0 draw with Valencia at Elland Road meant we had it all to do in the return leg. Before then, however, was the small matter of a Premiership game at Highbury. Jeff and I decided to stay in London after that game and meet up with Mick Hewitt and the rest the following day at Gatwick Airport. On the Saturday night we joined a number of the

London Leeds fans and a smattering of others from up and down the country in The Duke of York pub at King's Cross. Dave and Jenny from Croydon invited me and Jeff to stay with them. So after a few more beers we all set off to their house. It was like home from home and on the Sunday morning Jeff, Dave and I popped down to his local for a few beers during which Jenny joined us to announce: 'Lunch will be ready in half an hour.' After lunch and a glass of wine we got a taxi to the airport, met up with the lads, and were on our way back to Spain. Along with hundreds of other Leeds fans, we had plumped for Benidorm as our base camp. It wasn't long before we had dumped our bags in the hotel and had converged on the famous Yorkshire Bar. It also wasn't long before we were singing our hearts out with Loll, Noggin and Kev Snaith.

On the day of the match we drank in the bars around Valencia seafront, which was teeming with Leeds fans. I had a beer with Tony Denton from Kippax, who was there with Phil Roberts and Alison Mooring. Alison had lost her husband, Neil, a little over a year earlier. Neil too had been a big Leeds fan all his life and I attended his funeral and then a small ceremony at Elland Road where his ashes were scattered at the side of the Leeds dugout. Another good friend of mine, Steve Franklin, was also laid to rest at Elland Road, after a moving ceremony led by his best friend Tim Harland. This is always at the back of my mind when people talk about leaving Elland Road. I don't think Steve or Neil, or any other Leeds fans for that matter, would be too pleased to discover they are asleep beneath a supermarket or a warehouse and that the ground has been moved five miles away.

Drinking in the centre immediately before the game, UEFA had one more trick up its sleeve. Leeds' passage to the semi-final had been plagued with dubious decisions both on and off the field. Barcelona had been given four extra minutes out of thin air at Elland Road, allowing them to grab an equalizer. Lazio had been given a free-kick on the edge of the Leeds penalty area after a Leeds player, Alan Maybury, had been viciously scythed down. Lazio equalised from the free-kick.

And in the second leg of the semi-final of the biggest club competition in the world, a trophy we had been cheated out of in

Paris 26 years earlier, it seemed UEFA still hadn't given up on us. They had reviewed an incident in which Lee Bowyer had allegedly stamped on an opponent in a previous game at Elland Road. Bowyer was level at the top of the 2001 competition's Golden Boot table with six goals, which must have rankled. They seized upon the alleged stamp as an ideal opportunity to remove Bowyer from that list – he was banned for three games, with immediate effect. UEFA also issued a statement telling Leeds 'not to appeal against the decision, as they would only increase the ban if they did'. Scandalous. I spoke to BBC's Harry Gration about the decision and he too was mystified and outraged. I also later received an email from Martin Samuel at the *Daily Express* claiming that Leeds had been 'very hard done by by UEFA throughout the competition'. And so we were. Our European dream ended that evening as Valencia beat a below-par Leeds 3–0.

As if to rub salt in our wounds, the referee allowed a goal by Juan Sanchez, who deliberately punched the ball into the net past Nigel Martyn.

Afterwards I had a beer with Mark and Janet Belshaw from Wellingborough. Mark was recently confined to a wheelchair, but, aided by his wife Janet, never misses a game.

- 21 -

Mad Dogs and Mushrooms

A lot of my friends don't go to matches. You can be a Leeds supporter without going to the matches. There's so many people hate Leeds, as long as you've got it in your heart, you're a Leeds fan in my book.

When I retire it'll be to Key West – or Whitby. There's a Leeds coach that passes through there.

The start of Leeds United's 2001–02 UEFA Cup campaign coincided with the tragic events of 11 September in New York and Washington.

By a strange coincidence, Leeds had again been drawn against Maritimo of the Portugese holiday island of Madeira – who had been the opponents in the same stage of the same competition three seasons earlier, when the second, away leg, had been George Graham's last game as Leeds manager. Leeds won that with a penalty shoot-out but I remember the trip for an equally dramatic moment. Our flight landed at Funchal Airport the night before the game but after one or two drinks on board John Green and I were not exactly match fit. Incredibly, leaving the plane, we both lost our footing and went flying down the steps to the runway like world bobsleigh champions. Luckily for me I was sat behind John and he broke my fall, but as we reached the bottom at speed the tarmac broke John's head and he spent his first night in Madeira in hospital with a few stitches for souvenirs.

In 2001 the first leg was an away tie and we were due to fly from Heathrow on 12 September. Ironically, Spoon had been due to fly to America on the same day from the same airport but her flight was cancelled due to the atrocities so she stayed at home. We got a little bit further but were still only half way down the motorway when news reached us that our flight, and indeed game, had been cancelled also. Our airline informed us that our tickets would be valid when the fixture was rescheduled. This turned out to be a week later on 20 September.

Mindful of my last visit here, I took the aeroplane steps very carefully when we finally reached Madeira. The island is popular among British pensioners and on the night of the game, many of them turned up to see Leeds play at the small Estadio dos Barreiros. It was like a scene from *Cocoon* watching all these sprightly 70 year olds shouting and bawling at the referee. Elsewhere in the stadium a group of Maritimo supporters hung a big flag which read: 'Fuck You Bin Laden!' Leeds went down 1–0 that night, but eased their way through at Elland Road in the return leg to win 3–1 on aggregate.

France was the next destination and we opted to travel by coach to the game in Troyes. As usual I went with Hewitt Tours and on the day of the game around 1,000 Leeds fans gathered in the main town square. Leeds narrowly squeezed past their French opponents 3–2, but a comfortable 4–0 at Elland Road had ensured that Leeds would be in the hat for the next round, eventually being paired with Grasshoppers of Zurich. In Zurich I had a few beers with Procky and Macca from Oxford and Kev Morgan, Pete Varley and Clark 'Clarkey' Richardson from Lancaster. Webby, Ray and the Doctor soon joined us and told us that Stan, the man in charge of the visiting Leeds police contingent, was there to work in liaison with the Swiss police and was patrolling the bars. There had been a few scuffles between Leeds and Zurich fans, but nothing major. The Doctor doesn't particularly like Stan and refers to him as Marigold after the black character who appeared in *Till Death Us Do Part* tormenting Alf Garnett. Leeds triumphed 2–1 in the Hardturm Stadium, progressing 4–3 over the two legs.

The next round produced another relatively short coach journey to Holland, where PSV Eindhoven were the opponents. The Dutch had only entered the competition after the third round, dropping down from the Champions League.

We were based in Amsterdam and Leeds fans were there en masse. The familiar sight of Leeds flags hanging out of hotel bedroom windows greeted us everywhere we went. A good performance by Leeds saw the team grind out a 0–0 draw. Hopes were high for a more productive performance in the return leg at Elland Road but we knew too that Leeds would need to be wary of conceding a potentially calamitous away goal. Which is exactly what happened.

The Leeds manager David O'Leary had done a good job since he took over from George Graham in 1998 but it has to be said that he seemed to struggle towards the end of his time in charge. I believe he was tactically unaware in a lot of situations, none more so than that second leg at Leeds. Both teams had once again failed to score and with extra time looming his side got sloppy and allowed PSV to score a late goal which gave them victory. Leeds United's European exploits were at an end once again.

After the game I found my thoughts drifting back to the first leg in Holland and even further back to previous games in Europe. The flags that had accompanied Leeds United around the continent were prominent in my mind. The biggest was the ever-present 'Maverick Whites' banner – an enormous flag made by Leeds fans of the highest order, ably led by Lee Farrer.

The 'Tadcaster Whites' was carried by top fans Kayzo, Baz Swan, Budgie, Richard Knight and Chris Morris. I thought of flags bearing the names of Kippax, Beeston, Hunslet, Halton Moor, Harrogate – and many more – that had adorned the foreign perimeter fences. Alongside these were countless flags heralding support from Leeds fans in all parts of the country: the South-west and Wales, East Anglia, Blackpool, Scotland, Wellingborough, Lancaster, Oxford, London and the Isle of Wight. For all of these and many more not mentioned, I began to feel so let down by the team – a feeling shared by a good friend of mine standing beside me. Baz Copley, from Sherburn, was one of the original Kippax members way back in 1978 and the disappointment had been etched deep into his face earlier that evening in Holland.

These dedicated supporters of the club they love have, just like myself, travelled all over Britain and the world to watch Leeds United. I salute every single one of them. And I despair when certain people who are paid extremely well choose to criticise and in many cases, ridicule, the loyal people who pay for the privilege of watching these same people carry out their profession.

After the PSV defeat, O'Leary claimed that he could see that his team were having a problem competing in midfield. O'Leary never used to fill his bench with substitutes, in fact he very rarely used any. But one of the players sat beside him on the bench that evening was none other than David Batty, back for his second spell at the club. The best midfielder we possessed. The few times I met and spoke with O'Leary I found him to be a very pleasant fellow indeed and during a difficult period in 1999 I wrote to him, urging him to keep going because I was certain things would soon get better. I received a reply within days, thanking me for my support. But I do feel that he gradually began to lose his grip on the situation. I remember an incident at Everton in 2002. Leeds fans, upset at seeing O'Leary's assistant Eddie Gray slowly being edged out, began chanting Gray's name. The manager saw this as a direct attack on Brian Kidd. There were a small number chanting against Kidd but most of the chants were of 'What the fuck is going on?' and 'Eddie Gray'.

Since the appointment of Kidd, O'Leary began to spend less time on the training pitch to concentrate on other things. Play on the pitch clearly suffered as a result. The fast, free-flowing football previously displayed by Leeds disappeared and was replaced by frequent long balls and unnecessarily defensive tactics.

The day after the incidents at Everton, O'Leary came out and slammed Leeds fans for their action. Kidd, apparently, offered to resign. But Leeds players Alan Smith, Nigel Martyn and Rio Ferdinand called a press conference in what I perceived to be a poor and staged attempt at a show of solidarity with the manager.

More significantly, O'Leary claimed he would be returning to the training ground with immediate effect. He stressed, however, that it was purely his decision and that he had not been influenced in any way by the fans. It is worth noting that during the players' little speech and O'Leary's comments, Eddie Gray was never mentioned. In fact, while Brian Kidd features quite heavily in O'Leary's infamous book *Leeds United On Trial*, Eddie Gray receives very little acknowledgement.

Finally on this subject, at the end-of-season friendly at Barrow that summer I was standing with Kev Morgan and other members of the Lancaster whites when we were approached by chairman Peter Ridsdale and asked to refrain from chanting the name of Eddie Gray. Make up your own mind.

Much water has gone under the bridge at Elland Road since then, and most of it turbulent. At the start of the 2002–03 season, Terry Venables was named as manager. Before the end of it, he had gone. In May 2003, Eddie Gray and Brian Kidd were sacked by the club. Somebody else will surely some day write a book about it all. Me, I think I'll pop down the road for a slurp and remember the good times – like the pre-season tour Leeds undertook in 2002.

I have been on some brilliant trips around the world with Leeds United, but the pre-season tour of 2002 was by far the best.

Twelve of us flew from Stockport Airport (formerly known as Ringway) early one July morning and ten hours later we landed in Hong Kong. Leeds weren't playing there, but we had decided to have a few nights in the city before moving onto Hangzhou in China for the first game. Hangzhou is twinned with Leeds and the Leeds City Council were instrumental in arranging the game with local side Green Town. Leeds United had kindly offered to provide us with tickets for the three-game tour and on a hot steamy afternoon we headed for the players' hotel to collect them.

In the hotel bar, with tickets in hand, we were joined by LUSC treasurer, Roy Schofield. After a chat Keith Gaunt and I strolled over to the hotel shop and were immediately accosted by first one, then seven excitable Chinese girls waving autograph books at us. None of them could speak any English and so explaining that neither of us were actually professional footballers proved futile. In the end Keith and I shrugged our shoulders, pulled in our beer bellies and began signing the books. As we did so, Eddie Gray walked past unnoticed; he smiled at us, winked and disappeared.

Hours later we were sat in the sports bar beneath the stadium half watching some replays of English matches on the pub television. Little Mick suddenly shouted, 'That looks like Leeds!'

It was – and the broadcast was not recorded highlights but live – because the organisers felt the ground was full enough, the game had kicked off 15 minutes early! We gulped our beers and rushed upstairs to our seats. Leeds ran out easy winners, 5–1, and we resumed our drinking in various other bars. Among us was Coke, a Leeds fan out of the top drawer who hails from Wellingborough and never misses a game, and who was proving quite a source of attraction to the Chinese. He weighs in at around 30 stone and this caused much fascination among the slightly built locals.

In the early hours of the morning we moved onto a music bar where Coke, Jeff Verrill and Dick Fenwick and I took a table next to the stage where a duo were performing and ordered some food. Now Coke can eat like I've never seen anything eat in my life and after polishing off a huge meal he still wasn't full so he ordered another plate of chips. With the music playing in the background the three of us couldn't help but smile as our waitress returned, unable to stifle a giggle, to place yet another plate in the centre of the table.

Coke leant over and popped one of the chips into his mouth. As he did so, over the sound of the music, I heard a small creak and then a loud crash as Coke and his chair collapsed onto the floor. Through tears of laughter I watched as the music stopped and six members of staff scurried around Coke trying to get him back onto his feet. Others brought Coke a giant chair that resembled one of those huge wooden benches seen outside seaside amusement arcades.

From China we flew on to Sydney and then Melbourne for the second game against Chilean side, Colo Colo. We made a British pub called The Elephant And Wheelbarrow our daytime 'local' and at night adopted Club UK as an after-dark haunt. They were both close to our hotel. The night before the Colo Colo game some of us went to the famous Melbourne Cricket Ground (MCG) to take in an Aussie Rules game. Inside we noticed Alan Smith and other Leeds players had done the same. After the two-hour game we settled in a busy little Irish bar in the city centre. One of our fellow travellers was Neil Smurthwaite from York, who for obvious reasons gets called Smurf, but for our little trip he was known as Tommy Tourist as he took upon the job of discovering places of interest, other than bars, but not quite with the same appeal. When match day arrived we happily quaffed large quantities of ale with hundreds of Leeds fans from all over Australia as a mixture of ex-pats and a healthy number of Aussie Leeds fans descended on the city. In reaction to the recent sale of Rio Ferdinand to manchester united, one English Leeds fan, Craig Gill, from the Adelaide Leeds Supporters Club carried a large flag with the words, 'Rio is Scum and he knows he is' emblazoned across it, photos of which appeared back in England.

I also came across many people with Kippax connections. Alan, an old workmate of Steve Wills from Kippax. Paul Hargreaves, who knew Mark Birch from Kippax. It's a small world, but I wouldn't want to paint it! Also in our presence were two men from Oxford in fancy dress – a large kangaroo aka Macca and a very bizarre 'Robin' whose secret identity was Dave 'Procky' Procter.

There should have been a Batman, too, but an Oxford lad known as Moose had collapsed in the toilet. Moose never made it to the game or even the third and final game of the tour in Bangkok. He simply disappeared and Macca and Procky had to leave his passport and belongings from his room with Melbourne police. He was found days later wandering the streets unaware of where – or indeed who – he was. Later in a bar outside the stadium in Bangkok Macca and Procky were greeted by the sister and brother-in law of Moose. They had flown from Sydney to surprise Moose. 'We've got a surprise for you, too,' said Macca, 'He's in hospital back in Melbourne.' Even now although he is fully fit, his illness remains a mystery.

Our party arrived in Bangkok around one o'clock in the morning and after dumping our bags in our rooms, we were sitting outside a bar chatting with some locals. As we did so I looked down the street and thought I saw an elephant. I looked down at my beer and then looked up again and it had gone. Maybe I was over-tired. But as Coke, Jeff and Little Mick laughed at me a large trunk crashed through the bushes that surrounded the beer garden, followed by a 12-foot elephant. The locals knew him and we were told to give him some money. Plucking a 100 baht note (worth about 80p) from my wallet, I held it up and the elephant took it in its trunk and passed the note back to its owner. In return it was given some bamboo shoots and a glass of beer. Once fed and watered it disappeared into the night.

Later that day we met up with Ian 'Pool' Hewertson, the very loyal Leeds fan from Blackpool. Pool regularly travelled with 'The Kippax' in the early '80s and still attends every game. In the ground for the match that day I was in the toilets when an old friend, Nigel, walked in. I hadn't seen him since I and some of the other lads had helped him out as a gang on the streets of Sofia late one evening a couple of years ago attacked him. He was now living in Thailand, teaching English. Like I said, it's a small world.

The day after a 2–1 win over the local Bangkok side I found myself sitting alone outside a bar called Rumours near our hotel. I was getting pestered by a little fellow in a *tuk-tuk* – a small scooter-type taxi with a small cab on the back. He wanted to take me somewhere – anywhere. We had all been laughing the previous day when Coke and Hector from the Chiltern Branch had squeezed into the back of one of these *tuk-tuks*. Coke pinned Hector into the corner as he shuffled in arse first and immediately, the front wheel left the ground as the slender driver frantically bounced up and down in a vain attempt to balance things out. After a ten-yard struggle, Coke was told to get out. No easy task. Eventually in front of a large crowd that had gathered to watch, Coke slumped to the pavement, flat on his back, puffing and panting.

Meanwhile, my driver wasn't taking no for an answer and I agreed to let him take me on a 'tour' for only 100 bahts. As he drove he rattled on to me about something but over the noisy traffic I couldn't hear a word. Soon we stopped outside a tailor's shop. I realised then in return for taking me to this shop for 'only ten minutes' he would receive a voucher for a gallon of petrol from the owners that would keep him on the road for days. I got a tour of the city and a visit to a tailor's where, I was assured I wouldn't have to buy anything! So with my 'donkey's ears' firmly fixed upon my head, I walked in.

The second I entered, I was swamped by eager staff waving samples of material and brochures.

'Now Sir, what sort of suit would you like, Sir?'

I was dressed in an old T-shirt and shorts so must have looked like I needed one. Except the temperature outside was nearing 100 degrees. I was just about to say 'Bollocks!' when I heard the magic words.

'Would you like a drink Sir? Water . . . Beer?'

I ordered a cold beer and sat flicking through a brochure. I ordered a second beer then left with their business card, promising I would be in touch with my order, and got back in the *tuk-tuk*.

By the time I was in my third tailor's I had this trick down to a fine art. 'I'm returning in a few weeks to Bangkok for a wedding,' I would explain. 'I will need four tuxedos for my party.' OK, it was a tad cruel, but I was thrown in at the deep end and had to survive.

With my driver's circle of tailoring associates seemingly exhausted, he said, 'Would you like a massage?'

I nodded and joked that I'd prefer it from a woman. Although this seemed to go straight over his head we drove up a side street and within seconds I was sat on a sofa with 'Mamma' the 'leader of the ladies'. With a beer in my hand I stared at 3 tiers of 40 girls behind a large glass screen, all looking back at me. The ones on the left I was told were priced at 2,000 bahts each and the ones on the right were priced at 2,500 (about £20). The girls on the left side looked to be mostly crosses between Fatima Whitbread and Lenny Henry. Those on the right were too beautiful to describe. Eighty pair of eyes watched as I opened my second can. Eventually I told 'Mamma' that it would be unfair on the others to just single one out. So after my beer I waved goodbye to the sobbing, heartbroken girls and left.

My driver then took me to a couple of jewellers and a souvenir shop before dropping me off at my hotel. He was delighted with his petrol vouchers and I with my free beer. I offered him 200 bahts, which he refused and said, 'You do me big favour today. Thank you!'

The following night we bid farewell to the girls at Rumours, Puy, Kai, Sam and the others. We left them all with Kippax T-shirts and a white rose. It was 1 August – Yorkshire Day. We had a final pint with the elephant and were off.

When we eventually landed back in England, Tommy Tourist informed us from his notebook that we had covered 32,000 miles in two and a half weeks. I have a Ford Transit that's done less.

My first phone message back, however, was from Collar. John West's wife Debbie, only around 30 years old, had collapsed and died that very day.

How is it that something so good can be followed very quickly by something so bad?

One of my local pubs in Kippax is The Moorgate. After all the travelling I go back there and feel at home once again. The lads in The Moorgate taproom are a great bunch. I spend many long hours in there with them analysing and re-living Leeds United performances ancient and recent. Tom and Mick go back longer than me. Kanu, Noel Osty, Daz, Math, Picky and Rich are more recent Leeds recruits but still know their stuff. I've always time to chat to Cliff, too. Cliff is the best darts thrower in the place even though he is partially blind. Having said that, I prefer to talk to him when he's not playing darts. Just in case.

The Moorgate taproom is similar to an old-fashioned working men's club. Many punters have their own seats and woe betide anyone else who sits in them. There are two barstools, 'Rev' always sits on the far one, surrounded by Dave, Tony and Vic. Paul Brookes always sits on the near one, flanked by Phil Raper. On match days, on the dot, the 'Proverbial Pensioner' Bill Robinson, will walk in with the aid of his walking stick and order a pint. He too has his own seat and en route to that particular seat he will engage at least three regulars with his antagonistic views on a recent Leeds football story. When he reaches his usual corner, he smiles to himself as he sits down. He then takes his first drink and enjoys an argument, caused by him only seconds earlier, as it unfolds before his very eyes.

I have been in the taproom and watched Bill at work when there is a game on television. With the exception of Baz Henshaw and his two offspring boys, all the lads are Leeds fans. The Henshaws support Liverpool, but it's not really life-threatening. I have often asked the lads what Bill is like when Leeds are on telly.

'He's a bastard,' says Andy Boyes, 'You know he's reeling you in, but you can't help but bite. He'll sit there pretending not to be the slightest bit interested, then he'll say, just loud enough so everyone can hear him: "What a load of rubbish. If he's a footballer – bah!"'

The lads will bite their tongues. Kanu opens his mouth to speak and Daz Gunga puts his hand on Kanu's shoulder, Kanu stays silent. Big John Bates feels relieved, he was just about to be drawn in himself. Bill will launch another attack.

'Alan Smith. He's crackers him! Can't kick a ball without kickin' t'man.'

Even laid-back, pipe-smoking Alan Dickinson can't let that one go. 'Tha's talkin' bollocks Bill!'

Bill smiles, he's caught another one. As the game goes on, Bill continues to fire in the odd remark, then just when everyone in the room has reached boiling point and is on the verge of explosion, he finishes his only pint, gets up and says, 'Night, lads.' If I ever return from a Leeds game and find Columbo in the taproom, I will know exactly what has happened.

There's another sidewinder who frequents our bar, Smiling Eric. He's a big Leeds rugby league fan and you could be discussing electrostatic precipitation on Venus and within minutes the conversation will be about rugby league. He is a master at it.

Eric usually comes in when it's much quieter. Like when a game is on Sky and we're all watching it on Ceefax.

A couple of years ago the brewery that owns the pub, Samuel Smith's, apparently to save money, ordered that Sky television be taken out. So, if I'm not out at the Leeds game, I regularly meet up with the lads to settle down in front of the television to watch whoever else is playing on Ceefax or, if we're feeling adventurous, Teletext. We've done it for so long now, we can actually see the players running around.

As the gossip is passed around about the latest scandal to hit Kippax, a dozen or so of us will stare avidly at the screen. We've done this for years and never thought much more about it. But when I invited Neil Jeffries, editor of the Leeds United magazine *Leeds Leeds Leeds*, in to have a pint with me and some of the lads he suggested we watch the scores on a different page number – for the vidiprinter version. That way we'd get to know the scores quicker and from every game. He'd obviously done this sort of thing before . . . Now we were very happy before his suggestion, staring up at the latest match scores, waiting for the pages to scroll over, and some of the lads did complain about the new method, but Neil was our guest and we humoured him. But after he'd gone we reverted to our original method. In The Moorgate we like things done the traditional way.

Do come and join us, though – all are welcome. Even fans of opposition clubs. Best to keep your new-fangled Ceefax ideas to yourself, though, eh?

We regularly have visits by West Ham fans. We were introduced to these fellas a few years back by Alan Osborne and have met up with them ever since either at Leeds or in London. They are led by one Dean Lainey, president of SHITS (Special Hammers International Travelling Supporters).

I reckon you need a sense of humour to be West Ham fans and over the years we have ribbed them mercilessly, mainly over them being a selling club. In 2003, it was time for them to get their own back. Dean, Richard, John and a Canadian called, confusingly, Rob The Yank all sat there and revelled in Leeds' recent 'bargain basement sales' which had seen us offload Bowyer, Dacourt, Fowler and Woodgate. It was enough to drive you to the Ceefax vidiprinter.

Sometimes, when a game really is too boring to stare at, we would put the page up with all that evenings fixtures on and all have a pound bet on the next goal. This method certainly kills all conversation as we all gaze at the screen waiting for a '1' to appear. Once it does, it is greeted by several moans and one cheer. The winner retrieves his money from the ashtray, it is filled up again and the staring continues till the next '1'.

Kev Higgins and Sean Plows once watched 45 overs of a Yorkshire and Lancashire match on Ceefax. The young folk of today simply do not know how to enjoy themselves.

There are other distractions, though. One evening we were staring out of the window (there wasn't a game that night) when we noticed a Jack Russell terrier. It was just sitting there looking back at us through the window. Some of the lads sometimes bring their own dogs into the taproom of the pub, so we thought it may be a bit on the frisky side. No one in the pub knew whose dog it was, but at eleven o'clock that evening it hadn't moved an inch. The following lunchtime we saw it again. After five days it was still sat there. As the days passed, we began to get to know it a little. It was reluctant, however, to be approached. But from a respectful distance the dog looked in good condition and around its neck its fur was flattened where a collar might once have been. Most Moorgate regulars settled on the theory that it had been dumped by its owner.

Every car that drove in or out of the car park was scrutinised very carefully by the Jack Russell while it remained cautious if anyone it didn't at least recognise came close. Finally The Moorgate landlord, Steve, gained its trust and took it to the vets. It received a full bill of health and Steve decided to call it 'Eddie' and keep it as a companion for his own dog. Eddie quickly settled in to his new home and we were relieved to see such a happy ending to the story. We'd grown quite concerned about the little thing. Steve's wife Jean smiled as she told us in the bar how Eddie now had his own basket and was very settled indeed. It drew a tear to the eye of even the hardest of the taproom lads. Kev, the local 'Demon' Barber and another dog owner, was gladder than most about the outcome for Eddie. Barry the Boat (a lad called Barry who owns a boat) looked down at his own dog Max and smiled affectionately.

Two weeks down the line we were all sat in the bar. Barry was there with Max and Kev had brought his dog, Holly. We'd been in a couple of hours when Eddie walked in. Max is very friendly and walked up to Eddie. But this was now Eddie's patch and he attacked poor old Max immediately. A violent fight ensued as the three dogs went beserk and everyone leapt to their feet to try to break it up. Barry managed to pick Max up but as he held him high in the air Eddie took a massive chunk out of Barry's right leg. In shock, Barry dropped the bewildered Max and the fight continued once more. Sean Plows ran around the bar chasing after Eddie, screaming at him to stop while waving a pool cue menacingly in one hand. It had little effect. Then, as the dogs parted, I managed to get Max to safety and held him against the bar. Someone else grabbed hold of Eddie. Barry was still running about cursing and limping when Eddie escaped again and came running back towards Max. This time Sean, still brandishing the pool cue, managed to head him off. By now Kev had managed to scramble his dog Holly up onto the juke box and out of harm's way. One of the lads, Math, had jumped up onto a nearby stool as if some sort of killer mouse was on the loose. He's not too keen on dogs, Math. But with Holly on the jukebox and Eddie and Max pinned down out of each other's reach, things began to settle down. Finally, Eddie was escorted away. Max had had enough and retreated under a seat. Holly was let down off the jukebox. Barry was wincing at a hole in his leg. Had all this mayhem really been caused by the same tiny pooch we all took pity on only two weeks earlier? It had.

Word of the dog fight has got around and on some evenings the taproom looks like the waiting room on Rolf Harris's *Animal Hospital* – except that all the dogs are pit bulls and Rottweilers plus a couple of gun dogs from the Seacroft area of Leeds.

People often ask me if I'll ever miss a game. Something that happened on the way to the match in Madeira probably offers the best answer.

We stopped at Northampton to pick up Ian 'Coke' Cockayne and decided to have breakfast at the same services. All seemed to be going well but shortly after tucking into my meal, a mushroom got stuck in my throat. I took a drink, but it would not budge. I could neither swallow or cough it out. I went into the toilet armed with two fingers to try a more desperate remedy, but the mushroom simply bedded itself in further. I began to panic.

Back at the restaurant till, the woman who had sold me the mushroom in the first place pointed to a man in a white shirt who she said knew first aid. Once the man in the white shirt had established that I'd been unable to throw up he told me to follow him back to the gents. There, in front of a crowd of amused friends and strangers, he told me to bend over the sink. Nibs has a filthy mind and started laughing immediately but the man in the white shirt simply attempted the Heimlich manoeuvre, grabbing me tightly from behind, lifting and squeezing hard.

'Is it moving?' he asked, in between loud grunts.

'Is it fuck!' I wheezed, with all the dignity I could muster.

He tried again. It was both very uncomfortable and hugely embarrassing to have a man I didn't know hold me in such a compromising position with so many people looking on, smirking.

'Bend over, then, we'll try again,' he said.

That was easy for him to suggest. I was more than a little embarrassed and had had enough. I told him I'd rather just wait for the mushroom to work its way down. He frowned, but wasn't taking no thanks for an answer. Disturbingly, he then stood really close to me, his hot breath in my ear.

'I really think we should try again,' he whispered, sternly.

That was enough for me. I'd rather choke. This bloke was a pervert. I was convinced he was enjoying this. I made a speedy exit. But on the bus I became seriously worried.

'Coke, I'm choking here, I think I might need to go to hospital . . .'

He laughed.

'No, I'm serious, it's not shifting and I'm really starting to worry.'

He looked at me and realised I was telling the truth. Then he looked at his watch.

'We can go to hospital if you like, Snake, but we're due at the airport in an hour . . .'

I weighed up my options. Death by choking or missing a Leeds match. It was no contest. The mushroom was bad enough but we had a plane to catch. And about an hour further down the motorway I finally swallowed the little bastard.